THE PARIS REVIEW

Founded in 1953.

The Paris Review is published quarterly by The Paris Review, Inc. Vol. 41, No. 151, Summer 1999.
Business Office: 45-39 171st Place, Flushing, New York 11358 (ISSN #0031-2037). Paris Office:
Harry Mathews, 67 rue de Grenelle, Paris 75007 France. London Office: Shusha Guppy, 8 Shawfield
St., London, SW3. US distributors: Random House, Inc. 1(800)733-3000. Typeset and printed in
USA by Capital City Press, Montpelier, VT.   Price for single issue in USA: $12.00. $16.00 in Canada.
Postpaid subscription for four issues $40.00, lifetime subscription $1000. Postal surcharge of $10.00
per four issues outside USA (excluding life subscriptions). Subscription card is bound within magazine. Please give six weeks notice of change of address using subscription card.   *While The Paris
Review welcomes the submission of unsolicited manuscripts, it cannot accept responsibility for
their loss or delay, or engage in related correspondence. Manuscripts will not be returned or
responded to unless accompanied by self-addressed, stamped envelope. Fiction manuscripts
should be submitted to George Plimpton, poetry to Richard Howard, The Paris Review, 541 East
72nd Street, New York, NY 10021.*   Charter member of the Council of Literary Magazines and
Presses. This publication is made possible, in part, with public funds from the New York State
Council on the Arts and the National Endowment for the Arts.   Periodicals postage paid at
Flushing, NY, and at additional mailing offices. **Postmaster:** Please send address changes to 45-39
171st Place, Flushing, NY 11358.

HAWTHORNDEN CASTLE
International Retreat for Writers

The International Retreat for Writers at Hawthornden Castle, Scotland was founded to provide a peaceful setting where creative writers can work without disturbance. The Retreat is open for ten months of the year to receive writers for four-week residencies. It houses five writers at a time, who are known as Hawthornden Fellows. The institution is international in character. Writers from any part of the world may apply for the Fellowships.

Drawings by David C. Wilson

To Apply:

Any creative writer who has work already published may apply for a Fellowship at Hawthornden. Applications are made for the following calendar year. The deadline is normally September, (the exact date will be found on the application form) and awards are announced in January. Applicants should write for full details to:

The Administrator
Hawthornden Castle
Lasswade
Scotland EH18 1EG

92ND STREET Y
Unterberg Poetry Center

THE VOICE OF LITERATURE

1999/2000 Season of Literary Readings, Lectures and Programs

AUTHORS APPEARING THIS SEASON INCLUDE (in order of appearance)

Thomas Keneally	Mary Robison	Rachel Hadas	Nuruddin Farah
Frank McCourt	Barbara Guest	C.D. Wright	Robert Stone
Adrienne Rich	Kenneth Koch	Kurt Vonnegut Jr.	Aleksandar Tišma
Elizabeth Hardwick	Sue Miller	Paul Auster	E.L. Doctorow
Sigrid Nunez	Barbara Gowdy	Maureen Howard	Paul Theroux
Darryl Pinckney	Richard Howard	Bárbara Jacobs	Vikram Seth
William Least	William Logan	Juan Villoro	Jayne Anne Phillips
Heat-Moon	V.S. Naipaul	Craig Raine	Norman Rush
Jonathan Raban	Edwidge Danticat	Adam Zagajewski	Denise Chavez
Frederick Barthelme	Allan Gurganus	Chinua Achebe	Terry McMillan

SPECIAL PROGRAMS INCLUDE

Shakespeare & the Actors: A Reading by Brian Bedford and Claire Bloom /
A Tribute to Ted Hughes / Carlos Fuentes on Jorge Luis Borges at 100 / A
Centennial Tribute to Hart Crane / *Portnoy's Complaint* at 30: A Reading and
Panel Discussion / A Tribute to Toni Cade Bambara with Toni Morrison and
others / Shakespeare & the Critics: A Conversation between Harold Bloom
and Frank Kermode / American Slave Narratives: A Reading by James Earl
Jones / Shakespeare and the Poets / A Tribute to Rainer Maria Rilke / Society
Unbound: A series of verse dramas, including Robert Lowell's *Prometheus Bound*;
C.K. Williams' *"The Bacchae" of Euripides*; and Tom Paulin's *The Riot Act, a
Version of Sophocles' "Antigone"*
Poetry readings are co-presented with The Academy of American Poets.

SERIES MEMBERSHIP: At $190, a Poetry Center Membership admits you to all
of the above readings, special programs and much more.

CALL (212) 996-1100 for a season brochure or to order tickets
UNTERBERG POETRY CENTER / TISCH CENTER FOR THE ARTS
1395 Lexington Avenue, NYC 10128 / www.92ndsty.org / An agency of UJA-Federation

Petaluma

1ST. AVE. AT 73RD. ST., NEW YORK CITY
772·8800

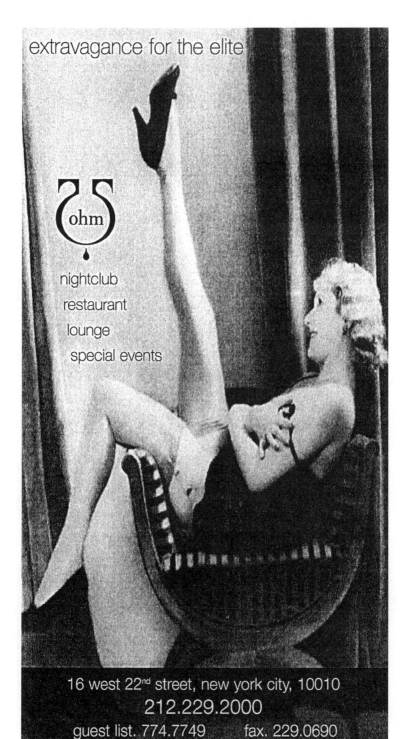

The Russian Samovar
Reading Series

256 West 52nd St.

Fall Readers

Charles Simic
Lucie Brock-Broido
Ann Beattie
Ruth Danon
Brenda Shaughnessy
Kate Walbert
Julia Slavin

Previous Readers

John Ashbery
Jonathan Galassi
Anthony Hecht
Amy Hempel
Mark Leyner
Norman Manea
J.D. McClatchy
Paul Muldoon

Richard Price
Francine Prose
Jim Shepard
Susan Sontag
Mark Strand
Rachel Wetzsteon
Charles Wright

7:00 pm   **Two Tuesdays a Month** $3.00

The Paris Review and Verse Theater Manhattan
are pleased to announce

THE PARIS REVIEW **VERSE DRAMA PRIZE**
Sponsored by Verse Theater Manhattan

THE PARIS REVIEW AND VERSE THEATER MANHATTAN WILL
AWARD A PRIZE FOR THE FINEST PREVIOUSLY UNPUBLISHED
VERSE DRAMA. THE PRIZEWINNING DRAMA WILL APPEAR IN THE
SPRING 2000 ISSUE OF THE PARIS REVIEW AND WILL BE GIVEN A
READING IN NEW YORK CITY BY VERSE THEATER MANHATTAN.
THE AUTHOR WILL RECEIVE A PRIZE OF $2000.

The Guidelines:
1. Manuscripts must be no longer than thirty pages.
2. Submissions must be original and unpublished.
3. Submissions must be typewritten and double-spaced.
4. Submissions must include a self-addressed stamped envelope for response.
5. Submissions should be sent to:
   Verse Drama Prize
   The Paris Review
   541 East 72nd Street
   New York, NY 10021
6. Submissions must be postmarked no later than November 30, 1999

The Paris Review

Editorial Office:
541 East 72 Street
New York, New York 10021
HTTP://www.parisreview.com

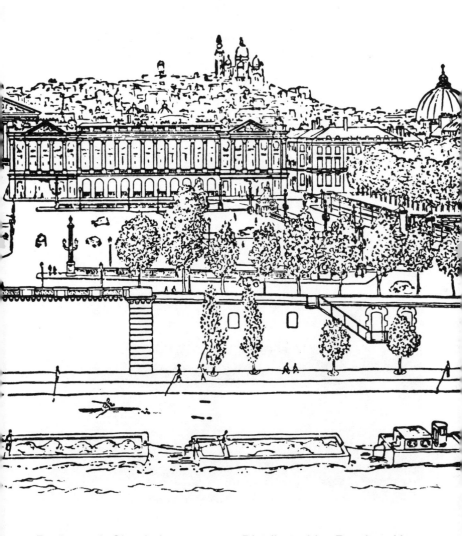

Business & Circulation:
45-39 171 Place
Flushing, New York 11358

Distributed by Random House
201 East 50 Street
New York, New York 10022
(800) 733-3000

Table of contents illustration by Valerie Sadoun,
acrylic on paper, 1999.
Frontispiece by William Pène du Bois.

Number 151

The Tale of the Unknown Island

José Saramago

A man went to knock at the king's door and said, Give me a boat. The king's house had many other doors, but this was the door for petitions. Since the king spent all his time sitting at the door for favors (favors being offered to the king, you understand), whenever he heard someone knocking at the door for petitions, he would pretend not to hear, and only when the continuous pounding of the bronze door knocker became not just deafening, but positively scandalous, disturbing the peace of the neighborhood (people would start muttering, What kind of king is he if he won't even answer the door), only then would he order the first secretary to go and find out what the supplicant wanted, since there seemed no other way of silencing him. Then, the first secretary would call the second secretary, who would call the third secretary, who would give orders to the first assistant who would, in turn, give orders to the second assistant and so on all the way down the line to the cleaning woman, who, having no one else to give orders to, would half-open the door and ask through the crack, What do you want. The supplicant would state his business, that is, he would ask what he had come to ask, then he would wait by the door for his request to trace the path back, person by person, to the king. The king, occupied as usual with the favors being offered him, would take a long time to reply, and it was no small measure of his concern for the happiness and well-being of his people that he would, finally, resolve to ask the first secretary for an authoritative opinion in writing, the first secretary, needless to say, would pass on the command to the second secretary, who would pass it to the third secretary, and so on down once again to the cleaning woman, who would give a yes or a no depending on what kind of mood she was in.

However, in the case of the man who wanted a boat, this is not quite what happened. When the cleaning woman asked him through the crack in the door, What do you want, the man, unlike all the others, did not ask for a title, a medal or simply money, he said, I want to talk to the king. You know perfectly well that the king can't come, he's busy at the door for favors, replied the woman, Well, go and tell him that I'm not leaving here until he comes, in person, to find out what I want, said the man, and he lay down across the threshold, covering himself with a blanket against the cold. Anyone wanting to go in or out would have to step over him first. Now this posed an enormous problem, because one must bear in mind that, according to the protocol governing the different doors, only one supplicant could be dealt with at a time, which meant that, as long as there was someone waiting there for a response, no one else could approach and make known their needs or ambitions. At first glance, it would seem that the person to gain most from this article in the regulations was the king, given that the fewer people bothering him with their various tales of woe, the longer he could

spend, undisturbed, receiving, considering and piling up favors. A second glance, however, would reveal that the king
was very much the loser, because when people realized the
unconscionable amount of time it took to get a reply, the
ensuing public protests would seriously increase social unrest,
and that, in turn, would have an immediate and negative
effect on the flow of favors being offered to the king. In this
particular case, as a result of weighing up the pros and cons,
after three days, the king went, in person, to the door for
favors to find out what he wanted, this troublemaker who
had refused to allow his request to go through the proper
bureaucratic channels. Open the door, said the king to the
cleaning woman, and she said, Wide open or just a little bit.
The king hesitated for a moment, the fact was that he did
not much care to expose himself to the air of the streets, but
then, he reflected, it would look bad, unworthy of his majestic
self, to speak to one of his subjects through a crack in the
door, as if he were afraid of him, especially with someone
else listening in to the conversation, a cleaning woman who
would immediately go and tell all and sundry who knows
what, Wide open, he ordered. The moment he heard the
bolts being drawn back, the man who wanted a boat got up
from the step by the door, folded his blanket and waited.
These signs that someone was finally going to deal with the
matter, which meant that the space by the door would therefore soon be free, brought together a number of other aspiring
recipients of the king's generosity who were hanging about
nearby ready to claim the place as soon as it became vacant.
The unexpected arrival of the king (such a thing had never
happened for as long as he had worn the crown) provoked
enormous surprise, not only among the aforementioned can-
didates, but also among the people living on the other side
of the street who, attracted by the sudden commotion, were
leaning out of their windows. The only person who was not
particularly surprised was the man who had come to ask for
a boat. He had calculated, and his prediction was proving
correct, that the king, even if it took him three days, was

bound to be curious to see the face of the person who, for no apparent reason and with extraordinary boldness, had demanded to speak to him. Thus, torn between his own irresistible curiosity and his displeasure at seeing so many people gathered together all at once, the king very ungraciously fired off three questions one after the other, What do you want, Why didn't you say what you wanted straight away, Do you imagine I have nothing better to do, but the man only answered the first question, Give me a boat, he said. The king was so taken aback that the cleaning woman hurriedly offered him the chair with the straw seat that she herself sat on when she had some needlework to do, for, as well as cleaning, she was also responsible for minor sewing chores in the palace, for example, darning the pages' socks. Feeling somewhat awkward, for the chair was much lower than his throne, the king was trying to find the best way to arrange his legs, first drawing them in, then letting them splay out to either side, while the man who wanted the boat patiently waited for the next question, And may one know what you want this boat for, was what the king did in fact ask when he had finally managed to install himself with a reasonable degree of comfort on the cleaning woman's chair, To go in search of the unknown island, replied the man, What unknown island, asked the king, suppressing his laughter as if he had before him one of those utter madmen obsessed with sea voyages, whom it would be as well not to cross, at least not straight away, The unknown island, the man said again, Nonsense, there are no more unknown islands, Who told you, sir, that there are no more unknown islands, They're all on the maps, Only the known islands are on the maps, And what is this unknown island you want to go in search of, If I could tell you that, it wouldn't be unknown. Have you heard someone talking about it, asked the king, more serious now, No, no one, In that case, why do you insist that it exists, Simply because there can't possibly not be an unknown island, And you came here to ask me for a boat, Yes, I came here to ask you for a boat, And who are you that

I should give you a boat, And who are you to refuse me one, I am the king of this kingdom, and all the boats in the kingdom belong to me, You belong to them far more than they belong to you, What do you mean, asked the king, troubled, I mean that without them you're nothing, whereas, without you, they can still set sail, Under my orders, with my pilots and my sailors, But I'm not asking you for sailors or a pilot, all I'm asking you for is a boat, And what about this unknown island, if you find it, will it be mine, You, sir, are only interested in islands that are already known, And the unknown ones too, once they're known, Perhaps this one won't let itself be known, Then I won't give you the boat, Yes, you will. When they heard these words, uttered with such calm confidence, the would-be supplicants at the door of favors, whose impatience had been growing steadily since this conversation had begun, decided to intervene in the man's favor, more out of a desire to get rid of him than out of any sense of solidarity, and so they started shouting, Give him the boat, give him the boat. The king opened his mouth to tell the cleaning woman to call the palace guard to come and re-establish public order and impose discipline, but, at that moment, the people watching from the windows of the houses opposite enthusiastically joined in the chorus, shouting along with the others, Give him the boat, give him the boat. Faced by such an unequivocal expression of the popular will and worried about what he might have missed meanwhile at the door for favors, the king raised his right hand to command silence and said, I'm going to give you a boat, but you'll have to find your own crew, I need all my sailors for the known islands. The cheers from the crowd drowned out the man's words of thanks, besides, judging from the movement of his lips, he might just as easily have been saying, Thank you, my lord, as, Don't worry, I'll manage, but everyone clearly heard what the king said next, Go down to the docks, ask to speak to the harbormaster, tell him I sent you, and that he is to give you a boat, take my card with you. The man who was to be given a boat read the visiting card, which bore the word *king* underneath the king's name, and these were the words the king had written as he rested the card on the cleaning woman's shoulder, Give the bearer a boat, it doesn't have to be a large boat, but it should be a safe, seaworthy boat, I don't want to have him on my conscience if things should go wrong. When the man looked up this time, one imagines, in order to say thank you for the gift, the king had already withdrawn, and only the cleaning woman was there, looking at him thoughtfully. The man moved away from the door, a signal for the other supplicants finally to approach, there is little point in describing the ensuing confusion, with everyone trying to get to the door first, but alas, the door was once more closed. They banged the bronze door knocker again to summon the cleaning woman, but the cleaning woman wasn't there, she had turned and left, with her bucket and her broom, by another door, the door of decisions, which is rarely used, but when it is used, it definitely is. Now one can understand the thoughtful look on the cleaning woman's face, for this was the precise moment when she had decided to go after the man as he set off to the port to take charge of the boat. She decided that she had had enough of a life spent cleaning and scrubbing palaces, that it was time to change jobs, that cleaning and scrubbing boats was her true vocation, at least she would never lack for water at sea. The man has no idea that, even though he has not yet started recruiting crew members, he is already being followed by the person who will be in charge of washing down the decks and of other such cleaning tasks, indeed, this is the way fate usually treats us, it's there right behind us, it has already reached out a hand to touch us on the shoulder while we're still muttering to ourselves, It's all over, that's it, who cares anyhow.

After walking quite a way, the man reached the harbor, went down to the dock, asked for the harbormaster and, while he was waiting for him, set to wondering which of the boats moored there would be his, he knew it wouldn't be large, the king's visiting card was very clear on that point, which excluded the steamships, cargo ships and warships, nor could it be so small that it would not withstand the battering winds or the rigors of the sea, the king had been categorical on that point too, It should be a safe, seaworthy boat, those had been his actual words, thus implicitly excluding rowboats, barges and dinghies, which, although entirely seaworthy and safe, each in its own way, were not made to plow the oceans, which is where one finds unknown islands. A short way away, hidden behind some barrels, the cleaning woman ran her eyes over the moored boats, I fancy that one, she thought, not that her opinion counted, she hadn't even been hired, but first, let's hear what the harbormaster has to say. The harbormaster came, read the card, looked the man up and down, and asked the question the king had neglected to ask, Do you know how to sail, have you got a master's ticket, to which the man replied, I'll learn at sea. The harbor master said, I wouldn't recommend it, I'm a sea captain myself and I certainly wouldn't venture out to sea in just any old boat, Then give me one I could venture out in, no, not one like that, give me a boat I can respect and that will respect me, That's sailor's talk, yet you're not a sailor, If I talk like a sailor, then I must be one. The harbormaster reread the king's visiting card, then asked, Can you tell me why you want the boat, To go in search of the unknown island, There are no unknown islands left, That's just what the king said to me, He learned everything he knows about islands from me, It's odd that you, a man of the sea, should say to me that there are no unknown islands left, I'm a man of the land and yet I know that even known islands remain unknown until we set foot on them, But, if I understood you right, you're going in search of one that no one has set foot on, Yes, I'll know it when I get there, If you get there, Well, boats do get wrecked along the way, but if that should happen to me, you must write in the harbor records that I reached such and such a point, You mean that you always reach somewhere, You wouldn't be the man you are if you didn't know that. The harbormaster said, I'm going to give you the boat you need, Which one,

It's a very experienced boat, dating from the days when everyone was off searching for unknown islands, Which one, Indeed it may even have found some, Which is it, That one. As soon as the cleaning woman saw where the harbormaster was pointing, she emerged from behind the barrels, shouting, That's my boat, that's my boat, one must forgive her unusual and entirely unjustifiable claim of ownership, the boat just happened to be the one she had liked too. It looks like a caravel, said the man, It is more or less, agreed the harbormaster, it started life as a caravel, then underwent various repairs and modifications that altered it a bit, But it's still a caravel, Yes, it's pretty much kept its original character, And it's got masts and sails, That's what you need when you go in search of unknown islands. The cleaning woman could contain herself no longer, As far as I'm concerned, that's the boat for me, And who are you, asked the man, Don't you remember me, No, I don't, I'm the cleaning woman, Cleaning what, The king's palace, The woman who opened the door for petitions, The very same, And why aren't you back at the king's palace cleaning and opening doors, Because the doors I really wanted to open have already been opened and because, from now on, I will only clean boats, So you want to go with me in search of the unknown island, I left the palace by the door of decisions, In that case, go and have a look at the caravel, after all this time, it must be in need of a good wash, but watch out for the seagulls, they're not to be trusted, Don't you want to come with me and see what your boat is like inside, You said it was your boat, Sorry about that, I only said it because I liked it, Liking is probably the best form of ownership, and ownership the worst form of liking. The harbormaster interrupted their conversation, I have to hand over the keys to the owner of the ship, which of you is it to be, it's up to you, I don't care either way, Do boats have keys, asked the man, Not to get in with, no, but there are store cupboards and lockers, and the captain's desk with the logbook, I'll leave it all up to her, I'm going to find a crew, said the man and walked off.

The cleaning woman went to the harbormaster's office to collect the keys, then she boarded the boat, where two things proved useful to her, the palace broom and the warning about the seagulls, she was only halfway up the gangplank joining the side of the ship to the quay when the wretches hurled themselves upon her, screaming furiously, beaks open as if they wanted to devour her on the spot. They didn't know whom they were dealing with. The cleaning woman set down the bucket, slipped the keys down her cleavage, steadied herself on the gangplank and, whirling the broom about her as if it were a broadsword of old, managed to scatter the murderous band. It was only when she actually boarded the ship that she understood the seagulls' anger, there were nests everywhere, many of them abandoned, others still with eggs in them, and a few with nestlings waiting, mouths agape, for food, That's all very well, but you're going to have to move house, a ship about to set sail in search of the unknown island can't leave looking like a henhouse, she said. She threw the empty nests into the water, but left the others where they were for the moment. Then she rolled up her sleeves and started scrubbing the deck. When she had finished this arduous task, she went and opened the sail lockers and began carefully examining the sails to see what state the seams were in after so long without going to sea and without being stretched by the vigorous winds. The sails are the muscles of the boat, you just have to see them swelling and straining in the wind to know that, but, like all muscles, if they're not used regularly, they grow weak, flabby, sinewless. And the seams are like the sinews of the sails, thought the cleaning woman, glad to find she was picking up the art of seamanship so quickly. Some seams were fraying, and these she carefully marked, since the needle and thread that, only yesterday, she had used to darn the pages' socks, would not suffice for this work. The other lockers, she soon discovered, were empty. The fact that there was no gunpowder in the gunpowder locker, just a bit of black dust in the bottom, which she at first took to be mouse droppings, did not bother her in the least, indeed there is no law, at least not to the knowledge of a cleaning woman, that going in search of an unknown island must necessarily be a warlike enterprise. What did greatly annoy her was the complete absence of food rations in the food locker, not for her own sake, for she was more than used to the meager pickings at the palace, but because of the man to whom this boat was given, the sun will soon be going down, and he'll be back clamoring for food, as all men do the moment they get home, as if they were the only ones who had a stomach and a need to fill it, And if he brings sailors back with him to crew the ship, they've always got monstrous appetites, and then, said the cleaning woman, I don't know how we'll manage.

She needn't have worried. The sun had just vanished into the ocean when the man with the boat appeared at the far end of the quay. He was carrying a package in his hand, but he was alone and looked dispirited. The cleaning woman went to wait for him by the gangplank, but before she could open her mouth to find out how the rest of the day had gone, he said, Don't worry, I've brought enough food for both of us, And the sailors, she asked, No one came, as you can see, But did some at least say they would come, she asked, They said there are no more unknown islands and that, even if there were, they weren't prepared to leave the comfort of their homes and the good life on board passenger ships just to get involved in some oceangoing adventure, looking for the impossible, as if we were still living in the days when the sea was dark, And what did you say to them, That the sea is always dark, And you didn't tell them about the unknown island, How could I tell them about an unknown island, if I don't even know where it is, But you're sure it exists, As sure as I am that the sea is dark, Right now, seen from up here, with the water the color of jade and the sky ablaze, it doesn't seem at all dark to me, That's just an illusion, sometimes islands seem to float above the surface of the water, but it's not true, How do you think you'll manage if you haven't got a crew, I don't know yet, We could live here, and I could get work cleaning the boats that come into port, and you, And I, You must have some skill, a craft, a profession, as they call it nowadays, I have, did have, will have if necessary, but I want to find the unknown island, I want to find out who I am when I'm there on that island, Don't you know, If you don't step outside yourself, you'll never discover who you are, The king's philosopher, when he had nothing to do, would come and sit beside me and watch me darning the pages' socks, and sometimes he would start philosophizing, he used to say that each man is an island, but since that had nothing to do with me, being a woman, I paid no attention to him, what do you think, That you have to leave the island in order to see the island, that we can't see ourselves unless we become free of ourselves, Unless we escape from ourselves, you mean, No, that's not the same thing. The blaze in the sky was dying down, the waters grew suddenly purple, now not even the cleaning woman could doubt that the sea really is dark, at least at certain times of the day. The man said, Let's leave the philosophizing to the king's philosopher, that's what they pay him for after all, and let's eat, but the woman did not agree, First, you've got to inspect your boat, you've only seen it from the outside. What sort of state did you find it in, Well, some of the seams on the sails need reinforcing, Did you go down into the hold, has the ship let in much water, There's a bit in the bottom, sloshing about with the ballast, but that seems normal, it's good for the boat, How did you learn these things, I just did, But how, The same way you told the harbormaster that you would learn to sail, at sea, We're not at sea yet, We're on the water though, My belief was that, with sailing, there are only two true teachers, one is the sea and the other the boat, And the sky, you're forgetting the sky, Yes, of course, the sky, The winds, The clouds, The sky, Yes, the sky.

It took them less than a quarter of an hour to go round the whole ship, a caravel, even a converted one, doesn't really allow for long walks. It's lovely, said the man, but if I can't get enough crew members to work it, I'll have to go back to the king and tell him I don't want it any more, Honestly, the first obstacle you come across and you lose heart, The first obstacle was having to wait three days for the king and I didn't give up then, If we can't find sailors willing to come with us, then we'll have to manage alone, You're mad, two people on their own couldn't possibly sail a ship like this, why, I'd have to be at the helm all the time, and you, well, I couldn't even begin to explain, it's madness, We'll see, now let's go and eat. They went up to the quarterdeck, the man still protesting at what he called her madness, and there the cleaning woman opened the package he had brought, a loaf of bread, hard goat's cheese, olives and a bottle of wine. The moon was now but a hand span above the sea, the shadows cast by the yard and the mainmast came and lay at their feet. Our caravel's really lovely said the woman, then corrected herself, I mean your caravel, It won't be mine for very long I shouldn't think, Whether you sail it or not, it's yours, the king gave it to you, Yes, but I asked him to give it to me so that I could go in search of an unknown island, But these things don't just happen from one moment to the next, it all takes time, my grandfather always used to say that anyone going to sea must make his preparations on land first, and he wasn't even a sailor, With no crew members we can't sail, So you said, And we'll have to provision the ship with the thousand and one things you need for a voyage like this, given that we don't know where it might lead us, Of course, and then we'll have to wait for the right season, and leave on a good tide, and have people come to the quay to wish us a safe journey, You're making fun of me, Not at all, I would never make fun of the person who got me to leave the palace by the door of decisions, Forgive me, And I won't go back through that door whatever happens. The moonlight was falling directly on the cleaning woman's face, Lovely, really lovely, thought the man, and this time he didn't mean the caravel. The woman did not think anything, she must have thought all she had to think in those three days during which she would open the door now and then to see if he

was still out there, waiting. There wasn't a crumb of bread
or cheese left, not a drop of wine, they had thrown the olive
stones into the sea, the deck was as clean as it had been when
the cleaning woman had wiped a cloth over it for the last
time. A steamship's siren let out a potent growl such as
leviathans must have made, and the woman said, When it's
our turn, we won't make so much noise about it. Although
they were still in the harbor, the water lapped slightly as the
steamship passed, and the man said, But we'll certainly sway
about a lot more. They both laughed, then fell silent, after
a while one of them suggested that perhaps they should go
to sleep, Not that I'm particularly sleepy, and the other
agreed, No, I'm not either, then they fell silent again, the
moon rose and continued to rise, at one point the woman
said, There are bunks down below, the man said, Yes, and
that was when they got up and stepped down to the deck,
where the woman said, See you tomorrow, I'm going this
way, and the man replied, I'm going this way, see you tomorrow, they did not say port or starboard, probably because
they were both new to the art. The woman turned back, Oh,
I forgot, and she took two candle stumps out of her apron
pocket, I found them when I was cleaning, but I don't have
any matches, I do, said the man. She held the candles, one
in each hand, he lit a match, then, protecting the flame
beneath the dome of his cupped fingers, he carefully applied
it to the old wicks, the flame took, grew slowly like the
moonlight, lit the face of the cleaning woman, there's no
need to say what he thought, She's lovely, but what she
thought was this, He's obviously got eyes only for the unknown island, just one example of how people can misinter-
pret the look in another person's eyes, especially when they've
only just met. She handed him a candle, said, See you tomorrow, then, sleep well, he wanted to say the same thing, only
differently, Sweet dreams, was the phrase that he came out
with, in a little while, when he is down below, lying on
his bunk, other phrases will spring to mind, wittier, more
charming, as such phrases should be when a man finds himself

alone with a woman. He wondered if she would already be asleep, if it had taken her long to fall asleep, then he imagined that he was looking for her and couldn't find her anywhere, that the two of them were lost on a vast ship, sleep is a skilled magician, it changes the proportions of things, the distances between them, it separates people and they're lying next to each other, brings them together and they can barely see one another, the woman is sleeping only a few yards away from him and he cannot reach her, yet it's so very easy to go from port to starboard.

He had wished her sweet dreams, but he was the one who spent all night dreaming. He dreamed that his caravel was on the high seas, with the three lateen sails gloriously full, cutting a path through the waves, while he controlled the ship's wheel and the crew rested in the shade. He couldn't understand what these sailors were doing there, the same ones who had refused to embark with him to go in search of the unknown island, they probably regretted the rough irony with which they had treated him. He could see animals wandering the deck too, ducks, rabbits, chickens, the usual domestic livestock, pecking at the grains of corn or nibbling on the cabbage leaves that a sailor was throwing to them, he couldn't remember bringing them on board, but however it had happened, it was only natural they should be there, for what if the unknown island turned out to be a desert island, as had so often been the case in the past, it was best to play safe, and we all know that opening the door to the rabbit hutch and lifting a rabbit out by the ears is always easier than having to pursue it over hill and dale. From the depths of the hold he could hear a chorus of neighing horses, lowing oxen, braying donkeys, the voices of the noble beasts so vital for carrying out heavy work, and how did they get there, how can they possibly fit into a caravel that has barely enough room for the human crew, suddenly the wind veered, the mainsail flapped and rippled, and behind was something he hadn't noticed before, a group of women, who even without counting, must be as numerous as the sailors, are occupied in womanly tasks, the time had not yet come for them to occupy themselves with other things, it's obvious that this must be a dream, no one in real life ever traveled like this. The man at the ship's wheel looked for the cleaning woman, but couldn't see her, Perhaps she's in the bunk to starboard, resting after scrubbing the deck, he thought, but he was deceiving himself, because he knows perfectly well, although again he doesn't know how he knows, that, at the last moment, she chose not to come, that she jumped onto the quay, shouting, Good-bye, good-bye, since you only have eyes for the unknown island, I'm leaving, and it wasn't true, right now his eyes are searching for her and do not find her. At that moment, the sky clouded over and it began to rain, and, having rained, innumerable plants began to sprout from the rows of sacks filled with earth lined up along the sides of the ship, they are not there because of fears that there will not be enough soil on the unknown island, but because in that way one can gain time, the day we arrive, all we will have to do is transplant the fruit trees, sow the seeds from the miniature wheat fields ripening here, and decorate the flowerbeds with the flowers that will bloom from these buds. The man at the ship's wheel asks the sailors resting on the deck if they can see any uninhabited islands yet, and they say they can see no islands at all, uninhabited or otherwise, but that they are considering disembarking on the first bit of inhabited land that appears, as long as there is a port where the ship can anchor, a tavern where they can drink and a bed to frolic in, since there's no room to do so here, with so many people crowded together. But what about the unknown island, asked the man at the ship's wheel, The unknown island doesn't exist, except as an idea in your head, the king's geographers went to look at the maps and declared that it's been years since there have been any unknown islands, You should have stayed in the city, then, instead of hindering my voyage, We were looking for a better place to live and decided to take advantage of your journey, You're not sailors, We never were, I won't be able to sail this ship all alone, You should have thought of that before asking the king to give it to you, the sea won't teach you how to sail. Then the man at the ship's wheel saw land in the distance and tried to sail straight past, pretending that it was the mirage of another land, an image that had traveled across space from the other side of the world, but the men who had never been sailors protested, they said that was where they wanted to disembark, This island's on the map, they cried, we'll kill you if you don't take us there. Then, of its own accord, the caravel turned its prow towards land, entered the port and drew alongside the quay, You can leave, said the man at the ship's wheel, and they immediately all trooped off, first the women, then the men, but they did not leave alone, they took with them the ducks, the rabbits and the chickens, they took the oxen, the donkeys and the horses, and even the seagulls, one after the other, flew off, leaving the boat behind, carrying their nestlings in their beaks, something never seen before, but there's always a first time. The man at the ship's wheel watched this exodus in silence, he did nothing to hold back those who were abandoning him, at least they had left him the trees, the wheat and the flowers, as well as the climbing plants that were twining round the masts and festooning the ship's sides. In the rush to leave, the sacks of earth had split and spilled open, so that the whole deck had become a field, dug and sown, with just a little more rain there should be a good harvest. Ever since the voyage to the unknown island began, we have not seen the man at the ship's wheel eat, that must be because he is dreaming, just dreaming, and if in his dreams he fancies a bit of bread or an apple, it would be pure invention, nothing more. The roots from the trees are now penetrating the frame of the ship itself, it won't be long before these hoist sails cease to be needed, the wind will just have to catch the crown of the trees and the caravel will set off for its destination. It is a forest that sails and bobs upon the waves, a forest where, quite how no one knows, birds have begun to sing, they must have been hidden somewhere and suddenly decided to emerge into the light, perhaps because the wheat field is ripening and needs harvesting. Then the man locked the ship's wheel and went down to the field with a sickle in his hand, and when he had cut down the first few ears, he saw a shadow beside his shadow. He woke up with his arms about the cleaning woman, and her arms about him, their bodies and their bunks fused into one so that no one can tell any more if this is port or starboard. Then, as soon as the sun had risen, the man and the woman went to paint in white letters on both sides of the prow the name that the caravel still lacked. Around midday, with the tide, The Unknown Island finally set to sea, in search of itself.

—translated from the Portuguese
by Margaret Jull Costa

Three Poems by Anne Carson

My Show

I was born in the circus. I play the flat man.
  My voice is flat, my walk is flat, my ironies
    move flatly out to sock you in the eye.

Hands, feet, vowels, hair, shadow, feelings of community,
  strings (you do not see) all flat.
    The epic model I guess I'll

pass over, Homer likening stalemate in war to a carpenter's
  chalkline. My flat world cost only $2 to view
    at first, later this price like others went up.

Brute natures and angles in transparent draperies all alike
  enjoyed the show. Flowers fell
    transparently off them as they entered my tent

where air was of course planar. In some other world they
  could have stayed organized but something about me
    cast their placards down (flat, yes):

Brechtian. See a flat rat escape that one-dimensional skull.
  And then, and then, what whispers there.
    Your agony, mine, in the fully consensual design

of this play of light—you crowd of missing ones,
  return the ball to me! whispers, whispers and her voice
    (she never arrives) froze on the knock.

Flat thunder, all my heart, you might use Brahms behind it.
  Dull, whitish, deadly as a carpenter's chalkline.
    Not Beethoven—Beethoven I cannot flatten.

Nothing for It

Your glassy wind breaks on a shoutless shore and stirs around
the rose.
Lo how
before a great snow,
before the gliding emptiness of the night coming on us,
our lanterns throw
shapes of old companions
and
a cold pause after.
What knife skinned off
that hour.

Sank the buoys.
Blows on what was our house.
Nothing for it just row.

Her Beckett

Going to visit my mother is like starting in on a piece by
Beckett.
You know that sense of sinking through crust,
the low black *oh no* of the little room
with walls too close, so knowable.
Clink and slow fade of toys that belong in memory
but wrongly appear here, vagrant and suffocated
on a page of pain,
Worse
she says when I ask.
And as in Beckett some high humor grazes
her eye—
"we went out rowing on Lake Como"—
not quite reaching the lip.
Our love, *that half-mad firebrand*,
races once around the room
whipping everything
and hides again.

Three Poems by Terese Svoboda

Euridice Abandoned in the Caves of Hades

You hire a guide. See several waterfalls,
a dock for a boat, and, indeed, a boat.
You rock to a shore where bats rise as gulls.
Or fall. Such silence. You keep your head low,
wade black pools, one for each of the senses.
You light cigarettes, unnerved, defenseless
in the blue of that smoke. You see the roots
of trees, your sisters' hair unpinned, you see
it leads out. The sky! Then the guide rapes you,
steals your purse and disappears. You really seethe.
Oh, god. Even Orpheus has lost it.
You can hear him through the rock, if that *Shit!*
is him shouting. You say, Let the stones drip
their milk. You'll sing louder, sing till you drop.

Anticipating Grief

It is both the coffin-worn hammer
and the hassle we walk under,
sans spouses, those shields
and mirrors of the family fantasy.

It is both, and we cry as if truth
changes when wet. When we speak
into the long tunnel ahead, we are heard
but the hearing takes time, maybe

we will die first. Oh, who can
die first? It's another family game,

each with his own blank screen.
When some echo of triumph

leaks back to where the spouses
wait, it's mixed with
an Esperanto of guilt
they invent, feet tapping.

Pool Tale

At bottom, a drowned harvester.
Sure as the spent soap slick
across the pool's deep side.

They scaled the fence, men
so black with dirt night itself
slid in with them. They came out

marked white where their hats cut,
when they came out. If you dove—
and we didn't—in the dark

to the bottom, you'd touch
the brick that held down
the drain, and the hands,

waving slow, the way they did
leaving town, the wheat
in our bins, the chaff drifting.

Michael Benedikt

Professor Albert Einstein Allegedly Commits a Crime; &, of the Difficulty of Finding a Jury of His Peers

1.

The idea of being tried by "A Jury Of One's Peers,"
Which, as we all know, is the pillar & pride of our American
    system of jurisprudence, among others,
Is, of course, a nice idea, & fine!

—But what if, during his later lifetime, a crime had allegedly
    been committed, by the late, great, Dr. Albert Einstein?

2.

Yes! What if, say, around 1950—while trying to hammer
    out the final ramifications of "Einstein's Theory of
    Relativity,"
Which, for the greater good of Humankind, definitively
    expanded Humanity's view of the entire Universe (!);
& With the good Doctor in an exceedingly excited state,
    perhaps virtually bordering on the hysterical

Professor Albert Einstein had committed, theoretically, what
    some people just might consider—& what some people
    just might not consider—
To be Manslaughter, or (heaven forbid!), even murder?

3.

Yes! What if, at some crucial Inspirational Moment, Professor
    Einstein had became uncharacteristically impatient with

some inept assistant who thoughtlessly spilled a cupful of
coffee all over a pageful of highly significant footnotes,
Thus distracting that great scientist, & teacher; & preventing
him from making a climactic "Quantum Leap";

—& What if Professor Einstein had then, in disgust, irately
thrown a clipboard into the air, in the general vicinity of
that poor man's head
Thus, by accident, alas badly denting it (the clipboard); &
alas, just in passing, also severely damaging that poor
man's nose;
& What if later on (perhaps partly due to a medical
misdiagnosis by some shortsighted, third-rate physician
who pooh-poohed the injury & prescribed only just enough
aspirin to stop a headache),
That poor man had, overnight, gone & bled to death?

—The quality of even our most extraordinary "Blue-Ribbon-
Juries" notwithstanding,
I wonder how our American legal system would like to try
taking something like *that* one on for size?

4.

In that particular case, the selection of jurors, of course,
would surely have had to continue for months, if not for
years & years
In order to find Prof. Einstein the necessary "jury of his peers";

—The likes of Max Planck, Niels Bohr, Lee de Forrest, &
Robert Oppenheimer; & probably the ghosts of Galileo &
Isaac Newton as well,
Would surely have had to have been among the peers to sit
on that particular panel!

5.

Of course, with respect to the very gentle, & mild-mannered
  Professor Einstein, the situation described above is purely
  hypothetical!; &, as I've said, is also historically unfactual,
& Besides being somewhat preposterous, is doubtless
  somewhat impish; & rather darkly playful

—I'm aware, for example, that it could have been thought
  up by any reasonably intelligent & speculatively-minded
  12-year-old who wasn't brought up to think like a sheep
Or, perhaps (come to think of it!) by any reasonably
  intelligent & speculatively-minded 12-year-old who *was*
  brought up to think like a sheep

Yet who managed, somehow, to discount it.

6.

Still, sometimes I truly wonder: What about the handling
  by any ordinary jury, of really Exceptional Individuals,
  generally?

—After all, it's one thing for lots & lots of school-age children
  in the USA today, to sit around under watchful
  educational eyes
In, say, the falling-apart chairs at, say, the deteriorating desks
  of some of the more miserably inadequate public schools
  we can, alas, find today, here in the USA;
&, Under the direction of some harried, hugely-over-
  burdened, yet doubtless fundamentally well-meaning
  schoolteacher who is sincerely intent on upholding The
  American System of Public Grade-School Education, &
  (however mediocre) of everything else entrenched &
  traditionally American, at all costs;

For those kids to write pious essays loaded with all kinds of
  misspellings glorifying how—so as to make sure that some
  relatively ordinary alleged miscreant, in some relatively
  commonplace legal case, received something like "a really
  fare trial"—
John Doe or Joe Schmoe was duly tried by "The Butcher,"
  "The Baker," & "The Candlestick-Maker;"

& It's another thing to imagine our—or any other legal
  system for that matter—even *beginning* to deal
  appropriately with a genius of the caliber of an Einstein
Who—if he allegedly committed a crime & theoretically had
  to go to court because of it—
Obviously ought *not* to be tried by "The Butcher," "The
  Baker," & "The Candlestick-Maker," but instead (to say
  the very least!)
By "The Anthropologist," "The Sociologist," "The
  Psychologist," & "The Astrophysicist"

—Unless of course The Astrophysicist happened to be one
  of those shortsighted, envious types of people
Who'd like to see an Einstein condemned in any event,
Just to get rid of "The Professional 'Competition'." . . .

7.

Yes, sometimes I truly wonder: What about the dilemma,
  trialwise & in practical terms, of *anyone* who happens to
  be even the least bit unusual, & rare, & (relatively
  speaking) Exceptional;
& Who, even if he or she *didn't* happen to be formally on
  trial—& if your average, conventionally envy-prone, &
  alas, all too often super-anti-intellectual American had
  anything to say about it—
Might have to go to jail & spend the rest of his or her life there!

—Or who, worse yet, might not even be deemed worthy of
living at all anymore
When duly beheld in the dimly viewing eyes of people whose
tolerance of even *minor* diversity or originality in other
people is so often so conventionally & so automatically
utterly zilch & *nil*,

That even I, for one, find it scary!

8.

—Yes!: trialwise, & in practical terms, what often happens
then, I wonder, to that really fine Federal judicial concept
Which says that, in America, for example, & in a Court of
Law, all people are entitled, right off the bat, to "The
Benefit of The Doubt";
& Which also asserts that people aren't supposed to be
thought poorly of, & disapproved of, much less be viewed
with prejudice beforehand, or regarded as automatically
guilty

Until such time as they *may* be proven not innocent!

9.

—But to come back to our exceptionally rare, & exceptionally
unusual Einstein: with him, there's also the fact to take
into account that (aside from being a genius & all that)

Professor Einstein, in his later years, like many other
Professors, whether absentminded or not, had the habit
of garbing himself quite often quite "comfortably," in
highly informal, or even old & somewhat worn-out
clothing,
So that he sometimes resembles, in his later photographs
especially, a rather worn-out, wrinkled, & disreputable
old duffel bag;

& Of course, as we know, most people tend ordinarily not
to think so well of a man or a woman if they simply don't
dress in a way that happens to impress others

—By wearing (for example), recently shined shoes; a clean
white shirt; a neatly pressed suit; & a bright (or better yet)
brand-new tie. . . .

Campbell McGrath

Atlanta

Airborne it's like a dream. It's dreamy. It's for
all the world like something
ants have made, something gigantic fomented
and foisted upon us by ants, clearings and houses, these
anticipatory trees and roads, the extremely
antic squiggles and zigzags traced
among the selfsame trees with a convincingly
antlike insouciance and sense of random
and undirected energy.
                              Ah, but of course
ants are anything but random!
                                        Thank you,
as always, Herr Insekt Doktor, but I'm
articulating the exact and random essence of the ant,
as evidenced by this rolling plateau of pine trees and
    houses en-
acted thereon. It's in the driveways
and ant-farm cul-de-sacs, gargantuan parking pads c-
antilevered to the sides, egg-spore sugar pods the pools
adaptively resemble, spackled like pinto beans
atop this fungal suburban
agraria. From four-door oaks are sexy hatchbacks
acorned, sand traps and little-league diamonds
abiding like jewels,
absolutely at odds with the mountains
as they gather in stark, elephantine folds
above the adamant plateau.
                                    Ah, but the
ant is a mover of mighty mountains,
a builder, a strongman,
a toter of grains!

Ahem, yes, thank you
again, dear Doctor, but I can see for myself
authorial scribblings of the wild jungle
ant below, disfigurations of dirt bikes
and wanton ATVs, runes inscribed so precisely
at random, indeed,
abject epitome of high ant society
adreaming honeyed crumbs on the banks of
an antebellum river.
                    Friend, this antebellum
ant by the riverside is
a myth. Perhaps you are thinking of the notorious
bee?
        Behold, I speak of the ant!
Behold, I bear witness to the ant!
Behold, I journey unto the City of Ants!

City of Ants wherein the beatitude of the airwaves is of
    an anthill!
City of Ants wherein the hermeneutics of the tribe is of
    an anthill!
City of Ants wherein the articulation of commerce is of an
    anthill!
City of Ants wherein the golden apple of compassion is of
    an anthill!

City of Ants! City of Ants!

Atlanta,
baby,
City of Ants!

Gary Fincke

The Eternal Language of the Hands

The surgeon Celsus, at the time of Christ,
Said the right hand should operate
On the left eye, the left hand should invade
The right. He meant the interns to practice
From the weak side like switch-hitters,
An old strategy which makes us smile,
But the smug health of the moment
Turns a page in the book of longing:
I looked left, then right, at the pictures
My father showed me: the husband, the wife,
Through five generations that ended
In German scrawled unintelligibly
Across the back. I was young enough
To believe, because he had lived
With grandparents who spoke privately
In German, he would translate the three pairs
Born somewhere other than Pittsburgh.
I expected a second language to
Enter me like the left-handed layup
I practiced each day, but he said German
Was forbidden like taking the Lord's name
In vain, that he'd shaken off *Kraut* and *Hun*
And *Heine*, slurs I'd never hear because
We'd changed. He might as well have tried,
Like some, swallowing a child's raw heart
For beauty and love. Consider
How many cataracts Celsus removed,
Inserting his needles, nudging them
Off-center like windblown grit. Left, then
Right-handed, thousands of years before
The surgeries we wait for. My father

The baker rolled sandwich buns with both hands
At once, circles so tight you couldn't tell
Which had been formed from the left or right.
Like Celsus removing clouds and teaching
Those miracles to disciples
In the eternal language of the hands.

Peter Davison

Little Death

I escaped, spinning off
   to heaven knows what
      location, eluding

control, threatening
   to relinquish: to end up
      bland, inert.

Without intake how should I not
   become my own dull
      monument, lie

immobile, cold as winter dirt, in-
   communicado? Unless I
      exert effort

my presence could harden into
   dead stone. *Yet mark this*: I must and will
      continue. Chest

heaves. Limbs lengthen. Head
   hums with vestiges of
      memory that pick up the scent

of desire. Body starts
   breathing. Listen!
      Bloodstream thumps

once more, tingling. Before
   I can so much as stir,
      my hair
      resumes growing.

A Shelby Foote manuscript page. About his penmanship he said: "I took a German course which included German script. I found a way to make no two letters look alike. You can't mistake an n *for a* u."

Shelby Foote

The Art of Fiction CLVIII

Although best known for his monumental trilogy The Civil War: A Narrative *(1958, 1963, 1974), Shelby Foote's preferred genre is the novel. Much as his hero, friend and fellow Mississippian William Faulkner created Yoknapatawpha, Foote imagined Jordan County. Writing five novels in five years, Foote recounted the Delta county's history and described every strain of society—a God-haunted hardscrabble farmer, a doomed black horn player, wealthy planter families*

in a state of advanced moral decline—in Tournament *(1949),*
Follow Me Down *(1950),* Love in a Dry Season *(1951) and*
Jordan County: A Landscape in Narrative *(1954). His fourth
novel,* Shiloh, *(1952) dedicated to his boyhood friend Walker
Percy, in which fictional characters appear beside historical
figures, follows the events and recorded dialogue of the actual
battle and foreshadows the epic history of the war which
would take him two decades to complete. His last novel,*
September September *(1977) is set in Memphis in 1957, when
racial tension threatens the city. All the novels reflect a deep
understanding of the way history shapes and warps individual
lives. Overshadowed by* The Civil War *in the States, his novels
have been best-sellers in Italy and France, where he is considered an heir to Faulkner.*

*Shelby Foote was born in the river town of Greenville,
Mississippi in 1916, the descendent of a planter who gambled
away his land and fortune. A formative influence was the
Greenville resident William Alexander Percy, a planter and
poet who brought young Walker Percy and his brothers to
live with him after they were orphaned. Had he and Walker
Percy not become friends, Foote has said, it's likely that
he might never have become interested in literature. Foote
followed Percy to the University of North Carolina, where he
spent most of his time in the library, devising his own curricu-
lum of history and literature. He left after two years. He
worked for Hodding Carter's* Delta Star *before joining the
Mississippi National Guard in 1940. He served as an artillery
captain in Northern Ireland but was court-martialed and dismissed after driving a jeep over the fifty-mile limit to visit
his Irish fiancée. Back in the States, he worked in New York
for the Associated Press and served briefly in the U.S. Marines
in California. In 1945, he returned to Greenville, worked at
a radio station, then quit to write full-time after selling a
story to* The Saturday Evening Post. *In 1954, he moved to
Memphis, which he calls "the capital of the Mississippi
Delta."*

For the last thirty-three years Shelby Foote and his third wife, Gwyn Rainer Foote, have lived in a rambling brick Tudor house shaded by magnolias and poplars on a street of grand homes built during the glory days of cotton trading at the turn of the century. Dressed in his regular writing attire, pajamas and bathrobe, Foote opened the door, a rambunctious chocolate Lab retriever named Bird barking and leaping behind him. With his trim gray beard and mustache and thick gray hair parted in the middle, Foote resembles a Confederate general. He has an aristocratic drawl reminiscent of Southern orators: "Jordan," he pronounced "Jurden." Gwyn Foote, a slender Memphis native wearing slacks and a blouse, can be found most anytime at her chair in a large living room reading stacks of contemporary fiction. The interview was conducted in his office at the far end of the house, a large room with an oriental rug, a double bed, a fireplace and pictures of his children on the mantle; bookshelves line portions of the room. There are a replica of Picasso's Guernica *with a WWII rifle mounted in its center, his helmet from the war on a shelf and a wooden model of a German* Stukka *hanging from the ceiling on a string in the attitude of a dive bomber. A poster of Proust looks down on a small desk with a typewriter. Pinned to a board over his main desk are quotations, a picture of Elvis and the outline of his long unfinished novel of the Delta,* Two Gates to the City. *During the interview, Foote sat at his desk or paced to and fro in his slippers, frequently refilling his pipe from a humidor with a mixture of Half & Half and Edward G. Robinson tobacco.*

In 1997, Donald Faulkner and William Kennedy interviewed Foote for the New York State Writers Institute in Albany, New York.

INTERVIEWER

With what instrument do you write? A word processor?

SHELBY FOOTE

I use a dip pen. Everybody on earth used to have one. They were in every post office in the land. I like the feel that

a pen or pencil gives you, being in close touch with the paper
and with nothing mechanical between you and it. The very
notion of a word processor horrifies me. When I've finished
a draft, I make changes in the margin. Then I make a fair
copy. I also edit the fair copy somewhat when I type it on
big yellow sheets so I can see it in print for the first time. I
correct those outsized yellow sheets, then retype them on
regular 8½ x 11 pages for the printer. I've had poet friends
tell me they never type a poem until they are really satisfied
with it. Once they see it in print it is very different from what
it was in longhand. It freezes the poem for them.

INTERVIEWER

I've heard that during the middle of writing *The Civil War*
you bought all the dip pens left in the United States.

FOOTE

My favorite pen-point manufacturer had all but gone out
of business—Esterbrook. I was running out and fairly desperate. On Forty-fourth Street just east of the Algonquin Hotel,
on the other side of the street, there used to be an old station-
ery shop, all dusty and everything, and I went in there on
the chance he might have some. He looked in a drawer. He
had what I wanted: Probate 313. I bought several gross of
those things, so I've got enough pen points to last me out
my life and more. Another problem is blotters. When I was
a kid, and when I was writing back in the forties, on into
the fifties, you could go into any insurance office and they
had stacks of giveaway blotters for advertising.

INTERVIEWER

What precisely is a blotter?

FOOTE

This is a blotter [*pointing*], and if you haven't got one
you're up the creek. You use the blotter to keep the ink from
being wet on the page. You put the blotter on top and blot

the page. I was talking about blotters in an interview, what a hard time I had finding them, and I got a letter from a woman in Mississippi. She said, "I have quite a lot of blotters I'll be glad to send you." So I got blotters galore. Ink is another problem. I got a phone call from a man in Richmond, Virginia, who had a good supply of ink in quart bottles. I got three quarts from him, so I'm in good shape on that.

INTERVIEWER

Do you reckon you're the last writer to be using dip pens in the United States?

FOOTE

There's probably some other nut somewhere out there doing it.

INTERVIEWER

Is it true that you spend the whole day in pajamas?

FOOTE

I live in pajamas. Sometimes I don't have anything on but pajamas three or four days in a row. If I'm not going out, why get dressed?

INTERVIEWER

So, you spent twenty years in pajamas writing *The Civil War?*

FOOTE

Spent much of it. I'm also very fond of nightshirts—old-fashioned, long-sleeved nightshirts. I'm recreating Balzac.

INTERVIEWER

Did you suffer from postpartum depression after you finished *The Civil War?*

FOOTE

Gibbon talks about finishing *The Decline and Fall*, saying how he had mixed emotions—liberated and very happy to have brought it to a close and to have lived long enough to wind it up. Then he became very sad, as if he'd lost an old friend. I felt all those things. It was a strange feeling. But I knew the last line from the time I started the book.

INTERVIEWER

What was the last line?

FOOTE

" 'Tell the world that I only loved America,' he said." *He* was Jefferson Davis.

INTERVIEWER

When you were writing *The Civil War*, which is some million-and-a-half words long, did you type the whole manuscript up yourself?

FOOTE

Twice. I've never had anything resembling a secretary or a research assistant. I don't want those. Each time I type, it gives me another shot at it, another look at it. As for research, I can't begin to tell you the things I discovered while I was looking for something else. A research assistant couldn't have done that. Not being a trained historian, I had botherations that led to good things. For instance, I didn't take careful notes while reading. Then I'd get to something and I'd say "By golly, there's something John Rawlins said at that time that's real important. Where did I see it?" Then I would remember that it was in a book with a red cover, close to the middle of the book, on the right-hand side and one third from the top of the page. So I'd spend an hour combing through all my red-bound books. I'd find it eventually, but I'd also find a great many other things in the course of the search.

INTERVIEWER

Where was the searching done? Libraries?

FOOTE

No. Mostly books right there at hand, a couple of hundred of those.

INTERVIEWER

How about revision?

FOOTE

I don't have to revise at the end; I revise as I go along. I might change commas around or something, but very little is left to do. Revision is heartbreaking. I just don't like it. Walker Percy was the exact opposite. He said if he knew how a story was going to turn out he wouldn't be interested in writing the book. Of course, this was sort of a joke, but he really meant it partway. For everyone a book is a search and, hopefully, a discovery.

INTERVIEWER

I've heard that when the third *Civil War* volume was finished and you turned it in, it went straight to typesetting without being copyedited.

INTERVIEWER

So did volume two. I had a funny experience with copy readers back at the outset. They worship reference books and dictionaries and all that ticky kind of thing. We had a sure-enough expert for volume one. He complained that I was using the phrase *by ordinary* instead of *ordinarily*. He said, "That's incorrect. You shouldn't do that." I said, "No, I've heard that and used it all my life." He said, "That doesn't keep it from being wrong." I said, "Well, let's look." I opened the *Webster's Unabridged* and went to *ordinary*. Under it, it said "By ordinary—Shelby Foote." That convinced him.

INTERVIEWER

So he didn't try to change anything after that?

FOOTE

No. Random House stopped using him after that.

INTERVIEWER

Do you consider yourself a novelist or a historian?

FOOTE

I think of myself as a novelist who wrote a three-volume history of the Civil War. I don't think it's a novel, but I think it's certainly *by* a novelist. The novels are not novels written by a historian. My book falls between two stools: academic historians are upset because there are no footnotes, and novel readers don't want to study history. It doesn't matter who's a professional historian and who's not: Herodotus, Thucydides and Tacitus weren't professionals—they were literary men. They considered history a branch of literature; so do I, to this day.

I am what is called a narrative historian. Narrative history is getting more popular all the time, but it's not a question of twisting the facts into a narrative. I maintain that anything you can learn by writing novels—by putting words together in a narrative form—is especially valuable to you when writing history. There is no great difference between writing novels and writing histories other than this: if you have a character named Lincoln in a novel who's not Abraham Lincoln, you can give him any color eyes you want. But if you want to describe the color of Abraham Lincoln's, *President* Lincoln's, eyes, you have to know what color they were. They were gray. So you're working with facts that came out of documents, just as in a novel you are working with facts that come out of your head or most likely out of your memory. Once you have control of those facts, once you possess them, you can handle them exactly as a novelist handles his facts. No good novelist would be false to his facts, and certainly no historian

is allowed to be false to his facts under any circumstances.
I've never known, in at least a modern historical instance,
where the truth wasn't superior to distortion in every way.

Everything I have to say about the writing of history was
summoned up by John Keats in ten words in a letter, more
or less like a telegram put on the wire nearly two hundred
years ago. He said: "A fact is not a truth until you love it."
You have to become attached to the thing you're writing
about—in other words, "love it"—for it to have any real
meaning. It is absolutely true that no list of facts ever gives
you a valid account of what happened. The bare-bone facts
are what you use to shape your description of what happened.
There are those historians who, I'm afraid, all too often think
that good writing gets in the way of the history. In other
words, you hide the facts behind blankets of prose. I believe
the exact opposite. I believe that the facts told with some art
are true narrative, which you then absorb into your being
and understanding as well as you do a great novel, whether
it's a short one like *Gatsby* or a long one like *Remembrance
of Things Past*. That's the way I feel about writing history.
Now it sounds as if I'm making an all-out attack against
academic historians. I *am* making some attack on them for
their lack of concern about learning how to write. It is as if
they thought it an onerous waste of time, which they might
better spend doing research rather than learning how to write.
The result sometimes is a prose that's so dismal that the
footnotes are not an interruption but just a welcome relief.
And we've all run across that.

I recently had a nightmare experience of being one of three
judges of what's called the Parkman Prize. Parkman happens
to be my favorite American historian because he fits the description I have given as to what a historian ought to be. I
received 208 books, all in their shiny jackets, published the
past year. I found all but two of them barely readable. That's
a shocking thing. It was because of the writing. It's also
because of me. As I get older, I care less and less what happens
in a book. What I care about is the writing—how it's told.

I read words and I don't see a scene going on as if I were at a movie; I want to see how these words are shaped and how they intertwine and what the sounds are next to each other, how they rub up against each other, along with the distribution of commas and semicolons. If it sounds like I'm making an attack on academic historians, the real truth of the matter is that these historians, whom I'm excoriating to some extent, have very little use for me. In fact I could not do a thing without them. I'm enormously indebted to these fact-gatherers, these perceivers of scenes, these perpetrators of scenes. They do a good job of that. I just wish more of them spent a bit more time learning how to write, learning how to develop a character, manage a plot.

INTERVIEWER

Do you have any historians whom you consider good writers?

FOOTE

I mentioned Parkman. He's a really good writer. There are a number of good historians with whom I don't agree but who are good writers. One was an historian at the University of Wisconsin named William Appleman Williams, more or less a Marxist, but a good writer. I always enjoyed reading him.

I don't mean to downscore everybody in the field, but some of the best historians with regard to communicating facts are dreadful writers. I find them close to unreadable except in the way of research. I'm also worried about something going on now—the use of word processors and computers to gather information. It might be mighty nice to push a button, get all the facts about the casualties in Fredericksburg or whatever, but it's been my experience that you are skipping two very valuable things. One of them is that it's been my experience that the more trouble I have learning something, the longer it stays with me; and the easier time I have learning it, the faster it leaves me. So if the information comes flashing across the screen, it goes in this ear and flies out the other by the time I've punched the button. That worries me. I worry about the authenticity of the material under this new thing where you're punching up information. It's as if you have more use for an index finger than you have for a brain. Somebody told me what great fun it is to be in a chatroom. It seems to me an inordinate waste of time, not to mention a bore.

INTERVIEWER

How did you start as a writer and how did you start to write novels?

FOOTE

I edited my high-school newspaper—I did poetry and editorials and everything else on it. I must have done a good job because it won the national championship for the best high-school newspaper in the United States. That came as a big surprise, right there in Greenville, Mississippi, population 15,000.

I think a large part of what made me whatever I am is the fact that I'm an only child. My father died just before I turned six years old, so I've been to a considerable degree on my own. I was a latchkey kid before there were any latchkey kids, and I liked it. Cast on my own resources, I began to read very early and with great pleasure. I read pretty good stuff in addition to terrible stuff. The most illuminating thing that ever happened to me in those early days was winning as a Sunday-school prize a copy of *David Copperfield*. Now, I'd read *Tom Swift* and earlier Bunny Brown and his sister Sue, then moved on to the Rover Boys and Tarzan. But here came *David Copperfield*. I was dismayed that it was about six-hundred pages long. But when I began to read I got so caught up in it—when I finished it, I realized that I'd been in the presence of something realer than real. I knew David better than I knew myself or anyone else. The way Dickens told that story caught me right then and there.

INTERVIEWER

Was reading *David Copperfield* an early catalyst for making you a writer and not just a reader?

FOOTE

I absolutely think so. I didn't react immediately, but eventually it made me want to do what Dickens had done—make a world that's somehow better in focus than real life, which goes rushing past you. He showed me how to do it, too.

INTERVIEWER

Could you have learned that in a creative-writing course?

FOOTE

I think creative-writing courses are a dismal waste of time. In the first place I don't think creative writing can be taught. I think it's very good if it makes you work; that's the only virtue I see in it. But I think to correct a writer's mistakes in a schoolmasterly way is to short-circuit the process. Writers have to discover their own mistakes and correct them for it to have real meaning. But the *David Copperfield* experience is with me to this day.

INTERVIEWER

How would you define that . . .

FOOTE

It's this ability to move *inside* people the way you can't move inside them in real life. You can't even examine yourself as well as Dickens examines David—David's life—by selecting certain parts of it to stress. Another master of what I'm talking about is Marcel Proust, who looks like he's just fooling around, when in fact he knows exactly what he's doing. Through digression after digression he's moving that story forward, nonstop, start to finish. That fascinated me.

Were you writing short stories in college?

I went to school in September, 1935. By September of the
following year things were heating up in Europe. Absolutely
no doubt that there was fixing to be a war in Europe. It was
obvious to me that it was coming and I knew too that we
were going to get into it, so I went home. During the two
years I was in college I had a story in almost every issue of
the literary magazine. At home, during that waiting period—
waiting at first for the war to start, and then for us to get
into it, too—I wrote the first draft of my first novel, *Tournament*. When Hitler went into Poland I joined the Mississippi
National Guard, which mobilized a year later. I spent the
next five years in the service, reading almost nothing except
army materials, learning how to be a soldier. It was an interesting time.

When you were in the army, did you do any writing at all?

I did some reading. I carried Freeman's *Lee* with me and
Henderson's *Jackson* all over the country. I was in the field
artillery and you're no good without your gun, and if you
don't have a truck with you, you can't haul your gun—so
you had plenty of room to carry these things around, and I did.
I liked the army. It was so different from any life I'd lived
up till then. That was before I ran into all kinds of trouble
from not being able to take authority from anyone anywhere.
I got into constant trouble. I finally worked up to sergeant
and got busted back to private. Then I went off to Officer
Candidate School, came out a second lieutenant, made first
lieutenant, made captain, then had a run-in with a staff
officer in Northern Ireland. I got crossways with a lieutenant
colonel on staff for making him apologize to a soldier for

cursing him. He laid for me and finally court-martialed me and I got sent back to the States and dismissed from the army. They didn't call it "dishonorable" then; they called it "other than honorable." I got back to the States and I worked on a local desk at AP for four or five months, and the war was heating up all the time. I couldn't stand it any longer, so I went down and joined the Marine Corps.

The marines had a great time with me. They said, "We understand you used to be a captain in the army. You might make a pretty good marine private if you work at it." I was in the Marine Corps a little less than a year so I didn't have enough time to get in any trouble. I would have gotten into trouble there eventually, although it's not easy to get into trouble in the marines; they take that kind of thing in stride and they don't have any objection at all to someone being somewhat crazy. Marines are mostly that way; they seem to prefer it.

Something kept me from getting my head blown off. Maybe the trouble in Northern Ireland kept me from being killed during Normandy. I was sent to combat intelligence school at Camp Lejeune and we were trained in all kinds of things. The rumor was, and I believe it was true, that we were going in on rubber boats at D-2 in Formosa, which means I most certainly would have gotten my head blown off. But they dropped the atomic bomb and put an end to the war. There's a lot of talk now about a guilt trip over dropping that bomb. Anybody who was in the army or the Marine Corps when they dropped that bomb never heard such hurrahs in his life.

INTERVIEWER

You have a reputation, across your biography, of being a bit hotheaded at times.

FOOTE

I always had trouble with authority. I never wanted anybody to tell me what I can and can't do. Imagine feeling that way in the army.

Was army service valuable to you?

FOOTE

Absolutely. All types and conditions of men. A certain hilarity of the night life—get drunk, have fights, all that stuff. Hunting was important to me at one time in my life. I haven't been hunting in twenty years. The last time I went I couldn't hit anything, so it's just as well. You really have to do that pretty steady to be any good at it—like Billy the Kid practicing. He'd get on his horse and ride along a road between fences with birds on them, and as the birds got up he'd shoot. I don't know how many of them he hit, but that was his practicing. One time Faulkner asked Howard Hawks, "Am I a better bird-shot than Hemingway?" Hawks said, "No, you're not, but my wife Slim's better than either of you."

You've heard that thing about Faulkner and Clark Gable haven't you? Howard Hawks was taking Faulkner out on a quail shoot and came by to pick him up a little before dawn to get to where they were going by first light. Clark Gable was in the car, and Faulkner in the backseat. As they rode along, Gable and Hawks got to talking. Gable said, "You know, you're a well-read man, Howard. I've always been meaning to do some reading. I never have really done it. What do you think I ought to read?" And Hawks said, "Why don't you ask Bill back there. He's a writer, and he'll be able to tell you." Gable said, "Do you write, Mr. Faulkner?" Faulkner said, "Yes, Mr. Gable. What do you do?"

INTERVIEWER

When you came out of the service, did you go back to *Tournament?*

FOOTE

Before we mobilized I put the manuscript of *Tournament* up in my mother's linen closet, and I got it out after the war. I saw something in there that I thought would make a

good story—it's about a Confederate veteran major who dies
during a Mississippi flood and they don't know how to bury
him. In any case, I took that section and I sent it to *The
Saturday Evening Post*. They took it, *boom*, like that. It was
twenty-two pages long and they paid me $750 for it. That
was a lot of money in those days for a beginning writer. I
thought, If I write one forty-four pages long maybe they'll
give me $1,500 for it. So I wrote a story forty-four pages
long—it's now in *Jordan County* and it's called "Ride Out."
I sent it to them and almost by return mail the fiction editor,
a man by the name of Stuart Rose, wrote me and said, "I don't
know whether this is a long short story or a short novelette and
I don't care." I got a check for $1,500 for it. I was pleased
with that, God knows. But I got to thinking, It's not supposed
to be like this; this is not the way you learn how to be a
writer. So I wrote one sixty-six pages long to see if I could
keep this thing going—it was a story that became half of the
novel *Love in a Dry Season*. I sent it to the *Post* and there
was no answer for about two weeks. The letter from the editor
said, "We regret to inform you that *The Saturday Evening
Post* doesn't publish stories about incest." That was the end
of my relationship with the *Post*. I was sort of relieved. I had
a strong feeling that it was not supposed to go on like this.

INTERVIEWER

You would have gone on to eighty-eight pages?

FOOTE

Right. But I knew all along it wasn't supposed to be this
way. These checks were coming in the mail and I wasn't
experiencing any of the trials and tribulations that were supposed to teach you something. So I was greatly relieved that
they finally turned something down. Then I buckled down
and wrote the novel *Shiloh*. By then I had an agent. He took
it to Dial Press and they liked it very much but said it wouldn't
sell. Did I have something else in mind? And I said, "Yes.
There's a novel called *Tournament* I'm thinking about writ-

ing." I told them what it was about; they said it sounded great and they gave me a $1,500 advance. So I went home and took it out of the linen closet again and really went through it. I had some problems with it. It'd been so loaded with influences by Thomas Wolfe and William Faulkner and other people that I really had to take a lot of that out and add things. Wherever I encountered any Proust influence I enlarged it. When I saw a Faulkner influence I reduced it. The Tom Wolfe influence I took out altogether. Then I patched the whole thing back into shape. That was my first novel. My second was *Follow Me Down*, my third was *Love in A Dry Season* and then eventually *Shiloh* came crippling in—finally got to where it could be published. After that came *Jordan County*, a collection of stories connected to each other that tried to explore a Mississippi Delta county. A present-day story starts it off and then it goes all the way back to Indian days. In other words, I tried through these stories to explore how a place became what it became—I consider it a sort of novel with place as the hero and time for the plot.

INTERVIEWER

You never really had a dry season then as a writer?

FOOTE

I had a dry season after I finished the Civil War narrative. I was either in a stage of exasperation or I felt there was nothing left to write. By a sort of secondary inertia I wrote *September September* a couple of years after I finished the war narrative. But then I intended to go back to this big novel that I had begun before I started the war.

INTERVIEWER

That's Two Gates to the City?

FOOTE

Yes: Two Gates to the City. It's about a family. It's not a saga but it's about a family, in much the same way as *The*

Brothers Karamazov is about a family. Those twenty years didn't exhaust me physically but they exhausted me from wanting to do another long work. Walker Percy said that writing a novel is like suffering from a terrible disease for a certain period of time. Then when you finish you get well again. Something like that was going on. I still may do it.

Getting old has way more virtues that it has faults, if you leave out the pain you might suffer if you have some serious injury. But I take great pleasure in being able to look back on things. I remember certain little scenes that are almost meaningless, like Thomas Wolfe coming up the library steps while I was coming down, being with William Faulkner and talking to him about his work, all kinds of things. I remember a sky without a jet trail. I remember Joan Crawford dancing. I remember Roosevelt's fireside chats and people sitting in front of the radio, like warming their hands in front of a stove. Everyone on the face of the earth has such remembrances if he lives long enough. I'm eighty years old now, which is almost inconceivable to me. I don't believe it for an instant.

INTERVIEWER

Could you describe the themes of your work? I know it's a rather broad topic to broach.

FOOTE

I'm not sure about themes except something so large as the basic loneliness of man. That's always there. But always, anything I write takes place at a certain time and a certain place. I think time, era and place—geographical location—are very, very important to me and what I'm doing. I wrote a story called "Child by Fever" and the critical time is 1910. It was a hell of a time. A black man won the world championship of boxing. Halley's Comet came along. The Russian ambassador's wife smoked a cigarette in the White House, and Taft struck the match that lit it, right there at the dinner table.

INTERVIEWER

Mark Twain died.

FOOTE

Right. A host of other things, and all of those are part of the story. They peg it down.

INTERVIEWER

So time and place anchor . . .

FOOTE

Right. So you can see why I have so little trouble transitioning to history; history was always a part of what I was doing. In any work of art, I want to know where I am and when it is; and if I don't know, I feel uneasy. I guess I have trouble with *Waiting for Godot* because it doesn't matter when or where it is.

INTERVIEWER

Could you talk a bit about your time with Faulkner and what he told you about writing, about his own work?

FOOTE

For one thing, I saw Faulkner actually reading a book only once in my life. I spent the night at his house, and we had dinner together and after dinner he went out by himself into the library there and sat down and was reading. I came out and spent a little time with him. He was reading *Bugles in the Afternoon* by Ernest Haycox. It was the only book I ever saw him actually read, although he was indeed a well-read man. He'd read a great deal, and it shows in his work. Some of his denials, such as his not having read *Ulysses*, are utterly absurd. He had read *Ulysses* to the depths. Once, in an unguarded moment, he expressed a great admiration for Proust, though he would ordinarily say, "I've never read anything like that." This is foolishness. Faulkner did not like to be questioned by people he didn't know and who didn't know him. His reaction was to lie to them: "If you're going to do this, I'll simply lie to you." The first interview he ever had, so far as I know, was in a publication long gone called

The Bookman. This was back in the early thirties. He was
making home brew in the kitchen and he was barefoot. A
reporter asked him about his family life. He said that his
mother was a Negro slave and his father was an alligator.
That's an example of what he was doing in those days. But
he was an outgoing, friendly man, once it was established
that you were friends and understood each other and above
all that you didn't want anything from him. He didn't want
anybody to want anything from him, anything including
taking his picture or anything else. He just didn't like that.
He considered it an intrusion on a privacy he valued. But he
was an interesting man. He told me any number of stories.
Some of it was embarrassing because he told me things he'd
already written, like one from "The Bear" about the bear cub
going up the tree when the train came by. So I didn't know
whether to say "Yes, I read it," or to laugh politely. I wound
up laughing politely.

INTERVIEWER

He once told you about who his great influences were, did
he not?

FOOTE

No, but we talked about that. I told him flatly that, in
my mind anyhow, the modern writers who influenced him
most were Joseph Conrad and Sherwood Anderson. Then I
made the joke that my influences were Proust and him, Faulkner, so I had every reason to be a better writer than he was
because my influences were better than his influences. He
laughed at that, and was kind enough to refrain from pointing
out that the person being influenced was also a factor in
this equation.

There was a great deal of protective pretense, I call it, in
Faulkner. Half the time he was in raggedy clothes. He liked
them. They were comfortable. But every now and then he'd
turn out just as spiffy as could be with the English tweeds.
He wore his handkerchief up his sleeve like an Englishman,
a feather in his hat.

INTERVIEWER

I saw those photographs near the end of his life when he was with the horse. Unbelievable tattered clothes.

FOOTE

That's right. That old coat. That tweed coat.

INTERVIEWER

When you talked to him about his work, did he ever talk to you about—apart from the influences—what he did and how he did it?

FOOTE

He wouldn't take it apart, but I remember I was with him just after *A Fable* came out and I said it gave me a great deal of trouble because in all of his books there was a tremendous amount of coincidence. Somebody would start from one end of the county, somebody from the other, and they'd meet and have a fight—meeting by accident. But in *A Fable* it seemed to me people were acting out roles that didn't exactly fit their personalities. I said the suicide of that young aviator who burned his jacket in the trash can didn't seem to me to be a necessary suicide. He was just unhappy the war was ending without his having a chance to fight in it, but it didn't really seem to me necessary for him to kill himself for the loss. He said, "Do you remember his name?" I said, "Yeah, his name was David." He said, "Do you remember his last name?" I said, "No, I don't." He said, "His last name was Levine. Don't you see?" I said, "No." He said, "He's one of the four Jews in *A Fable*. The story turns on those four men." I said, "Thanks for the information," which meant nothing then and still means almost nothing. But he would go to that extent if he trusted you. He would not have begun to say that to somebody who he didn't know was genuinely inter- ested and who he knew was going to make explicatory use of it in a scholarly paper or something. He wanted the book to speak for itself. That's one of the few occasions where he did any explication of his work at all. To me, I mean.

INTERVIEWER

Could you describe the first time you met Faulkner?

FOOTE

Walker Percy and I were driving from Greenville, Missis-sippi, to Sewanee, Tennessee, where we often spent one or two months in the summer. I had read *Light in August* and was tremendously impressed by it. It was the first modern novel I read—a hell of a first one, too. From that point on, all through the thirties I was reading all the Faulkner up to then: *Doctor Martino, Pylon, Absalom, The Unvanquished.* So I said, "We ought to stop by Oxford and see William Faulkner." Walker said, "I'm not going to knock on that man's door. I don't know him." I said, "Hell, he's a writer. It's all right." (A remark I've learned to regret when it's applied to me in these later years.) So we drove over to where a double line of cedars ran along the brick walk to the doorway. We parked over to the side. There were about a dozen dogs there: a dalmatian, two or three hounds, some bird dogs and three or four fox terriers. I got out of the car and waded through all those dogs and went up to the front door and knocked. The door opened and there stood Faulkner. I said, "Mr. Faulkner, my name is Shelby Foote. I'm from over at Greenville and I was wondering if you could tell me where I can find a copy of *The Marble Fawn*." (I didn't want a copy of *The Marble Faun*; that was only a cover tactic. I wanted to say hello to Mr. Faulkner.) He said, "Well, I don't have one, but my agent Leland Hayward might be able to find you one." He said, "You over from the Delta, huh." I said, "Yeah." He said, "Come on, we'll walk down this way."

INTERVIEWER

Talk about Walker Percy.

FOOTE

We met when he was fourteen and I was thirteen. We were each others' closest friends for sixty years.

INTERVIEWER

What did you learn from him?

FOOTE

I had written five novels before Walker's first came out. I was not a mentor, but I had been through an awful lot that I wanted Walker to be aware of—the dangers of the publishing world and so on. In our letters, which recently have been published, I'm constantly telling him what to do and what not to do—that's a result of this five-book head start. Later it settled down to something else because Walker became in the next two or three decades a far better-known writer than I was. He won the National Book Award and respect all round. But that friendship meant a great deal to me. I learned a lot from Walker because he was interested in areas I had never known existed. I'd never read Kierkegaard or Marcel or Maritain or any of those. Still haven't read them, incidentally. I poke at them, but I don't get anywhere with them. Right up to the end, we got along fine. We knew what would make each other angry so we never mentioned those things except on purpose. We made a lot of trips together. Walker had a remarkable stubbornness that would come out sometimes. We got on an Amtrak train in Chicago, along with our wives, to go to San Francisco. You have this great plateglass window and, along the way, you really do see the deer and the antelope play. We got to Ogden, Utah, which is where they drove the golden spike. It was about eleven-thirty at night. The train stopped, and the engineers came through hollering, "All out, all out. There's an engineers' strike. Buses are waiting to take you to San Francisco." I began to scurry around, to get our bags straight so they didn't get lost in the shuffle, and Walker never moved from his bed. The conductor came around and said, "You'd better get up. This bus will be leaving soon." Walker said, "I'm not going anywhere. I've got a ticket that says you're going to take me to San Francisco." The man says, "Well, we're going to close down the air conditioner and turn off the electricity." Walker says, "If you do, I'll sue you for every cent the US government's got." So the man said, "Sorry, sorry, stay here." We stayed on the train. Everybody else got on the bus. The next morning early we got up and they had a minibus take us to Salt Lake City. We got on an airplane and got to San Francisco before the buses did. But this is the kind of stubbornness he had. I later found out he either had taken a powerful sleeping pill or a laxative, I'm not sure which. He was not about to get off that train onto any bus.

Walker Percy and I are very different writers. I do a strict outline, which helps me enormously. I always say if I were going to do a dance I would make sure that I had a good platform to dance on so I wouldn't worry about the thing collapsing. I do that on the novel, always leaving room for stretching things or making it shorter, or adding this or taking this out; I like a good outline to go with it. Walker, on the other hand, not only had no outline but he said, not entirely joking, that if he knew what was going to happen next he wouldn't be interested in writing about it. He wrote to find out what was going to happen, and then when he finished the first draft he really had to get to work because he had to go all the way back to find out how it had all started.

INTERVIEWER

How long does it take you to do an outline before sitting down to write?

FOOTE

Not long at all. I could do it on the back of an envelope, Lincoln-style. There is not a great deal of thought about theme and all that. It's all mechanics. You have this information that is to be released. In the writing itself is where you really bring it off. I learned a lot about the organization of material from Henry James. James actually wrote scenarios. We've got the scenario for *The Ambassadors*, for instance—15,000 words. Once he had his scenario, he flew by it.

INTERVIEWER

Which comes first, character or plot?

FOOTE

Character comes first. I separate the mass of novels into good and bad. A good book could be described as one about a man who, in a situation, does such and such. A bad book is about a *situation* in which a man does such and such. In other words, plot ought to grow out of character. You don't have to make up a plot. You have to have a person and place him in a situation, and a plot starts happening. When you take a person like Harley Drew in *Dry Season* and you introduce him into a Mississippi town, things are going to start happening. That's the way it should be, it seems to me.

INTERVIEWER

A character, in fiction, will take on a life of his or her own . . .

FOOTE

Absolutely. As they do in history. They come more alive for you and, therefore, for the reader. The character will do something, and you will say, "Hey, I hadn't expected him to do that. Why did he do that?" And then you find out why. Some things that sound unattractive can be attractive. Ulysses S. Grant, for instance, was never willing to accept blame for anything, under any circumstances. He would let no blame attach to him. He always blamed somebody who was alongside him or under him or over him. It becomes a key to understanding the strength of his character. He just didn't admit the possibility that anything could be his fault. That sounds unattractive, but it's quite attractive in Grant. It's so much a part of his character and part of his ability to be a great general.

INTERVIEWER

What about General Robert E. Lee?

FOOTE
The single greatest mistake of the war by any general on either side was made by Robert E. Lee at Gettysburg, when he sent Pickett's and Pettigrew's divisions across that open field, nearly a mile wide, against guns placed on a high ridge and troops down below them, with skirmishers out front. There was no chance it would succeed. Longstreet told him that beforehand, and Lee proceeded to prove him right. Having made this greatest of all mistakes, Lee rode out on the field and met those men coming back across the field—casualties were well over fifty percent—and said, "It's all my fault." He said it then on the field; he said it afterwards, after he'd gotten across the Potomac; he said it in his official report a month later. He said, "I may have asked more of my men than men should be asked to give." He's a noble man, noble beyond comparison.

INTERVIEWER
When researching *The Civil War*, you used the 128-volume—

FOOTE
The War of the Rebellion: A Compilation of the Official Records of the Union and Confederate Armies. It includes the field orders, battle reports, correspondence. It's a remarkable publication, and the one for the navy is equally good—there are about forty volumes of it. They're sometimes written under terrific pressure, and you can just *feel* what a man was going through.

INTERVIEWER
You mentioned historians in general. Who do you think are the greatest Civil War historians?

FOOTE
It's hard to say. Certainly the early ones like G.F.R Henderson, whose *Stonewall Jackson* came out around the turn of

the century, a biography of Nathan Bedford Forrest by John A. Wyeth, who had been a Confederate soldier. The modern historian who really started addressing the Civil War in a scholarly way is, of course, Douglas Southall Freeman, who wrote a four-volume biography of Lee and three volumes on Lee's lieutenants. They've got their flaws. Freeman's so much of a Virginian that he couldn't see anything but Virginia. He limited himself to writing about Virginia except when he sent Longstreet out for the fight at Chickamauga, and he made pretty much of a mess of that. He was so Virginia biased and his dislike of Longstreet was so strong that it warped his work. He's not a stylist. He writes sort of jogtrot prose, but once the reader becomes accustomed to it, it somehow seems just right.

INTERVIEWER

Do you think there's a bias in your history?

FOOTE

I like to think there's not. I've been complimented for an absence of bias; I've had people tell me that if they didn't already know, they couldn't tell whether I was a Northerner or a Southerner, but you can't help noticing that my heart beats a little faster when the Confederacy is out front. Bias is an interesting thing to try to deal with. It can make you work harder to be fair. There are two generals in the Civil War I acquired an increasing dislike for. One was Joe Johnston, a Confederate general. The other was Phil Sheridan, a Union general. At every chance I praised them. They were easy to praise because they were damn fine generals, both adored by their men, so that you always had that point to make. But Joe Johnston spent his whole life backing up. If he'd been kept in command while Atlanta was coming under siege, he'd have wound up in Key West complaining that something was rounding one of his flanks. And Phil Sheridan hated Southerners so much, he used to go around punching his fist into the palm of the other hand saying, "Smash 'em up. Smash 'em up." All the same, he was inspiring to his troops, and a hell of a fighter.

Had you been alive during the Civil War, would you have
fought for the Confederates?

No doubt about it. What's more, I would fight for the
Confederacy today if the circumstances were similar. There's
a great deal of misunderstanding about the Confederacy,
the Confederate flag, slavery, the whole thing. The political
correctness of today is no way to look at the middle of the
nineteenth century. The Confederates fought for some substantially good things. States rights is not just a theoretical
excuse for oppressing people. You have to understand that
the raggedy Confederate soldier who owned no slaves and
probably couldn't even read the Constitution, let alone understand it, when he was captured by Union soldiers and
asked, "What are you fighting for?" replied, "I'm fighting
because you're down here." So I certainly would have fought
to keep people from invading my native state. There's another
good reason for fighting for the Confederacy. Life would have
been intolerable if you hadn't. The women of the South just
would not allow somebody to stay home and sulk while the
war was going on. It didn't take conscription to grab him.
The women made him go.

What about fighting to end the institution of slavery?

The institution of slavery is a stain on this nation's soul
which will never be cleansed. It is just as wrong as wrong can
be, a huge sin, and it is on our soul. There's a second sin
that's almost as great, and that's emancipation. They told
4,500,000 people, "You are free, hit the road." And we're
still suffering from that. Three quarters of them couldn't read
or write, not one tenth of them had a profession, except for
farming, and yet they were turned loose and told, "Go your

way." In 1877 the last Union troops were withdrawn, after a
dozen years of being in the South to assure compliance with
the law. Once they were withdrawn, all the Jim Crow laws
and everything else came down on the blacks. Their schools
were inferior in every sense. They had the Freedmen's Bureau,
which did, perhaps, some good work, but it was mostly a
joke, corrupt in all kinds of ways. So they had no help. Just
turned loose on the world, and they were waifs. It's a very
sad thing. There should have been a huge program for schools.
There should have been all kinds of employment provided
for them. Not modern welfare, you can't expect that in the
middle of the nineteenth century, but there should have been
some earnest effort to prepare these people for citizenship.
They were not prepared, and operated under horrible disad-
vantages once the army was withdrawn, and some of the
consequences are very much with us today.

INTERVIEWER

Bedford Forrest's picture hangs on your wall. He was an
ex-slave trader, responsible for the Fort Pillow massacre of
captured black soldiers, and after the war deeply involved in
the Ku Klux Klan.

FOOTE

You could add that in hand-to-hand combat he killed
thirty-one men, mostly in saber duels or pistol shootings, and
he had thirty horses shot from under him. Forrest is one of
the most attractive men who ever walked through the pages
of history; he surmounted all kinds of things and you better
read back again on the Fort Pillow massacre instead of some
piece of propaganda about it. Fort Pillow was a beautiful
operation, tactically speaking. Forrest did everything he could
to stop the killing of those people who were in the act of
surrendering, and did stop it. Forrest himself was never a
bloodthirsty sort of man who enjoyed slaughter. He also took
better care of his soldiers and his black teamsters than any
other general I know of. He was a man who, at the age of

sixteen, had to raise six younger brothers and sisters after the
death of his blacksmith father. He became a slave trader
because that was a way of making enough money to support
all those people and to get wealthy. Forrest was worth about
a million dollars when the war started, an alderman for the
city of Memphis. He was by no means some cracker who came
out of nowhere. All writers will have great sympathy with
Forrest for something he said. He did not like to write and
there are very few Forrest letters. He said, "I never see a
pen but I think of a snake." He's an enormously attractive,
outgoing man once you get to know him and once you get
to know more facts. For instance, he was probably Imperial
Wizard of the Ku Klux Klan, but he dissolved that Klan in
1869; said it's getting ugly, it's getting rough, and he did
away with it. The Klan you're talking about rose again in
this century and was particularly powerful during the 1920s.
Forrest would have had no sympathy with that later Klan.
Last thing in the world was he anti-Catholic or anti-Semitic,
which is what that Klan was mainly in the twenties. I have
a hard time defending the Klan and I don't really intend to
defend it; I would never have joined it myself, even back in
its early days. But I don't know what you expected men,
having gone through four years of utterly savage war, to do—if
you expected them to come home and put up quietly with
the kind of occupation that happened in France after World
War II. The French Maquis did far worse things than the Ku
Klux Klan ever did—who never blew up trains or burnt
bridges or anything else; they didn't even have lynchings.
The Klan is as nefarious as you want it to be, but you have
to understand better what they did do and they did not do.
And the "massacre" at Fort Pillow, so-called, truly had better
be investigated more closely. When word of the massacre at
Fort Pillow got up to Washington, Lincoln wrote to Grant
and said, This is intolerable, I want whoever was responsible
for it punished. Grant passed the word along to Sherman. If
you know anything about Sherman, you know he would have
jumped on Forrest like a tiger if he'd been guilty. Sherman

never recommended anything along those lines. They sent a committee of Congress down to investigate Fort Pillow and they took testimony from people who were obviously lying their heads off, talking about people being buried alive, women and children shot while pleading for their lives. If you read a biography of Bedford Forrest, you'll get some notion of what a fine man he was.

INTERVIEWER

Is there too much focus on the military in writing about the Civil War?

FOOTE

Well, Forrest said war means fighting, and fighting means killing. The Civil War was simply a four-year military action. The causes were so nebulous and so diverse. Lincoln said plainly, "What I do about slavery I do because I want to win this war. If I could win this war by freeing all the slaves tomorrow, I'd do it. If I could win this war by keeping them all in slavery, I'd do that. I'd do anything to win this war." The emphasis was on war, "this mighty scourge." Almost everybody realized that the various bickerings and arguments and the fire-eaters in South Carolina and the abolitionists in Massachusetts, were sort of outside of things really. All they did was cause it. The real monster of the Civil War was that it cost us God knows what all, not only in young men, blue and gray, but in the recasting of what public life was going to be like. It brought a new cynicism in to us that we've lived with ever since. We began to appreciate scamps in politics, which we hadn't really done before. It was a military action and was to be studied as such—not neglecting the causes, not neglecting the arguments of what went on, but it's always primarily combat.

INTERVIEWER

As a Southerner, and with the benefit of hindsight, do you believe the South fought the war as well as it could?

FOOTE

No, nobody ever fights wars as well as they should have, especially in hindsight. But I do think that the South came closer to putting everything it had into that war than any nation I know of. So many things happened to show you how deep the commitment went. About the time that war started I think roughly eighty-five or ninety percent of the teachers in this country were men. After the war was over something like eighty-five to ninety percent of teachers were women. Those women who went through that war had to live in the modern world before there was a modern world. They had to take over jobs that they later would be clamoring for, but they had the responsibility on their hands and they did a good job, mainly, of running things. Now how you could ask a woman—my great-grandmother for instance—how you could ask her to run a plantation, keep up a thirty-two-room house with half the slaves gone and her husband off somewhere shooting and getting shot at. But she did it. I think Northern women did much of that too. The South was aggravated enormously by the effects of the blockade. There were little things that could run you crazy. You couldn't get needles to sew with; they used thorns and things. You couldn't get nails to keep your floors from coming loose or the roof from sagging in. There were many things that tried them awfully hard, not to mention marauding armies passing through killing all your chickens and pigs. It's been romanticized, but it's easy to do because it is highly romantic.

INTERVIEWER

I'm going to go back to what you said earlier about Lee. Lee had such a great track record at that particular time. Why do you think he made the choice regarding Pickett's charge given all of his long success?

FOOTE

This is another instance of life imitating art. Not only had he won those battles leading up to Gettysburg—Chancellorsville was only one month back—but the first day he nearly crushed the Union army. Then when that army grew and took position on that ridge he charged it on the second day and got all the way to the top. If he'd pushed further he'd have taken it. We go back to Greek tragedy now; the gods were leading him to destruction. That's not an overstatement. He never would have made this greatest of all errors without these greatly encouraging things that were happening one after another. He was facing much shorter odds than he had at Chancellorsville, where he won a great victory. He was just being pulled along. I don't claim that the gods made him mad in order to destroy him, but they did suck him in to committing this most grievous of all errors. It's almost unbelievable that it can be so in tune with Greek tragedy, but it is.

INTERVIEWER

You talk about the gods, and life imitating art. Is that alive in your cosmos?

FOOTE

Yes, I think that it prints things in your mind and clarifies them for you. It's very useful in doing that. I think that's one of history's main jobs—to let men know what happened, before, so they won't make the same mistake afterward. Also, the Romans believed history was intended to publicize, if you will, the lives of great men so that we would have something to emulate. That'll do as one of the definitions. It's really, really and truly, a search for truth. One of the greatest writers that ever lived is William Faulkner. And he's praised for a great many things. But what Faulkner could really do better than any writer I know, with the exception of Shakespeare—like in music you say with the exception of Mozart—Faulkner could communicate sensations, the texture of things. He could tell you what this feels like [*rubs his fingers on the table-cloth*]—that particular cloth, the way it rubs on your fingertips. He could make you feel it by describing it. That's our job. That's what you have to do, as Conrad said so often.

You have to communicate sensation, the belief in what life is, what it's about, and you do it through learning how to handle a pen. That's the reason why I have always felt comfortable with the pen in my hand and extremely uncomfortable having some piece of machinery between me and the paper—even a typewriter let alone a word computer, which just gives me the horrors.

INTERVIEWER

What makes a work survive?

FOOTE

I don't have much trouble giving an easy answer to that, which is—true excellence. Of course, you can be misled. When I was fifteen and starting out to read in earnest, everybody knew who the greatest writer in the world was—absolutely no doubt about it; he had no rival; his work was so pure, it could never perish—Anatole France, who is close to forgotten nowadays and probably deservedly so. Since the death of Tolstoy, France had been the leading writer in the world, the Western world anyhow. It's hard to say, but it seems to me that both Hemingway and, to a lesser degree, John O'Hara, are bound to come back. I'm far less sure about O'Hara than I am about Hemingway. But I'm absolutely certain of Hemingway's position in American literature. He's right up there with Twain and Faulkner.

INTERVIEWER

A great enthusiasm of American literature for a short period was Thomas Wolfe. How do you explain how everybody loved him with such passion at a certain moment in our history, and then suddenly nobody can read him anymore.

FOOTE

I'm not sure nobody can read him, because the people who read him with the greatest enthusiasm were young people. We were young when we read him, and when we read him it had a pure zest to it, larger than life. It was wonderful. He stated all the problems eloquently, or at least with verve and gusto, and he didn't give you any solutions. When you get older or you pass the age of reason—whenever that is—you begin to be more interested in things than just exclamations about ain't nature grand. That's what Rebecca West said about Goethe. She said it can all be summed up: "Ain't nature grand." But Rebecca West was ruled all her life by a consuming hatred of everything German, including Goethe. I like Rebecca West, though. *Black Lamb and Grey Falcon* is one of my favorite books.

INTERVIEWER

You mentioned John O'Hara.

FOOTE

I'm a big O'Hara fan. He's largely unread nowadays, alas. He wrote sixteen or seventeen novels, nearly all of them now out of print. *Appointment in Samarra* is in The Modern Library now, but the novel *From the Terrace*, which he considered his best work, is out of print along with the others, including the short-story collections. If Faulkner is our Dickens, O'Hara is our Trollope, and someday I hope he'll be recognized as such. Moreover, he is one of the few American writers who can write about women. Mostly we're not good at women. The biggest flaw in both Hemingway and Faulkner is that their women are scarcely women at all. Maybe we're going to get better, now that women have asserted themselves to the degree they have. But we have tended to romanticize them. Faulkner's very bad about it—and he's afraid of them, too.

INTERVIEWER

Did you ever meet O'Hara?

FOOTE

No, I never did. Always wanted to, and everybody tells me I was very fortunate not to. A most objectionable man, they say, but I don't think that would have bothered me. He had an experience I could have made him feel better about. When Faulkner was getting the Nobel Prize, Bennett Cerf had a small dinner party for him the evening before he left for Sweden. O'Hara and his wife were there. O'Hara was a very sentimental man in many ways. Philip Barry, the well-known playwright and a good friend of O'Hara, had given him an engraved cigarette lighter. O'Hara, in salute to Faulkner for winning the Nobel and for at last getting to meet and talk with him, said, "I have something for you." He gave Faulkner the cigarette lighter. Faulkner put it in his pocket without even a thank you. O'Hara's feelings were terribly hurt; he felt that Faulkner should have realized that this lighter meant a great deal to him. Well, I could have told O'Hara that of all the objects on the face of the earth Faulkner despised most, the worst was a cigarette lighter! He once said, "I cannot understand how Bennett could use one of those things. To light a pipe with a cigarette lighter, you might as well be smoking gasoline!" So if I'd met O'Hara, I could have told him that Faulkner was really quite considerate in not saying, "Get that goddamn thing out of my sight!"

Faulkner said a funny thing. He told Ben Wasson once, "All these people are talking about me having genius and all that. I don't know anything about that, but I can tell you one time I had genius and that was when I named these people Snopes." A writer is a little like a painter. You tell him that you admire his picture, and he'll stand there looking at it, and he'll say "Well, I like that part here," and he'll point to some little patch of nothing in one corner.

INTERVIEWER

In a letter to Walker Percy in 1951 you wrote, "I think the novelist's principal task is the communication of sensation. If he does this, and does it right, he has rescued something from time and chaos." Do you still feel that way?

FOOTE

Yes, I do. Sensation means to communicate the tactile nature of things. What's it like to walk out in the rain? Those things. Faulkner does it superbly.

INTERVIEWER
What about Hemingway?

FOOTE

There's an interesting difference between Faulkner and Hemingway. Hemingway, in *Death in the Afternoon*, says that he understood his mission as a writer from attending a bullfight in which there was a young fighter, a novice, in a cheap rented suit, out there with a bull, obviously scared to death, timorous and jumpy. The bull got the tip of its horn in his thigh just above the knee and ripped it all the way up and tore up this cheap suit and laid open a wound in which you could see the white bone and the red meat. In *Death in the Afternoon* (I'm paraphrasing) he says, I saw what my job as a writer was—to understand the essence of the emotion I felt when I saw that white bone and red meat. Faulkner, on the other hand, believed that the essence of emotions was a very complicated thing. He has Ratliff at some point in *The Hamlet* saying, "You can't tell a story and really communicate it. You've got to complicate it up. It ain't complicated-up enough." So here are two great writers with totally different notions about the basic nature of what they're trying to do, both realists but each in a very different way. Faulkner does it by communicating this tremendously complex combination of sensations, Hemingway by honing everything down to the essential pang. Faulkner in his Nobel speech says that you have to write about the heart, otherwise you're just writing about the glands. He said this with scorn. Yet Faulkner wrote about the glands better than anybody I know.

INTERVIEWER

What happened after *September September*? There's a long hiatus.

FOOTE

What happened after *September September* was the TV *Civil War*. For one thing, comparatively speaking, I got rich. That makes a difference. Artie Shaw once said that what you need to write the blues is no money in the bank and nobody loving you. Maybe writing prose is the same way, at its best.

At one point you said that you were going to write five novels, and then you were going to write five more.

I was going to write another five after taking a year, or maybe two years, off. Instead, I launched into *The Civil War* and spent twenty years on it. I would have written another five novels or so, at least, if I hadn't written *The Civil War*.

Has Hollywood ever beckoned?

I have always been aware of certain dangers. Stanley Kubrick wanted me to do a film script for him about a Civil War incident in the Shenandoah Valley. That was right after I had begun writing about the war in 1954. But I had conditions. The main one was that I wouldn't come to California, and the reason I wouldn't go to California was all that weather, all those beautiful women, all that money. I was absolutely certain I would disappear as if into quicksand; I'd be gone. With those three things holding me there, I certainly wasn't going to do any writing. So I said I'd be glad to do it, but I couldn't come out there. He said "It's no problem. We can meet in New York just as well." So I did the script for him. He never made the movie. He made *Lolita* instead and never looked back.

What was the script?

It was called *The Down Slope* and it's about John Mosby when Sheridan had Custer's division hang six of his rangers.

Mosby from then on, when he captured one of Custer's men, had him taken to a schoolhouse in the backwoods until he had about fifty of them. Then he had them line up and draw slips of paper out of a hat. Six of them would be hanged in retaliation. You can imagine the relief everybody felt who got a blank slip instead of a black dot. Then they discovered that one of the black-dot unfortunates was a drummer boy about fourteen years old, and Mosby said, "I'm not hanging no boys. Have them draw again." So they had to draw again. That was the plot. But Kubrick never made it.

INTERVIEWER

Have any of your books been made into a film?

FOOTE

September September was made into a movie called *Memphis*. It was made for television. Cybill Shepard starred in it.

INTERVIEWER

Was it any good?

FOOTE

It had its points. They left out everything that was best about the book and stressed everything that was least best—instead of bad, least best. And I was not happy about it but I don't take it that seriously. Anything they want to do with it is all right with me. On the screen, I mean—it's out of my league or control.

INTERVIEWER

You're a movie fan of a sort?

FOOTE

Oh yeah, all my life.

INTERVIEWER

What about the influence of film on your writing and on writing in general?

FOOTE

I think it's had a large influence on writers ever since the movies began. I read a piece once about Fitzgerald. Remember how *Gatsby* opens. The film comes on, moves over the lawn, and up that wall. That's a long shot—it's a camera shot. It's absolutely a straight camera shot. There's a great deal of that all round. Truman Capote picked up on it in a very canny way.

INTERVIEWER

You're at work now?

FOOTE

I've done a few things. I've done some introductions. I'm on the board of the Modern Library, where I've written an introduction to Stephen Crane's *Red Badge of Courage*. I've drawn up books that I hope they'll publish. Three short novels of Dostoyevsky, a three-volume Chekhov, two-volume Maupassant, arguments about including this, not including that. So I'm doing things. Many of the things having to do with the Civil War, I decline. I had a funny experience with that. I knew there was one thing I would never write anything more about and that was the Civil War. Not long after I finished the *War* and the dust sort of settled, I got a letter from *National Geographic* saying that they were doing a special on parks and Shiloh National Park was one of them and would I contribute 1,500 words? They'd pay me $3000. Well, for once in my life I wanted to make $2 a word, writing, and besides I could write Shiloh in my sleep; I had already written a novel and a straight historical book about it. I sat down and I got interested and wound up with 4,500 words. I sent it to them and I said, "I'm sorry part of this got away from me." And they wrote back and said "We're just absolutely delighted, but all the other pieces are 1,500 words. We can stretch to 3,000 words without too much trouble." I said, "Well that's no problem, send it back, I'll just cut it down to 3,000 words." So they sent it back. It's the first time I ever tried to cut anything, and I thought it would be easy.

You know: just take this out, and that and that. But every-where I cut it, it would bleed. So I sent it back to them and said, "I find that I can't cut this thing but surely you have people up there who know how to do this." Next thing I knew, I got galley proofs and found their method of cutting was to take the middle out of every other sentence. They broke its back. I had to rewrite the whole thing. I never worked so hard for $3,000 in my life as I did with that thing.

INTERVIEWER

But you got $2 a word.

FOOTE

Well, as a matter of fact I didn't because it was 3,000 words. Only one dollar a word. And all of this took me a month or so. I could've been parking cars and made more money than that, with far less strain on my crotchety dispo-sition.

INTERVIEWER

What kind of advice would you give young writers?

FOOTE

To read, and above all to reread. When you read, you get the great pleasure of discovering what happened. When you reread, you get the great pleasure of knowing where the author's going and seeing how he goes about getting there: and that's learning creative writing. I would tell a young writer that. Of course I would tell him: work, work, work, sit at that desk and sweat. You don't have to have a plot, you don't have to have anything. Describe someone crossing a room, and try to do it in a way that won't perish. Put it down on paper. Keep at it. Then when you finally figure out how to handle words pretty well, try to tell a story. It won't be worth a damn; you'll have to tear it up and throw it away. But then try to do it again, do it again, and then keep doing it, until you can do it. You may never be able to do it. That's

the gamble. You not only may not be able to make a living,
you may not be able to do it at all. But that's what you put
on the line. Every artist has that. He doesn't deserve a whole
lot of credit for it. He didn't choose it. It was visited upon
him. Somebody asks, "When did you decide you wanted to
be a writer?" I never decided I wanted to be a writer. I simply
woke up a writer one morning.

INTERVIEWER

I remember Saul Bellow once said, "You anoint yourself
as a writer."

FOOTE

That's right. One of the most remarkable jobs of becoming
a writer I ever heard of was done by one of my favorite writers,
Robert Browning. Browning decided at the age of fourteen,
I think, out of the clear blue sky, to become a writer. His father
had books all over the house anyway. He said, "If I'm going
to be a writer, there's certainly one thing I must do," and
then he proceeded to memorize Johnson's *Dictionary*—both
volumes, cover to cover. He has, next to Shakespeare, the largest
vocabulary of any English writer. Now that's *preparation*.

INTERVIEWER

Why do you write?

FOOTE

Freud says we write for three basic reasons: desire for fame,
money and the love of women. I don't argue with any of
those three. They're all there. Notice he didn't say a mumbling word about inspiration or duty or anything like that.
Desire for fame, desire for money and the love of women.

INTERVIEWER

Is this accurate in your case?

FOOTE

I wouldn't deny it an iota.

INTERVIEWER
Is there a fourth reason that Freud didn't name?

FOOTE
The joy of writing. To write well is a huge pleasure, and you feel awfully good doing it. One of the greatest enemies of happiness, of enjoying life, is the intrusion of loneliness. When you're most alone is in nausea: when you're throwing up you are alone on the face of this earth. The moment of orgasm is very lonely, too—a little island in the middle of nowhere. There are a lot of paradoxes involved. When you're working very hard you're not lonely; you are the whole damn world. I have a strong feeling that the very worst writing of all comes out of what's called inspiration. Good writing doesn't come from inspiration. It may spark you, set you off, but if you write under the influence of inspiration, you will write very badly—probably sentimentally, which is even worse. Inspiration certainly better not be governing the thing; you had better have learned your craft through very hard work, reading and writing, and cold observation. People say, "My God, I can't believe that you really worked that hard for twenty years. How in God's name did you do it?" Well, obviously I did it because I enjoyed it. I don't deserve any credit for working hard. I was doing what I wanted to do. Shakespeare said it best: "The labor we delight in physics pain." There's no better feeling in the world than to lay your head on the pillow at night looking forward to getting up in the morning and returning to that desk. That's real happiness.

—Carter Coleman,
Donald Faulkner,
William Kennedy

Mary Gordon

Prayers

For Liars

For makers of elaborated worlds, adorned and peopled by the creatures and the furniture of their inventions. For those who live as if the way things are were not enough and mean, by their words, to do something about it. For those who would protect the first beloved from the fresh reality of the second. For fabricators of plausible excuses that will save the fragile hostess's *amour-propre*. For ornamenters who cannot endure a history without clear heroes and sharp villains. For speakers of the phrases "it's a fabulous haircut" or "of course you aren't gaining weight." For forgers of Old Masters and fakers of *petites morts*. For advertisers presenting a Paradise that can be bought or cures passed quick, over the counter, sellers of temporary, unlikely, but not impossible hopes: the Brooklyn Bridge, the golf course in the swamp. Keep them from the terror of the hunted, the ring of hounds barking in the freezing air, "the truth, the truth, why can't you tell the truth for once?" Shelter them in their dream of an earth more various than our own. Preserve them from diseases of the tongue, the mouth, the lips. For Your sake, who have thought of universes not yet made, which rest, like lies, in the Mind of Your Infinite Love.

For Those Who Have Given Up Everything for Sexual Love

O Lord, fount of Desire and its source, have mercy on these Thy servants who have followed the words of their flesh in the innocence of its singleness. Who have acted in accordance with its urging and obeyed it in humility, bowing the knee before its strength, knowing it greater than their own. Who have, in unity with its precepts (believing they were spoken in Your voice), turned their backs on the sweetness of habit, lost the regard of their fellows, endured the world's shame, suffered remorse, the abandonment of those by whom they knew and named and recognized themselves. Who have refused the blandishments of prosperity, the comforts of home, the pride of faithfulness, the honor of the law.

Protect the reckless, for they gave everything in Your name, their losses have been great.

Keep them from the plagues that they could understand as punishment.

Vouchsafe that in the light proceeding from Your light, they may reap the rewards of their sacrifice and be repaid a hundredfold.

Grant that we who have lacked their courage may be strengthened by their example to pursue our partial loves with gladness and fullness of heart.

For Those Whose Work Is Invisible

For those who paint the undersides of boats, makers of ornamental drains on roofs too high to be seen; for cobblers who labor over inner soles; for seamstresses who stitch the wrong sides of linings; for scholars whose research leads to no obvious discovery; for dentists who polish each gold surface of the fillings of upper molars; for sewer engineers and those who repair water mains; for electricians; for artists who suppress what does injustice to their visions; for surgeons whose sutures are things of beauty. For all those whose work is for Your eye only, who labor for Your entertainment or their own, who sleep in peace or do not sleep in peace, knowing that their effects are unknown.

Protect them from downheartedness and from diseases of the eye.

Grant them perseverance, for the sake of Your love which is humble, invisible and heedless of reward.

For Those Who Devote Themselves to Personal Adornment

For office workers who have fallen into debt because they spend their salaries on dresses, for women who require regular appointments with podiatrists to compensate for the ravages of years on high heels, for the victims of disastrous plastic surgery, for those who deprive themselves of sugar, for invalids who rise from bed only to dress and make up and then fall back exhausted, for those who weep in front of mirrors, for those with great legs and bad tempers, for mutton dressed as lamb, for those who sweat and strain their muscles out of fidelity to the illusions of a form.

Spare them diseases of the skin and teeth, for in their sacrifice of time and health and friendship they have given hope to strangers whose hearts have been lifted at the sight of a line that finishes itself finely, of colors undreamed of by nature, of constructions which at once affirm and quite deny the body's range.

Bless them, because a change of fashion can allow us to believe there could just be, for all of us, a change of heart.

Grant this for the sake of Your love, which has adorned the mountains and created feathers and elaborate tails, O Lord, source of all that exists for delight only, for display only, suggestions, in the joy of their variety, of the ecstacy of light which is eternal, changeless and ever-changing.

For the Wasteful

O God, in Your benevolence look with kindness upon those who travel first class in high season, on those who spend whole afternoons in cafés, those who replay songs on jukeboxes, who engage in trivial conversations, who memorize jokes and card tricks, those who tear open their gifts and will not save the wrapping, who hate leftovers and love room service, who do not wait for sales. For all foolish virgins, for those who knowingly give their hearts to worthless charmers, for collectors of snowman paperweights, memorial cups and souvenir pens. For those who take the long way home.

We pray to You, whose love is prodigal, who multiplied the loaves and fishes so that there were baskets upon baskets left, who turned plain water into wine of a quality no one required, who gave Your life when You need only have lifted a finger, protect these, Your servants, from afflictions of the hand, cover their foolish bets and greet them with that mercy whose greatness is unearnable by calculation or by thrift.

For Those Who Misuse or Do Not Use or Cannot Use Their Gifts

For conservatory-trained composers of incidental music, for beauties run to fat, for the patrons of charlatans, for athletes who watch television, for poets who write commercials, for mathematicians turned card-sharks, for Legal Aid lawyers turned corporate counsel, for actors who are waiters, for wives who do not wish to stay at home, for cat-lovers afraid of mess, for paramours who fear transmittable diseases, for those who no longer go to auditions, for blacksmiths and letterpress printers.

Lord who created manna in the desert and who caused to flow the living springs, who made disciples of fishermen and tax collectors, and a king of a shepherd boy, grant these Thy servants the gift of new enthusiasms, protect them from diseases of the spine, so that they may turn and bend to glimpse Your Hand at the fork of roads not taken, at the tunnel's end.

Martha Silano

What I Meant to Say Before I Said "So Long"

for Dante Alfredo Silano

There will be spiders the size of your ears, drinks
that will make you stupid, matches you'll long
to strike; there will be mop-ups the size of Rhode Island.

Or you'll be driving at night beneath the cloud-hidden
     Perseids
but the car in front will lose a wheel, spray a million sparks.
The spider won't drop its strand above your bed,

but choose a far corner. Don't kill it.
What it spins will rival what (dewfully, sparklingly) hangs
from your neighbor's hedge. Your father loves

what shines—the flash in the pan, two-penny nugget
glint, what might lead him from buckets, latex, brush's
swish, loves the gleam that was you

in his eye. As a child he built fires beneath a rising
Dog Star, ignored the heat, his mother's *nos*,
heard only "go ahead, Matty-boy, my Tee-too, my Shaver,
     build

whatever you like." Loved what was left
when the brightness died, to fish the yard
for the stubs of rockets. What he kindled in Ash Flat—

eight miles from Evening Shade, the lift of earth
that is Ozarks—he feeds logs to now (last stop
before the flashing CHAINS REQUIRED), where the spark

between him and your mother . . . where you were born.
Ashland. Which must be why they named you
Dante, an unlit match held close

to a blaze, what it means to burn like hope.
He pans for gold, tells us by the crow's fly (by the eagle,
by the osprey), we're close to a mine, scars

in the side of a hill, close to where the flood of '64
tore the earth, unearthed the glimmers he dreams of.
He's got scars on his back and stretches of road

he can't recall, but don't be scared: all that firewater's
behind him, the bottomless tap, beer after golden beer. . . .
His love for explosives cost him all the gold

in the Applegate Valley, "Possession of a Firearm"
    emblazoned
on screens from Metuchen to Tucson—"a pellet gun; I shot
at the sky . . ." (not that we're here

forever, not that we don't live
in the shadow of live volcanoes, the chance
we'll wake to at least a dusting

of ash). "So long, trooper,"
I managed to say, your father asking
for Roman Candles, Dancing Bees, Flower Clusters,

"stuff that shoots out sparks." South of Eugene,
two hundred miles from your eager hands,
the sun through clouds a million motionless searchlights,

I began to fall in a trap. *Don't let boredom grip you
the way you gripped my finger. Let even the seemingly
starkest places yield you black-eyed Susans. Learn*

from the woman who with her entire body tells you,
"I've done all this." Since each of us will soon
be part of the meal, since we're more like tents

than mountains, and mountains disappear . . .
(spinning . . . sinking . . . fuel light
an ember . . . finally sputtering out).

Peg Boyers

Open Letter to Alberto Moravia

La Stampa, July 14, 1971

Dear Alberto,

It's true: I am a coward. The other night,
at dinner, I neglected to tell you how much
I detest your latest novel. Had you asked me,
I would have found a way to say something not
exactly false, but less than true: *You've done it again!*
A tour de force! But your thoughts were already
elsewhere, in Persia perhaps, or Turkey, where
your translators would soon greet you, whirling
at the airport with garlands and rare oils, adoring dervishes
ready to anoint you their new byzantine king.

Great One, Monolith
                    —*ormai amico dopo tanti anni*—
you still frighten me. Impatient mentor, enormous
nourisher: your power paralyzes. I owe you
my honesty, but I shrink from the physical you.
Forgive me this public confession.

Now that you are away in Arabia with an Arab,
I'll tell you what I think, here, in the newspaper.
They say a public place is always best
for the most intimate fights. Yesterday
I overheard a pair of estranged lovers at the corner
rosticceria as they hammered out the terms of their separation
while the waiter served them antipasto, polenta, osso bucco.
The civility of eating taming the occasion.
                    Aglio e origano, basilico
e pomodoro, would that you could flavor my words.

Alberto, you have lost your way—you, our *dopoguerra*
  beacon.
Publicity, that siren, has seduced you.
You have not only written a bad book;
you have betrayed your vocation.
You say the book's a comedy. It is not.
I hear no laughter here, only the inexorable grind of
  contrivance.

This book is a lie. It has no truths or truth.

False muse, get thee gone;
free the famous from his fame.

You will say that you worked five years to produce
this work, and I should grant you that. To which I answer:
five years writing are five years of pleasure.
Your reward is in the doing.

I am not *unduly harsh.*

Understand me: this is a love letter.
My criticism, my embrace.
You are the Original, I the copy.

You are evaporating, Alberto. Stop before you disappear!

You were always the most limpid, genuine, of men.
Now this persona studs
your soul like so many rhinestones.

Adorned one, adored one.

This crassness in you confuses.
This magazine self, the one
in the interviews, devours the serious core.

Conformista, Indifferente.

Come back.

This is my slap. Cry now to show me you breathe.

As always,
Natalia Ginzburg
Rome

Nairobi, Kenya

The sun is fierce over the slum of Kibera
and the iron roofs wrinkle into eyelids
sleepily tilting over damp mud walls.
When rain falls the water lasts forever;
mud greedily tugs the soles of our feet
and shifts beneath those lazy shelters,
restless and impertinent. Disease runs in rivulets
from north to south, and the sunflowers drown.

Long after the last drops have risen from the roofs
with a painless itinerancy of which we only dream
when the radio sings with a spun silver voice
floating upward like a twice-tossed coin,
or when we glimpse in the hollow of a spoon
a world less rapid, more embracing;
yes, long after the horizon has lapped up storms
the watery ground still tries to swallow our footsteps.

But there is no room for enmity in Kibera
that crowds children into their own songs about the moon
and narrows the stooped shoulders of the too-soon old.
The doctor tucks a ray of light into his bag
and considers how even the birds-of-paradise
know to scatter their seeds, not to suffocate
on their own black earth. By a thin-needled potion he hopes
to grant us eyes and teeth of a more nourished world.

Poverty expresses itself most keenly
in certain kinds of plenty. So alongside the last stop
begin the tables of dark green shoes, tire-soled sandals

and half cakes, as many as you can hold
for the last shillings in your pocket.
By now the buses are empty metal canisters.
What could justify leaving us here,
a great, hot bazaar at the turnaround?

When the sky has ducked back into conscienceless blue
and looks at us with the eyes of a rich man
(but today, tomorrow and the next day come
as if the rain just ended yesterday)
then we leave the radio on when we sleep.
As distant and more promising than the stars,
it promises forests and traveling cars,
and a world where the one voice, though faint, plunges deep.

Pear Man

One would give emeralds
for what was not bought from the pear man
who stood in hot, blank sunlight
of a late Sunday afternoon
that seemed finally to be putting on a hat
and lowering its eyes, touching the sea
with soles of old walking sandals.

He holds the fruit like a man accustomed
to selling irons and pots, or pens emblazoned
with unspecified flags; as if he can hardly guess
a salesman's words about them,
as if doubts still linger concerning "pears"
which doesn't suit their brown awkwardness,
how they tumble sideways left on their own.

You don't mean to turn around,
but he senses your interest more quickly than you

and holds out a bag of pears as if they were pearls:
something of bewildering value
with which he would sooner part.
Chuff-chuff go his shoes
against the pavement as he halts.

He will not tell: where he was born
lilies grow high as bus windows
and no one walks the street weekday noons
with doormats or jars of two swimming fish
doing that hawker's step of shuffling loneliness,
bearing hope, hope, hope so openly in—the bracelets,
the soap, boxes and brooms—one's own hands.

To the pear man, not unwise,
your back is inscrutable as many puzzles—
a person walking on, touched and determined,
as he, stalking back across the empty street.
"Dear Pear Man," you want to call,
but some impulse of ordinariness
does not allow that, and already

he has begun again to wait—not untroubled,
seeing how the day, too, strides off:
another kindly, disinterested personality.
Immutably alone, he tucks the pears
into crooks of his arms. He walks
outside tall shadows of the minarets,
and sunlight glints off his long-stopped watch.

Ostriches at the Border Crossing, June 14

Namanga

In the first place they would sustain themselves
on warm, sugary drink, as they imagine herons
and kingfishers do—confusing bodily elegance,

affinity to water, and fondness for jewel-like scales
with access to unreasonable luxury. Secondly,
they refuse to observe solemnity appropriate

to a site of physical boundary, running instead
around ends of the long gate, slipping through
ahead of buses, as if seeking to indicate

the timidity of an office embarrassed to stop them.
Then, they are unaffected by weather. Neither rain
nor sun pleases them especially, nor does heat

make them grumpy. Cold they've known only
by wandering in far foothills, the last one
to do this (maybe a hundred years ago) indicating

it seemed a lot of work for nothing. He survives
in folklore, and they don't climb much any more.
Finally, if you attend their annual contest

during warm months in a highland city, you'll note
a certain tenacity and mischievousness
in their approach to the world, mainly

how, impervious to the blandishments of man,
they step daintily over stones by all measures the same
as those they raced across yesterday at marvelous

rate for no reason except enjoyment of running.
Admire them sunning themselves while they regard
with wide eyes the host of impatient competitors

who implore them with strident outcry, waving
to emphasize exhortations. Oh, the ostriches
are wise to strategies of pleasure and resistance,

delighted by their audience in makeshift stands.
They anticipate return to the land of buses,
an imminent regrouping at the borderland.

Robin Davidson

Women Harvesting: Virgins, Widows, Wives

after Konrad von Hirsau, ca. 1200

It might be von Hirsau believed he composed
a celebration, these wood panels brushed
with egg and tempera, a medieval man's rendering
of the rich work of women in his world,
or he might be any century's man
harnessing the unruly longing beauty stirs
within him. Either way, he names them
after himself like daughters . . .

virgins, these young women not yet touched,
their bodies bundled like the sheaves
they carry, unbind only for each other.
Content with what they do not know,
their bodies are the swinging of the scythe,
they are the gathering
folds of their robes, they are the bending,
swaying of torsos, knees
yielding. Why need they resist,
these passing beauties whose arms
harvest slowly, one sheaf at a time?

And these women, widows, what are they
but resistance? They bend beneath
the scythe's weight, heave
a full season on their breasts,
keep, for companions, sisters and ghosts and stones.
They wear white . . . shrouds, larval veils.
They weep for their lost men, bereft

of shoulders, arms, those bearded faces.
Is this grief, to work alone, a woman among women,
the garden become a field, the field a landscape
of stone, or is this plenitude?
Do they smell of absence
or of the grain they harvest?

And I, wife and witness, turn to you
in the third panel, one man among wives . . .
Do you know the woman who works at your side,
the curve of her neck, the small shoulders,
or have you mistaken
the urgency of her voice, her body

for strength, good faith?
She stoops below a radiant tree,
bends and bends until her wrists can touch
her red shoes. No. From her back
a small tree grows white,
the possibility of radiance,
like the box of seeds she carries

at her right side. Surely you see this tree,
this abstract of a tree, the shadow
of what burns inside her. Open your hand,
lay your palm against her throat, release
the brown dress she wears like sheaves loosened,
falling, until the body's work dissolves,
a field on fire, a fiery harvest.

Charles H. Webb

Coach Class Seats

Each has a foot-square paper napkin stuck
to the headrest: a bow to budget travelers' sensibilities.
Too bad each square evokes a paper toilet seat:
a 747 full of people shuffling in, then settling down to reek.

At least my hair won't pick up grease
from God-knows-whom. At least I won't be colonized
by roaming lice, or forced to lie, in effect, cheek-to-cheek
with a stranger (though his brain contains the same serotonin,

dopamine and endorphins as mine, that mediate
the same trembling at takeoff, same intake of breath,
same slow relaxing of the hands on the armrests
as the plane climbs and the earth opens its green Atlas below).

No other head has ever been here, the squares state.
This experience is fresh, reserved for you.
The waiter changing the tablecloth before seating new
lovebirds where you've just proposed—

the nurse tearing a length of paper from the doctor's
table on which you've just heard terrible news—no,
you're not interchangeable, these gestures say. The way
that two-pound brookie sipped your Wooly Bugger,

then wrapped your line around a jutting root has never
in fishing history happened before today.
Your fingerprints: unique as snowflakes. Your lover's
kiss: nonpareil. You were the first, stepping onto your lanai

in Kona, ever to say, "Whoa, honey, look at that view!"
How cheap the thrill if everybody felt that way.
Of course they don't, these napkins say. In all the miles
this plane will fly, there'll never be a passenger to rival you.

Pictures of Chocolate
(four drawings in chocolate syrup)

Vik Muniz

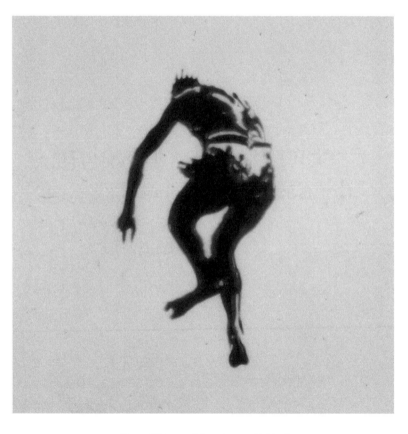

from *Chicago After Aaron Siskind*

Baudelaire

Action Painter

Action Photo

The Intervention

Kate Walbert

Anytime someone needs help but refuses to accept it, an . . . intervention is appropriate. Family and friends may initially be . . . ambivalent. Some may be afraid of the person, others may be angry. The goal is to move from this disorganized and chaotic state to a cohesive, focused group. —The Intervention Center

It was one of those utterances that sparkled—the very daring! Could you see us? Canoe shrugged, to be expected. After all, Canoe was our local recovering. Truth be told, it was she who left those pamphlets in the clubhouse next to the men's Nineteenth Hole.

Still, the very daring!

Intervention.

Canoe cracked her knuckles, lit a cigarette. We sat around her swimming pool absentmindedly pulling weeds from the flagstone. The ice of our iced tea had already melted into water and it was too cold to swim, besides.

"It's obvious," Canoe said, blowing. "He's going to kill himself in less than a month. I don't want that blood on my hands."

Who would?

He was someone we loved. Someone we could not help but love. A classmate of our ex-husbands, a past date. We had known him since before we were *we*, from the Sailors' Ball, or earlier summers. We loved his hair. Golden. The color of that movie actor's hair, the famous one. Sometimes we caught just the golden gleam of it through the windshield of his BMW as he drove by. Sporty. Waving. Green metallic, leather interior. Some sort of monogram on the wheel. You've seen the license plate? SOLD. A Realtor, but never desperate. Yes, he sold our Mimi Klondike's Tudor on Seven Oaks Lane with full knowledge of her rotting foundation. But desperate? No. Just thirsty.

"Intervention," Trudi Jones repeated. Canoe flexed her toes as if she had invented the word.

This a late summer day, a fallish day. Ricardo, the pool boy, swept maple leaves from the pool water, in this light a dull, sickly yellow. We watched him; we couldn't take our eyes off. Canoe interrupted.

"Actually, I shouldn't be the one explaining. There's someone from the group who's our expert. Paul Peters, actually."

Paul Peters? The lawyer? Paul Peters?

We spoke in whispers. Who knew who lived in trees?

Besides, he might drive up any minute. He often did. You'd hear the crunch of his tires on the gravel, see the flash of blond hair behind the windshield. These times you'd dry your hands on your shirtfront, check your face in the toaster. You wouldn't want to be caught, what? Alone? You let him in. He'd ask you to. He would stand at your door, behind your screen, wondering if he could. Of course, you'd say, though you looked a mess. If you were unlucky, the dishwasher ran. One of the louder cycles. If you were lucky, all was still—the house in magical order, spotless, clean. He surveyed; this his job. You never knew, he told you, when he might be needed.

You shivered. Him a handsome man. A man with the habit of standing close, his smell: animal, rooty—your hands after gardening. His straight teeth were white, though he didn't smile that way. His was a better smile, toothless, brief, as if he understood he had caught you with more than a wet shirtfront. You obliged the suspicion. You were always guilty of something.

Still, you showed him what you had done, were attempting. Recent renovations. Whatnot. A fabric swatch laid on the back of your couch. A roll of discount wallpaper for the powder room, shells of some sort. You'd been trying, you'd explain, to fix the place up. But things had gotten behind; time had slipped through your fingers. Your many burdens, etcetera.

He nodded, or did not. His was a serious business: assessing value. Worth.

A few days later Ricardo, the pool boy, served sandwiches. We had spent some time per Canoe's instruction contemplating the responsibility of our action: the absolute commitment, the difficulty, the discipline, the *sacrifice*. Esther Curran now sat among us. Someone had invited her. She was speaking of how he had sold her her Cape near Lighthouse Point and how she, Esther, was not a beautiful woman. Here Esther peeled the crust off her sandwich and looked away.

We sat around her in Canoe's wrought iron; it was too cold to lounge. The weather had suddenly turned, and the reason we sat around the pool at all was beyond us, unless it had something to do with Ricardo. We watched him receding toward the pool house then turned back to Esther.

This was the point, Esther was saying, though we may have lost it.

He had taken her hand. He had stroked it. He had told her of the possibilities. There wasn't much to be done—the demolition of the Florida room, a few shingles rehung, refurbishing the kitchen. Think of it, he had told her, and she had and here she was, she said. An owner of divine property.

We watched Esther with looks on our faces. We had never understood her. Rich as Croesus, she drove a Suburban and compared prices at the Safeway. Her husband William had died years ago, but she still referred to him as if he had run downtown for milk and would be back any minute. She allowed her hair to gray. She taught her grown children to curtsy when introduced and every Christmas made ornaments out of dead flowers. She often had paint on her hands and more than once had been escorted home, we understood, in the early hours of the morning, found wandering in robe and slippers on the old Route 32, luckily rarely traveled, for she could have been struck down as easily as a stray dog. Now here she was among us.

"*Intervention*," she said, "is not a word of which I am particularly fond." Esther cut her crustless sandwich into nine even squares. "William and I are of the live and let live philosophy," she continued, "but in certain unavoidable circumstances, such as the one we confront here today, I say, yes. I say, intervene." She picked up a square and we waited, thinking Esther might have more to add, but she simply smiled and popped it whole into her mouth.

"Frankly," Canoe said, this to Paul Peters, who had convened the meeting and sat at the edge of us in a deck chair, "I don't want to hear about him wrapped around a telephone pole. I wouldn't be able to live with myself."

Paul Peters nodded. He seemed to have little to say, too quiet for an interventionist, though Canoe insisted he was skilled in these matters. And we had read in the literature that we needed him: a leader, a discussion initiator.

"Understood," he said. He turned to me. This was unexpected. I am a back-of-the-class kind of student, a woman who likes to be left unseen.

"And you?" he said.

My mind frizzed in the way it does in these situations. "I feel the same," I said.

We agreed to meet the next day in the Safeway parking lot for a run-through. Paul Peters would play His part. Did we understand fully, Peters had explained, that this would be tantamount to ambush? There would be little time, he said. He will fight you. He will want to flee. He will deny your accusations. You will have to talk quickly. Under absolutely no circumstance can you allow him to leave the vehicle. (We had decided that this would be the place we'd find him.) When it is over, one of you will get behind the wheel and drive him to the Center. You will check him in. It has been arranged.

Paul Peters now sat in his Buick, the motor running. We saw him clearly though we pretended not to: this was part of the plan. We pulled in in Esther's Suburban and got out one at a time, no one saying a word. Canoe gave a short whistle and we circled the Buick, feeling the rush of the boarding-school escapade. What were we doing? Was anyone watching?

Paul Peters pretended not to notice. He was a poor substitute for Him, truth be told. He sat there in a gut-hold against the wheel, his fingers strumming. He smelled of gum or mints, of pretzels, of efforts to stave off tobacco. We knew him as a weak man. We knew him as a man who could be trusted. His wife Eleanor carried the look of the perpetually bored; his children were overachievers. You can only guess at the good-cheer stickers on the bumper of his Buick. He was a hedge trimmer, a leaf raker, a birdhouse builder; he was a man who never thought of selling. Every spring along the borders of the driveway to his house—a ranch just past the K & O Cemetery—he planted red and pink impatiens.

"Paul!" This from Canoe, acting surprised, our signal to converge. Paul looked up, turned off the engine. "Canoe!" he said, our signal to open his doors. Canoe had already slid in the passenger side, yanked the keys from the ignition. Our hearts beat too loud, drumlike. We were not used to intervening.

"What is this?" Paul said. "What's everybody doing here?" His talent was not for acting. He sounded like a commercial you might see on late-night television.

"We're here because we love you," Canoe said. "We're here because we care about your life."

We flushed. Who wouldn't? We didn't care for Paul's life.
We wanted Him. We wanted his smooth leather shoes, his
argyle socks, his blue cashmere, double-breasted coat. We
wanted his promise of future appreciation.

"What are you talking about?" Paul said, shifting around
to look at those of us in the backseat. Some couldn't fit and
leaned on the windows. "What's the big idea?"

We laughed; we couldn't help it. "Please, Paul," Esther
said to clue him in. "He'd never say *big idea*."

Paul gave us a look and turned back toward the windshield.
He composed himself, a man of infinite patience, then shifted
around again. "What's the meaning of this?" he said.

"The meaning," said Esther, "is concern. You are a sick
person. It's not your fault. You can't help yourself. It's ge-
netic. You need help. We're here to help you."

Some of us bit our fingernails.

Paul laughed like Bela Lugosi. "Sick? Me? What do you
mean by these unfounded accusations. I've never felt better.
I think you're sick. I think you are all suffering from a serious
mental-health problem."

This was going all wrong. No one sounded like a real person.

"What we're trying to say," said Bebe McShane, but she
didn't know what. Then came a long and awkward pause.
Canoe sighed, audibly. "Come on ladies," she said. "We've
gotten off on the wrong foot." Then she opened the passenger
side and got out, signaling for us to do the same. We did,
as Paul Peters waited, pretending, once again, that he had
just driven up.

Know that we are a close-knit community. We've lived
here for years, which is not to say that our ancestors are buried
here, simply, this is the place we have all ended up. We were
married in 1953. Divorced in 1976. Our grown daughters
pity us; our grown sons forget us. We have grandchildren we
visit from time to time, but their manners agitate, so we
return, nervous, thankful to view them at a distance. Most
of us excel at racket sports.

It is not in our makeup to intervene. This goes against the

grain, is entirely out of our character. We allow for differences, but strive not to show them. Ours are calm waters, smooth sailing. Yes, some among us visit therapists, but, quite frankly, we believe this is a passing phase, like our former passion for fondue or our semester learning decoupage.

We've seen a lot. We've seen the murder-suicide of the Clifford Jacksons, Tate Kieley jailed for embezzlement, Dorothy Schoenbacher in nothing but a mink coat in August dive from the roof of the Dew Drop Inn. We've seen Dick Morehead arrested in the ladies dressing room at Lord & Taylor, attempting to squeeze into a petite teddy. We've seen Francis Stoney gone mad, Brenda Nelson take to cocaine. We've seen the blackballing of the Stewart Collisters. We've seen more than our share of liars and cheats, thieves. Drunks? We couldn't count.

Still, he's someone we love. And, in truth, we love few.

Early the morning after our practice run, we met again at the Safeway. Canoe brought a thermos of coffee and we stood drinking from our Styrofoam cups in the early cold as if at a tailgate. It did seem a game, the weather, football weather, changeable, ominous, geese honking overhead, flying elsewhere. A strong wind set loose shopping carts in random directions, as if they were being pushed by the ghosts of shoppers past. Coupon offers and flyers of various sorts blew about as well. Canoe suggested coffee cake, but we declined. We were, on the whole, nervous. We enjoyed our weekly stocking up at the Safeway; we kept lists. But to linger in its parking lot we felt just shy of delinquency and a long way from Canoe's swimming pool and Ricardo's languid strokes. When we finally spotted Paul Peters' Buick turning in, our spirits had undeniably flagged.

Peters didn't seem to notice. "Ladies," he said, slamming the door, getting out. "Top of the morning!"

Was Paul Peters always working from some sort of script?

"Why the long faces?" he said.

"They'll get over it," Canoe said. She dropped her Styrofoam cup to the asphalt and crushed it, twisting her flat as if to stub out a cigarette butt. We watched, riveted. You do not need to tell us we were stalling. Canoe got into her Jeep and rolled down the window. "Understand," she told him. "They're not used to unpleasantness."

In truth, she was right. We have seen a lot, but know so little. How were we to learn? Years ago we were led down the primrose lane, then abandoned somewhere near the carp pond. Suffice it to say, there is little nourishment here and the carp have grown strange cancers. When we look in their pond we see them beneath our own watery faces.

But think of the consequence: His disappearance.

We piled in as instructed. We buckled our safety belts. We turned to Paul Peters, who stood in salute, and waved. Canoe gunned the Jeep. "Hi-Yo Silver," she said, and we were off, the plan to find him come hell or high water, to drive to the limits of our town, to cover his turf. We watched Paul Peters trail us in his Buick, his flaccid pink face in the rearview. We weren't nice. We made fun. We said how ordinary was Paul, how completely known. We said how He could flatten Paul Peters with one fist.

"Kaboom!" Trudi Jones shouted. And she meant it. "Kaboom! Kaboom!" She raised her fist and punched the air.

"Why the anger?" Mimi Klondike asked, as if intervention were catching.

Trudi Jones shrugged. "Felt like it?" she said.

Esther, we noticed, wasn't talking. She wasn't often among us, and now she might as well not have been. She sat in the back of the Jeep staring out the window, some kind of smock we wouldn't be caught dead in spread over her legs. She had letters in her pockets to people we had never met; her hair seemed generally unwashed.

"Esther?" Mimi Klondike said. "Why the long face?" Trudi Jones smirked, but Esther simply turned toward us. She might have been smiling, or this might have been her natural expression. Beyond her, our country—changing maples, stone walls, gravel drives, newly washed automobiles, children, horses, dogs—passed. But we were looking at Esther.

"I was thinking how lucky," she finally said. "I was thinking how lucky we are to be alive." Then she turned away. We drove in silence; what else was there to do? Time passed and we thought our thoughts; we thought of him. How he held a flashlight to our souls, our basements. How he checked for dry rot, carpenter ants, the carcasses of flying insects. In the darkness we saw him searching and we yelled down, Do you need a hand?

"Bingo!" Canoe shouted. She slammed the Jeep brake. "Bingo Bango!"

We leaned in, looking. "What?" we said. "Him?"

Yes, there: Pinned to the Cooper's chemicaled lawn, the sign: SOLD Realtors, freshly hammered to the ground. Beside it his BMW, forest green, buffed as his nails, stood idle in the Cooper's drive, arriving or leaving impossible to say. We knew Dick Cooper, on early retirement, dropped dead putting the eighteenth green. We knew Louise had thoughts of moving to Captiva, where her sister, Vivian, owned a condo. Still, we felt the jealousy of his transferred affections. Louise? we thought. Her?

"Keep calm!" Canoe shouted, veering in. Our hands were in our laps, our feet pushed against the carpeted floor, braking. Mimi and Trudi ducked on impulse. The rest of us stayed stock-still. We knew the plan; Paul Peters would stay behind, at a distance, there if needed, ready to follow in his car to the Center, to do the necessary paperwork to check him in. The approvals had been given, the gears were in motion.

Canoe parked the Jeep, jerked the emergency brake. This a stroke of luck, really. We might have found him nowhere. We might have been too late. Now here we were—sitting and listening to the ticking engine, watching the steam rise off the hood. The day seemed warmer, the gray breaking into blue, the sun a sudden glare. It shone off the chrome of his BMW, flashed in our eyes as if a badge he held up for protection. Was he there? Did we see him?

Canoe got out. She slammed the front door and sauntered over. She strode, Canoe, the toughest among us. We kept still. We waited for the signal: two coughs followed by a hand clap. This would mean he was in the vehicle and we should proceed as rehearsed. Mimi, still ducking, rolled down her window so we could better hear, but what we heard was an ordinary day: a dog barking, crickets, a siren at the far edge of town. In it Canoe's boots crunched gravel; Canoe knocked.

It should be said that in recent months he had acquired a new BMW. The latest model. Understand him as a lessor. In his profession, the importance of the vehicle is not to be underestimated. Every year he trades in. Still, the license plate remains: SOLD. The color, forest green. This one, however, has been slightly altered—the windows blackened, as if a rebuke to our constant attentions.

But he cannot escape us. We know his comings and goings, his ring size. We know at the Stone Barn he orders Manhattan clam chowder, a cup, and a BLT for lunch. We know his difficulty with languages, his general insecurity in all things pertaining to math. We know as a boy he watched the mayor hide the golden Easter egg then blatantly pretended to find it. We know he dreams of killing. We know he scratches himself in ugly places and picks his nose; that his breath is rank in the morning and he scissors black hairs from his ears and plucks his eyebrows and once, even, he purchased the dye that is sold in certain salons for men his age, though his nerve failed him and he tossed the box in the kitchen trash.

We know this and more: his bad back, his quenchless thirst. He is our faithless husband, our poor father. He is our bad son, our schemer, our rogue. He is our coward in the conflict, our liar. He has betrayed all he has promised.

Still, we love him.

"Must be in the house," Canoe shouts back to us. "Come on."

We go. We fan out. Our hearts taut drums. Our feet heavy. Canoe crouches ahead, then rounds the bend, breaking away from the cul-de-sac. We run after her and line up on either

side—Trudi at the far end, Mimi, the near. We cross our
arms over our chests and wait. Canoe tries the front door.
It's open. She pushes through. It is Louise Cooper's house,
but it may as well be our own—the powder room off the foyer,
Louise's monogrammed hand towels from her first marriage
turned inside out. There's ivory soap in the shape of shells,
dirtied from her gardener's hands. There's a chandelier that's
dusty, unused; unpaid bills on the secretary. A needlepoint
giraffe, weighted with sand, holds the den door open. Here
we'd find Louise's real life: her *TV Guides*, her tarnished
tennis trophies, framed photographs of her children with
outdated hairstyles. But we're not going there. We pause,
instead, in the empty foyer. What are we listening for? What
do we want?

And then we hear him. He is speaking in a low voice, a
whisper. It is a sound we'd recognize anywhere: the sound
of his prospecting. A cold call. Like the slap of waves in our
ocean, like a salt cure. He wants something. He is asking. To
all of us he has spoken in such a manner, kissed our fingers.
He has guided us through our living rooms, his hand on the
small of our backs.

"Shhhhh," Canoe says, as if someone has spoken. But no
one has said a word. We simply stand at the bottom of
Louise Cooper's staircase like bridesmaids waiting to catch
the bouquet, but we are not bridesmaids. We are women
near the end of our lives. We look up at nothing: the hallway,
the bedroom doors.

Still, his voice is everywhere. Which room? Which direction? Canoe climbs. We follow. At the top of the stairs, we
pause, waiting. Nothing. No sound at all but something just
below the surface quiet. What? Something so familiar: a
woman weeping? Our Louise? We walk down the hallway,
pushing at doors—there are so many empty bedrooms. This
one simply lit from the now-blue sky shining through its open
windows onto the poplin spread, pulled taut, pillows fluffed
as if expecting guests; the next one, the same. We move
quickly. We hurry. We push on doors, we open closets.

We do not find her until the maid's room. She sits on a
narrow cot among little—a wire-cage mannequin, a yellow-
painted dresser, a children's mirror. On the floor there is no
rug. If we were barefoot we would be splintered, but we are
not. We are shoed and zipped, buttoned and covered; this
we notice because Louise is not. She is without a stitch of
clothing, entirely nude.

She covers herself when we burst in, drawing her legs up
and around to cinch them. She is a ball of flesh, Louise
Cooper, leaking from the eyes. She does not need to ask to
know our mission; she points, weakly, in the direction of a
narrow staircase—the back way. Esther takes the lead and we
hurry, pell-mell, reckless. We sense there is little time and
so we tumble down the stairs, our flats nicking the soft wood,
our hands slapping cold walls. Released near the back door
into the open—the sudden fresh air, the sudden light—we
run. We tear. We might spread our arms. Fly.

Now can you see us?

We head out fast, our flats flapped off some way back,
eight pairs abandoned like sixteen blackbirds in a jagged
line, our soft soles hopscotching gravel, rock, then the grassy
stubble in the field behind the Coopers', Esther ripping the
just-red stalks from their roots, Trudi and Mimi holding
hands, running. We must find him, we know. We must
intervene. We do not want him wrapped around a telephone
pole. We do not want that blood on our hands. We must
save him, mustn't we? We must save him, quick.

But first, no. First, ourselves.

William Logan

The Shorter Aeneid

I. The Ship

> The Fighting Téméraire, _J.M.W. Turner_

The sunlight was like wire on the water,
that morning the ghost ship drove upriver.
The only witness was a Jersey cow.

Florid and testy, a miniature industrialist,
the steam tug spouted its fiery plume of smoke,
and on the banks the dead trout lolled,

beyond the reach of fishermen now.
From a distance the fish were bodies of sailors
after a great sea battle, when masts and spars

are matchsticks on the water; the mist
hovering over inlets, cannon smoke drifting
off the now-purple, now-green bloom of water.

In shadow a train inched over a brick viaduct
ruling the still-dark valley,
as aqueducts once ruled the dawn campagna.

The cows were Cincinnatus patriots:
they knew of being bred for slaughter.
The morning was a painting: the battered warship

hung with dawn lights like a chestful of medals,
the barren canvas of the Thames, empty out of respect,
the steam tug beetling to the breaker's yard.

The sun lay on the horizon like a vegetable.

II. The Train

The brackish green of poisonous shrub
took the window of the train like tapestry.
Hedgerows bristled, the jigsawed spines of map,

broken like the millefleur duchies of Europe.
How long had they fallen
on discontented earth, travelers

twisting their watches to catch the light?
Folded in your lap were headlines,
and as I slept in my tarnished suit

the decade vanished and we were strangers again.
None of the new-risen words had been broken.
Behind us lay a ruined city,

a Rome of chimneys the stalks of blown weeds.
Then I awoke, and you *were* gone, nothing on your seat
but the unread *Times*. I looked out the window

as we shunted through dressed-up, derelict stations,
past a dirt track climbing the humpbacked ridge,
fields of shattered poppies an Impressionist blur,

and then you swayed into the aisle, unexpected,
as we crossed a burned-out farm.
Your hair caught something flashing

at the beginning of evening.

III. Refugees

London, 1945

Two ravens flared across the blue-edged field,
political evening lit by veins of flint
as if each spark struck a single word

and night were a plowed dictionary.
They stood on the bomb-scarred platform
beside cardboard suitcases, the crowd milling

like named ghosts through the DNB; and then they walked
into the city as clocks chimed the dead hour.
Evening, the time between two worlds,

shivered down the naked barometer.
The gassy streetlamps glowed like mercury,
and over the chimneys of cobbled walks

swifts like Spitfires darted through clouds
of insects. Each brick house a sooty curtain
above a sprocketed bay. Odor of smoke and bacon fat.

Beneath iron gutters, the birds beat back their wings
and fluttered to clamorous nests. He leaned against her
in the hollow street, each bearded nest the mouth

of a language they could not understand.
They had entered that country with the money
of Jews, paper tags on their wool coats.

Only their passports remembered where they belonged.

IV. The Oracle of the Birds

What are the arms of exile, the oracle asked,
the shield of the mute or shell of the deaf?
Under the crossed necks of swans

that live but cannot speak, the rage of words
batters the brass gates of the throat.
Even one word can be a Trojan horse,

each damascened letter a drawn sword.
Words flower on the pool of the dead,
even one letter revelation in a threat,

revolution in a thread.
From the soil of crumbling London come,
as if from that other world,

the marble fragments of Augustan Rome,
each letter chiseled in the slow-motion of empire.
Speak, there was never time to speak

beneath the muffled motors of eternity.
Silence, there will be time enough for silence,
to be buried with the words unspoken,

your mouths stopped with cemetery gravel.
They are the purchase of history, icy in its ellipses,
its freeze-dried gallery of moments,

momentum in equal fear of past or future.

V. The Other World

In Venice I had seen that other world,
the prewar world of water,
lights of decaying palazzi floating

ghostlike, eerie as fish, in the drowned canals.
The opera house burned like a candle,
and through its open windows

glared an almost-sky almost innocent.
That dark morning history was made elsewhere,
I stood, uncertain of my path,

watched by a lounging Englishman
beneath the hotel's rusted sign,
a tiny compass in his cupped palm:

"Aeneas, throw away your canvas map.
Here in our drained canal, the houses lull
on limestone rotted by retreating tides,

the pleasure of palazzi on the mud,
the black wake of the gondolas, oaring past
to songs their fathers' fathers sold to tourists,

though finally none are tourists here. Each night,
the singer's little gasp and clutch of pain
float to the upper windows, like an aria.

The mud below still casts the doge's bones.

VI. The Other World

"I'll guide you through a labyrinth of names
you would not recognize, familiar ghosts
lost to the city of glass, city of water,

where the Rialto's history is engraved
within the cheesy mortar of the stone,
each choked canal a circle of the dead.

You cannot see the starving corpses stand
up to their necks amid the pea-green sewage,
their toes like snails upon the leathery slime.

Tourists are rowed among them as if blind.
The starving cats can see, see the old doge
towed on his barge, the gilded trumpets blaring,

the painted sailcloths taut against the breeze,
his sails the flayed skins of his enemies.
He judders across a bay of flailing arms

pleading pardon from the burning sea.
Each watery hour they drown in the lagoon,
invisible to all the chittering crowd,

to all except the quayside's six-toed cats.
On tiptoe in Armani suit, the doge
scatters his blessings and indulgences,

the black confetti of his government.

VII. The Other World

"Our air is stained in phosphorescent burning,
the glow of Mestre's factories alight,
the flare of gas across the storage tanks

on midnight's dreaming skin, the veined pollution
in the draining stones, where the cold acids tear
holes in the eyes of marble, and carbon inks

tattoos upon the shoulders of the gods.
Beneath these gods I stole my foreign name,
ever to wave my diplomatic passport

across the borders of the other world.
I knew the empire from the emperor,
who pensioned me upon hexameters

to script the gods their VCs in the war.
The empress wore an India on her crown,
and Africa adorned her swanlike neck.

America was a second-best tiara.
My soul debates the world in a hearing aid.
On starless nights the dead men strut

backward along the course of filled canals,
their heads above the pavement, moaning, moaning
their bargain grievances and antique pain.

They rate two stars within your Baedeker.

VIII. The Other World

"Due north the jagged street of traitors lies,
where men tear out their tongues, and there we cross
the alley of assassins, where the stones have eyes.

Put your thumb into the politicians' drain,
plugged with the guts of fish. Beyond this wall,
in bricked-up campi where a plane tree grows,

the old stars breakfast on their old reviews.
The two ghosts you have come for cannot speak.
The woman turns her face away and laughs.

The old man counts his rosary of debt
beside the Grand Canal. Most of the dead
have nothing left to say to those alive.

Last you must cross the campo of Marco Polo
who saw the godlike khan amid his tents,
who walked the trackless waste, knew burning gods,

saw catwalks in Milan and Rome, an F-16
writing its landlocked battles on the air,
the glowing ruby of the microchip,

who after decades lying among the living
returned to this archipelago of lies.
Some say he never left Albania.

Some say that China was just poetry.

IX. The Other World

"Within these garden walls, a Persian cat
descended from the sacred cats of Rome
gave Eve the fish of wisdom and our sins.

Venice rewrote the book of Genesis.
The waters of the flood rise from these drains;
the dove of Noah sees, atop the ocean's slur,

the Campanile lift its angel like a buoy.
The rushes of that barren islet steal
the orphan Moses to the doge's arms,

and here the *acqua alte* parts at his hand
to drown the Austrian privates as they sleep.
Where Cain slays Abel on San Marco's steps,

beneath the horses of Apocalypse,
the bloodstained *pavimenti* heave and split.
Now Joseph's colored bathrobe is on sale

behind the plate glass of Missoni's shop;
and off the street of arrowmakers lies
the temple of American Express,

where the lost souls redeem their ancient pledge.
Each church a Calvary, each black canal a hell."
Then my stooped guide, who'd known the emperors,

walked through Fortuny's silks and disappeared.

X. The Book of Genesis

Where Cleopatra reigned, Liz Taylor danced
and Chaplin practiced Hitler's mincing step
while Charlton Heston crooned in the voice of God.

Bright with a vat of foam, like God He worked,
covering the floor as if with an ocean of surf,
the Venetian come to clean the soiled carpets.

A death foretold. Breathing heavily, as if the eighth day
of creation could make the sinning world clean again,
He moved His hand over the darkness of the kilim,

the hum of His machine a fatal tide.
No ark this time with its quarrelsome crew,
no pairs of animals, predator locked up with prey,

nothing within the devil's rage of temptation,
nothing that might go wrong in the aftermath.
Evil? said the actor at the end of the film.

I think it has something to do with free will.
Brow furrowed like a water-god's, the Venetian was gone,
sweating and overweight, His tie crooked,

still like a god, though old like a god,
as if He had known all this before.
His brushes were worn down to stubs.

He suffered along with the cleaning.

XI. The Book of the Gecko

Night. The color of battle. Written across the moon,
a gecko takes a burning moth in its mouth.
You lie across Procrustes' bed,

beneath the cotton disarrangement of sheets.
The words you take into your mouth
don't sound like words. That night in Venice,

you stood within the charred conch of La Fenice.
Sunday morning, in dawn's bright order,
each church we entered was a cold, dangerous world,

its shedding plaster walls a map
of the unknown: fallen worlds, here and there
revealing the filthy lath all worlds are plastered on.

You could not find your way back,
back to the gold boat hammered thin
with its threadlike gold oars; back to the mosaic boat

mortared to the ceiling of San Marco,
the boat in which they smuggled the corpse of St. Mark
packed in a barrel marked pickled pork;

back to the rocking, dark traghetto prowling
the waves at its decaying dock. The weather fair,
the distance across the water far, too far.

Words, words, naked as prey to predator.

XII. Measure for Measure

The ornamental plum frizzled into daylight,
dank, pinkish, slightly scorched blossoms
floating, alien as Shakespeare's money

on the exchange boards of shuttered banks.
They fell in still life, snow in a woodblock print,
dappling the mottled carp in kept ponds.

The plum married the plum of another country
above the dead empire of ferns,
their curled skeletons a row of bishop's croziers.

Unseasoned cold, searing as summer heat,
had borne away the surface of the garden,
each wart and crevice apprentice to the new world.

Three days of cold, and Christ's roses would not rise again,
taken from the life in the old phrase.
The lost house was cold, cold in the guarded spring,

Queen Anne's lace laced up in Queen Anne's style.
You were burning in the surfaces,
and beneath green water a face peered up at me.

What is timeless, the glebe cow or the monument?
Already fiddleheads uncurled above the waste
and termites sang like dryads in the wood.

The garden had to be rebuilt like a city.

Three Poems by Christian Nagle

Gold

Swallowed by blood-red vinyl of the hotel lounge,
I drain the last of a grasshopper—my first cocktail,
ever. You loosen your tie, Dad, glare at headlines
in ruby-glass light; we're welcome strangers
on the homeward leg. *A business trip*, I'll explain
to dumbstruck Miss Rowe after days of truancy,
to Geneva. And, true, I'm the greenhorn yankee crawler

who missed the swimming gala not for Lindt,
nor shushing and booming in the Matterhorn's shadow.
Rather, I've vanished in a vault with Krugerands
bright as chocolate money, bars that impress
my downy thighs to the bone—hardly the bricks
of Goldfinger's Fort Knox, but smaller, like boxes
of .45 bullets, like the dictacorder in your pocket.

A nine troy ounce chain shackles your right wrist,
an inveterate, shiny Rolex your left.
Crème de menthe breaks out on my forehead.
Soon you will have an occupation I can name.
You click out a pen and scratch a note (the moral
of our story). Three days ago I might have wondered
what it said, but now I am busy with the straw.

Convexed in my tumbler, you become a giant.
Father, I'm as immortal as you now
I've seen our throne-room, a standard
stable in its drum of silence. A decade hence,
you'll return to Alexandria, a Pharaoh whose chariot—

an ashes-of-roses Cadillac—drifts tombward. There,
ungilded, a bust looks blindly for its fortunes.

The bar has come alive. Sidelit, you order
another Johnny Red, but already your image blisters
in my acid, virgin drunk. Your black-as-gold-dust hair
begins to smoke. It is November, '74.
You unlink your cuffs and Oman's crest
furls twice in Saville Row cotton. A smile flickers
from your odd occlusion. *Ready to turn in, son?*

We boil out of here at 0700. At 1,000 Celsius,
cavities surrender their nuggets, rivulets
from your mouth; 5,000, and the puddles under
radius and ulna go the way of cyanide, a gas.
But for now we burn with Rome, Paris and Saint Joan,
inertly, while on Lake Geneva, the fountain keeps
aspiring above its peak, five parts per hundred million.

Foreigners: Homage to Elizabeth Bishop

> *Heavens, I recognize the place, I know it!*

Palermo. Along the dock, boys greet our boat,
turn cartwheels for five lire coins (inferior
brass I try bending with my teeth, once),
push tours of the island's baroque interior.

"What kind of an Italian will you make?"
Father squeezes my hand as if it's a matter
of importance but there appears no inky red stamp
in my passport. So, to the hydrofoil. Up a ladder

we embark again, scan the unsettled
channel for what castaways call signs of hope:

smokestacks, a finger of land. *Cigarette?*
American cigarette? English soap? . . .

A peddler lurches down the aisle. He's seventy,
at least, and frayed like a Sicilian shawl.
Marlboro! . . . Yardley! . . . These foreign expressions
fall from his mouth and we are certain he will fall

with the weight of luxuries. Past freighters,
we skip towards the boot. Where we've been
is now a wake trailing off in a white hook
to snag the horizon; the air is cut with brine.

In a year, my brother and I will presume upon
our neighbors with near-Roman accents, be seen
as visiting pretenders whose makeshift crowns
are bowlcuts bleached silver by the local *piscina.*

But for now, no forward window. What's coming?
An American club where the pianist plays rags
and the walls are glossed with ghosts from before
the last war, a forty-eight-star flag

dwarfing the bandstand. The Old World
sleeps after lunch, buries our apprehension,
another tumbled column. Here, "immediately"
means "sometime," life in suspension

like the Kenwood stereo at home, on strike
for an adaptor. The sky narrows its possible blue.
In Rome, at last, my mother gives her tourist
garb to the neighbor's daughter. "Can you—"

Possa usare? . . . Soon, she will harbor
a passion for imagined scenery,
paint Milan as an old market, Tuscany's "mountains"
behind a branch of lemons, pregnant with greenery.

The Vines

for my father

The cardinal's cursed us with another spring
and the vines awake to exercise their rights,
nearly burying the side wall: full, gorgeous,
uneven, bewildering. Yearly, with shears,

one ladder, beer for breakfast, we come to stem
this heaving shag of greenery, thin croziers
clutching the outskirts. Wising up to our mission,
sparrows flutter, inscribe a certain doom.

No one could hate us more than the birds will.
Your undershirt goes in a flash, a flag importing
surrender (in fact, just one short break at noon).
Spirals of gray hair decorate your burl.

Mortar, resigned to its particular fate,
has crumbled in the preternatural grip.
The "battleship" is mortal after all.
Even the nails are loosening, clearly frail.

Clouds uninviting, you scale the ladder—bent,
it seems, on some end well beyond the roof.
Veins stand out on your legs, tortuous, blue
as rivers glimpsed from countless miles above.

You're all job now. While water stripes the shoulders
of unopened bottles, you cut the stalks,
call them *the devil's notion of paradise* . . .
At least no future sins can torture us.

I spell you and the house begins to clear,
masonry showing its relief in sunlight.
Each motley brick alters—but doesn't gray
always intend silver, umber oxblood?

My feet are unfamiliar with the rungs.
Beer-tipsy, I conjure Troy—men spiriting
up into that lethal belly—and almost fall;
the balance of the siege is yours alone.

Fanatic to closure, you consign a nest
of bluish jay eggs into the hyacinths.
The mourning dove looks down, oblivious
(you've surgically preserved her window haunt).

At last there's nothing left we can destroy,
uncover or dispose of. Garbage bags
covet their refuse, gorged but oddly light.
The victorious creeper comes to nought again.

High in our thorny locust tree, a finch
loots the abandoned crow's nest. Do we care?
Like seasoned admirals on the afterdeck
we laugh at nothing, drink, admire the work.

1) This is the better version, I think. 2) I'm a little doubtful but not why (and how) is the rising? 3) I realize that many translators go this way, but the rest don't. And it may create a false impression — that O. and P. remain quiet and all night .....

23. 9

but you and I, and a single handmaid, Actoris,
the [~~slave~~] ‹servant› my father gave me when I came,

cf. †. 786

who kept the doors of our sturdy, well-built room--
You've [~~won~~] my heart--my hard heart--at last!"
  ‹conquered›   [~~maybe~~]

    The more she spoke the more a deep desire for tears
welled up inside his breast--he wept as he held the wife
he loved, the soul of loyalty in his arms, at last . . .
Joy, warm as the joy that shipwrecked sailors feel
when they catch sight of land--Poseidon has struck
their well-rigged ship on the open sea with gale winds
and crushing walls of waves, and only a few escape, swimming,
struggling out of the frothing surf to reach the shore,
their bodies crusted with salt but buoyed up with joy
as they plant their feet on solid ground again,
escaped the worst at last--so joyous now to her
[~~that sea-hell far behind--~~]   ‹mind (2›
the sight of her husband [~~rising~~] in her gaze
that her white arms embracing his neck
‹would never for a moment›
[~~not even now would ever~~] let him go . . .
Dawn with her rose-red fingers might have shone
upon their tears, if with her glinting eyes
Athena had not thought of one last [~~touch~~] ‹thing›
She held back the night and night lingered long
at the Western edge of the earth while in the East
she reined in Dawn of the golden throne at Ocean's banks,
commanding her not to yoke the windswift team that brings men
        light,
Blaze and Aurora, fresh young colts that race the Morning on.
‹Yet now (3›
[~~At length~~] Odysseus, man of exploits, said to his wife,
"Dear woman, still we have not come to the end
of all our trials. One more labor lies in store--
boundless, freighted with danger, great and long--
and I must brave it out from start to finish.
So the ghost of Tiresias prophesied to me,

[not then, not now, would ever let him go.
  down all the years would ever let him go.]

A manuscript page from the Odyssey. *This passage is from the reunion of Odysseus and Penelope in Book 23.*

Robert Fagles

The Art of Translation II

Robert Fagles and I met several times in his office at Princeton, where he is Arthur W. Marks '19 Professor of Comparative Literature, to discuss our forthcoming interview at the Unterberg Poetry Center of the 92nd Street Y. White-haired, tall and spare, he moves with the air of preparedness, flexibility and covert attentiveness of someone who, I correctly guess, has played a lot of tennis. His conversation is flecked with stanzas of poetry and quotations he values, often from W.H. Auden, whose lines he quotes as if he were reverting to a private native tongue. His manners are fine in the way that Americans, having not yet evolved a word, still inappropriately describe as courtly, a word that misses the lack of ostentation and the deliberate grace that are at the heart of democratic elegance.

His office is stark on first impression, but comes to seem increasingly peopled, in part because most of its ornaments, like the poster of a mosaic Orpheus singing the beasts into harmony, are gifts from other people—the sign of a man for whom partnerships and collaborations are cherished matters, an ideal temperament for a poet-translator. On his work table are several photographs, a sculptural valentine from his wife Lynne, and an origami bird, fashioned from her program by a blind student of his at a performance of Aristophanes' The Birds. *Nearby is an open paperback version of Virgil's* Aeneid, *his next translation project. The poster on the far wall is of the image he submitted for the cover for his* Iliad, *a bronze votive offering of a fierce warrior from 500* B.C. *A table opposite him holds a tape player, on which he reviewed the raw tapes of the actors Derek Jacobi and Ian McKellen performing his translations of the* Iliad *and the* Odyssey *respectively, "listening for a kinship in the cadence of what they were trying to read and what I was trying to write." This must have been a task of joyful absorption for someone who never forgets that Homer was a singer, and was himself an amateur singer. The tape player concentrates the atmosphere of the office, which has something of the shell-like ambience of a recording studio, a space artfully hollowed to create the best acoustics for the concert of voices Fagles is working to bring to life.*

A pair of regal Gothic Revival windows, which used to remind his young daughters of a king and queen, look out on a tree-filled courtyard and on Nassau Hall, where the Continental Congress met during the American Revolution. Placed parallel with the windows, resting on a stand, is the mammoth, "inevitable" Liddell-Scott, as Fagles calls it, the standard Greek-English lexicon, the great open dictionary seeming like a stately window itself, opening onto an incalculable number of views.

INTERVIEWER

I thought we would start with the classic Homeric question, in the words of Queen Arete from the *Odyssey*, "Who are you? Where are you from?"

ROBERT FAGLES

Well, I'm the son of a lawyer and an architect, and I grew up outside of Philadelphia, in a household beset by my father's illness and filled with my parents' kindness. I'm an only child, and that's a curse and a blessing both, according to the old wisdom, and it's true. I was educated in public schools in the Philadelphia suburbs, then I went to Amherst College for undergraduate work, and Yale for graduate work, in English, and I've been teaching literature at Princeton since 1960, where I'm a "lifer," and lucky to be one, too. There I live with my wife of more than forty years—the greatest luck of all—and there we've raised two daughters. They cover the real world, one's a physician and the other a businesswoman, while I've been hiding out in Homer for the last twenty years.

INTERVIEWER

Was there anything in your childhood that was a bridge to Greek?

FAGLES

Probably what I was reading, and what my mother read me as a child. Many kinds of adventure stories on the one hand—Kipling, Robert Louis Stevenson, James Fenimore Cooper (when I could understand him), Jack London—and on the other, the newspapers, full of breaking news about the world at war. Adventure and violence, something like the *Odyssey* and the *Iliad*, perhaps, and so a kind of bridge-in-the-making to Homer and both his poems.

INTERVIEWER

You did graduate work with a great Alexander Pope scholar, Maynard Mack?

FAGLES

He was a superb mentor (and still is) for many reasons. He would draw my eye to the fine points of Pope's great translation of Homer and then expand into Pope's entire epic vision, his notion of what Homer's all about. Thanks to Maynard, I came to realize, early on, that Pope's *Homer* is really an original English poem on the order of Dryden's translation of the *Aeneid* and Milton's *Paradise Lost.* An important lesson, I think, and not only in literary history; it may have prompted in me a kind of epic ambition that I've tried to follow ever since.

INTERVIEWER

So you came to Greek really as a young adult?

FAGLES

I began the language late . . . my junior year of college. English friends will always scold me for not having come from the womb fluent in ancient Greek. So I've always felt behind and struggled to catch up. That's not false modesty. It's just a fact.

INTERVIEWER

Do you think that Greek and Latin should be taught as a matter of course in the high schools?

FAGLES

I certainly do. And if we can't do that, by all means let's teach Greek and Latin literature in translation. And if the translations are worth their salt, they just may win recruits to learn the old languages themselves.

INTERVIEWER

Your first volume of translations was *Bacchylides*, the choral-lyric poet. Published in 1961, followed in succession by the *Oresteia*, a volume of your own poems, Sophocles' *Theban Plays* and then Homer. There's a natural progression from lyric to tragedy to epic.

FAGLES

Yes, by virtue of twenty-twenty hindsight, I suppose, not by some determined plan. Now that I look back on it, I see that I began with lyric poetry, moved to choral-lyric, which forms the spine of Greek tragedy, then to what we think of as our first tragedy, the *Iliad*, and then to its necessary sequel, the *Odyssey*, its comic sequel—not in the sense of something side-splittingly funny but as a *commedia*, a story of adversity overcome, a song of things harmonious and normal, set to rights.

INTERVIEWER

You acknowledge Robert Graves in your introduction to *Bacchylides*. What was your connection to him?

FAGLES

Oh, just a passing in the night—and a folly of youth. I was translating Bacchylides, and I felt kind of good about it, for no very good reason. So I sent a draft to Robert Graves on Majorca, an idiotic thing to do, chutzpah of the worst sort. And back it came, almost by return mail, with a letter from the master pointing out a lot of errors I had made, things gone wrong in tone or sense, and he signed off by saying, "Excuse me for looking a gift horse in the mouth, but a bit of dentistry won't hurt." I writhe every time I think of it, but I'm grateful for it too, and so it goes.

INTERVIEWER

Have connections with other poets been important to you?

FAGLES

Very much so. I've been blessed with a lot of poet friends, privileged to eavesdrop on their sense of enterprise, vocation. Just to name a few . . . Bill Meredith—and what good news it is that Bill has won the National Book Award for his collected poems—and Ted Weiss, Carolyn Kizer, Maxine Kumin, Richard Howard, Dan Halpern, John Hollander, William Merwin,

Paul Muldoon, Rachel Hadas, C.K. Williams . . . I could go
on and on. Two of the poet-translators have been particularly
helpful. Robert Fitzgerald was a friend, and he confirms our
notion of what an epic poem might be like in modern English.
The other is Edmund Keeley, a friend who is the American
voice of the great modern Greek poets, especially Seferis, who
owes so much to Homer. And last I'd mention Jim Dickey,
whom I knew but only in the last two years of his life. There's
something about the rugged daring of Dickey that I've always
admired, and the few letters that passed between us mean a
lot to me.

INTERVIEWER

And what was the occasion of your first translation from
Homer?

FAGLES

I can practically date it for you, more than twenty years
ago. My mother died in 1976, and it fell to me to fit together
a kind of service for her, some readings, some sentiments,
some tears. The first thing that leaped to mind is a memorable
moment in the *Odyssey*. Odysseus hasn't seen his mother for
twenty years, and he'd left her quite alive in Ithaca before
he went to Troy. But after the war he goes to the underworld
and finds her ghost and sees at once that she belongs to the
world of the dead—a world "embraces cannot bridge"—while
he, alive and breathing, is severed from her. That's the text
I thought might be the best for the occasion, so I tried my
hand at turning it from Greek to English.

INTERVIEWER

You've cited W.B. Stanford's work on the *Odyssey* as an
important influence and said that he told you in County
Wicklow of a path back to the roots of Homer. What was
that path?

FAGLES

Stanford was a fine commentator, on Aeschylus as well as
Homer, and a good friend. We worked on the *Oresteia* to-

gether, and we saw eye to eye about those plays. He felt that the route back to Homer, the source of tragedy, lay in trying to capture Homer's energy, momentum, performative aspect. That sounded right to me, and it was something I pursued.

INTERVIEWER

So you began your Homer project with the *Iliad*, which you published in 1990. I'm curious about how long it took you for each epic.

FAGLES

I think a little over ten years for the *Iliad* and a little under ten for the *Odyssey*.

INTERVIEWER

Those are good Homeric numbers. Can you talk a little bit about the role of Bernard Knox, the classicist whom you describe as your collaborator in these books?

FAGLES

I've been responsible for the translations and Bernard for the introductions and the notes, yet we've passed our writing back and forth, offering suggestions. Bernard is not only a collaborator but my former teacher and now a comrade— though I probably shouldn't use the word for my friendship with an old soldier, a very seasoned one at that. I have never known combat—lucky me—and war is only a dim, vicarious experience for me. To work with Bernard on a translation of the *Iliad*, to receive his comments line by line, shaped the entire poem for me. From my careless use of the word *murder*, for what one soldier was doing to another—when Bernard caught me short and said, "You know, it's really not mur- der"—to Homer's entire vision in Bernard's eyes, the tragic vision of the *Iliad*, the comic vision of the *Odyssey*, especially as we see it in the remarriage of Odysseus and Penelope. From start to finish Bernard's help has meant the world to me. Lawrence of Arabia said that Homer was "more an aspiration than a person. I aspire most fervently in him." I feel the same way about Bernard Knox. He embodies the great classical ideal—"a man of words and a man of action, too."

INTERVIEWER

There was also an impact on your imagination, a sense of having just missed combat in a war?

FAGLES

Yes. This may sound a little far-fetched, but it's something that's been on my mind for many years. Ever since my parents read the papers to me and I could follow the European and Pacific theaters of World War II, I've hankered to be a soldier—if only in that war, a war worth fighting, and winning, too—and I've been fascinated as well as repelled by the notion of mortal combat. Translating the *Iliad* was, in some distant, protected way, a way of entering combat, experiencing what many other friends, somewhat older than myself, have known.

INTERVIEWER

You also spoke about imagining the American Civil War as a path into Homer's song.

FAGLES

Very much so, and largely because of Shelby Foote's three-volume narrative of the Civil War. When I began translating the *Iliad* my friend George Garrett asked if I knew Foote's great work. "No," I said, and he replied, "Well, drop everything and read it!" At the end of Foote's labors—a magnificent piece of writing—he credits Homer as a model for his volumes. And when I think of that "defining moment" in American history I think of a sentiment expressed by Oliver Wendell Holmes (in his Memorial Day address in Keene, New Hampshire, 1884): "Through our great good fortune, in our youth our hearts were touched with fire. It was given to us to learn at the outset that life is a profound and passionate thing." That's Homer through and through.

Can you take us through a sample working day on one of these translations?

FAGLES
I have a merciless internal clock that wakes me up rather early and gets me to my desk by seven-thirty or so and puts me to work on Homer. The work itself? The easiest thing to say is here, on one side, I'd have the Homeric texts and commentaries and lexicons, and on the other, as much as I could manage of English and American poetry, in my head or in an open book—say, Derek Walcott's *Omeros*. There are about 2,700 years that separate the two traditions, and the trick (and the hard labor) is somehow to bring the two together. What I always do is read the Greek aloud until I begin to feel or find some English lurking between the Greek words, between the Greek lines, and I keep on mumbling like a maniac: *Andra moi ennepe, Mousa, polutropon, hos mala polla / plangthê, epei Troiês hieron ptoliethron eperse* . . . "Sing to me of the man, Muse, the man of twists and turns / driven time and again off course, once he had plundered / the hallowed heights of Troy." The two passages are hardly equal, obviously—Homer's infinitely greater—but trying to work from the Greek lines some English cadence of my own, trying over and over, would consume about three hours every morning. I once drove Robert Fitzgerald back to the Newark airport after he gave a reading in Princeton, and I said—fatuously, when he was halfway through his *Iliad*— "it's an awfully long poem, isn't it, Robert?" And he replied, "Yes, Bob, but I wake up every morning with Homer as my companion. That's the privilege." I know exactly how that feels now. It's quite a privilege, and one you hate to leave.

INTERVIEWER
Robert Fitzgerald, your predecessor in these translations, said that his guide was to remove anything transient from the language, that the test of any given phrase would be, "Is

it worthy to be immortal?" You have said that your aim was to bring to life as many voices as possible. Can you talk a little bit about your sense of Homer as performance?

FAGLES

I think it has a lot to do with voices. As I read Homer, he's a remarkable combination of the timeless, immortal phrase, and of the timely, too, and he's meant to be heard, not read. "*Homer* makes us Hearers"—in Pope's fine formulation—"and *Virgil* leaves us Readers." The *Iliad* is more than half dialogue, direct discourse; the *Odyssey* more than two thirds. Both are very dramatic poems, in other words, filled with many voices. It's as if Homer were a ventriloquist, projecting his voice into the voices of dozens of people living within his poems. That's one of the most important things to capture—if you can—the dramatic sense that he conveys. Whole books (Books Nine and Twenty-four of the *Iliad*, Nineteen and Twenty-three of the *Odyssey*, the reunion of the king and queen) could be lifted out of the text and placed directly on a stage. They're plays waiting to be performed.

INTERVIEWER

Do you think it's this conception of translation as performance that differentiates your work from your predecessors' versions?

FAGLES

I can't say, or at least I'd rather not. I can't believe that any translator ever set about to write an unspeakable Homer—though I think that Chapman came quite close! But whether mine is more speakable than other translations, I'd rather leave that for others to decide.

INTERVIEWER

Until roughly the 1950s Homer in English had been a pretty British fellow.

FAGLES

That's true.

INTERVIEWER

Is he having an American incarnation now, and why is that?

FAGLES

He's still a pretty British fellow. (Any Brit will tell you!) In fact, much of Homer's currency derives from Christopher Logue's epiphanies from the *Iliad*, and the strong prose translations by E.V. Rieu, revised by his son, and Walter Shewring. The English tend to take their Homer straight, in prose. We tend to like our Homer in verse. That may explain, in fact, why American translations of Homer are in style these days. We don't want to subject a great ancient poem to what Fitzgerald would call "the betrayal of prose." We want our work to be in partnership with Homer's poetry—in poetry that's in some way comparable (never equivalent!) to the matchless Greek original. I think it's through that effort, trying to turn Homer into poetry, that we just may come a little closer to Matthew Arnold's unforgettable touchstones: Homer is simple, direct, swift and, above all, noble. So Homer's becoming more and more a Yank these days. At least I'd like to think so.

INTERVIEWER

One of the traditional problems for a Homer translator has been that rapid movement from the sublime to the low, from Olympus to pails of milk with flies swarming around them, which made Pope wince.

FAGLES

And he couldn't handle it very well, either . . .

INTERVIEWER

Has being an American poet given you a different perspective on that and maybe even been an advantage?

FAGLES

I think it's been an advantage. We are more agile in climbing off our high horse than some other practitioners of English. We like a full run in tone from the high to the low. Robert Frost might even be, I think, what you call a tutelary spirit. There are many things in Frost that come to an American Homerist's aid. One is his bluntness. That does well for the *Iliad*, I think. His kind of earthy, ironic savvy has a lot to do with the pastoral parts of the *Odyssey*, especially with the long powwows between Odysseus and the pigkeeper. When we're writing well, and talking well, there are parts of American speech that are rough and ready on the one hand, "high, wide and handsome" on the other—strong with a kind of burly courtesy. When I think of those American tones and turns of speech, I think they might serve Homer rather well.

INTERVIEWER

For me that's been one of the freshest and most daring elements of your translation—the refracting of Homer through American voices and, in some ways, the jettisoning of Shakespeare, whose echoes are so strong in other translations, especially Fitzgerald's.

FAGLES

I tried, in fact, to stay away from Shakespeare. The Shakespearean gesture might be too literary, stilted, too "poetic." Homer is more down-to-earth than that. I'd like to persuade a reader that Homer is not a writer, strange as that may sound. There's something paradoxical about reading Homer in a book. He's meant to be heard—performed, not savored in your brown study, where you can mull over the same passage time and again. Nothing should get in the way of Homer's immediacy, his headlong pace.

INTERVIEWER

On the other hand, has the lack of tradition in American poetry as public speech been a hindrance?

FAGLES

There's probably no tradition of public speech as poetry, but there's a lot of public speech in this country that verges on poetry. I'm thinking of Lincoln, of course, and Frederick Douglass too, and all the voices resonating throughout Ken Burns's *Civil War*. We're not short on a commanding kind of oratory. I think again of Oliver Wendell Holmes.

INTERVIEWER

Can you give us a metaphor for the role of a translator with regard to his poet: we have prison; we have marriage; we have ghost and medium?

FAGLES

Let me tackle them all and give each one a twist, if I may. Being a translator is to be a prisoner, all right, a prisoner of Homer, which is not such a bad thing after all. I mean, if you're a "lifer" with Homer, Homer has the gift of setting you free, on occasion, releasing you into a larger form of utterance than you'd ever imagined for yourself. Was the next metaphor a marriage?

INTERVIEWER

Yes.

FAGLES

Marriage. It is a kind of marriage, often on the rocks, I must say, when the days go hard and the work won't come and you can't hear Homer for a moment. But it can be a good marriage, too, I think. I remember the line in praise of marriage that Odysseus says to Nausicaa—"two minds, two hearts that work as one." That, too, can be the relationship between a translator and his great original, if you're lucky. What was the other? Ghost . . .

INTERVIEWER
Ghost and medium.

FAGLES
Ghost and medium. Indeed, you're a kind of ghost writer. I remember George Steiner's bon mot: "when a translator looks behind him what he sees is a eunuch's shadow." I'm a little unclear about the physiology here but I surely know the feeling. You're bloodless, to some extent. A ghost writer for the great master, it's true. Yet you're also like those ghosts in Homer's underworld. You're sipping the magic blood that can animate you, give you a voice in fact. So it's a kind of necessary dying, as Keats would put it, "dying into life."

But my favorite metaphor for the relationship is that of actor and role to play. You need to perform Homer, in your own day and age. I'm always asking myself: "If Homer lived in the nineties, how would he say this or that?" Well, given the limits of our language, not to mention our sensibility, he probably wouldn't have mentioned the "wine-dark sea" or "the dawn with rose-red fingers," let alone a one-eyed cannibal or a witch that turns men into swine or, most miraculous of all, a marriage that survives twenty years of separation! But, at the same time, Homer might insist on those miracles even in the nineties. And so, as an actor with a role to play, you experience a kind of contraction and a kind of release as well. And if you feel the limits and the liberation fully enough, you stand a chance, as the good cliché would have it, of "bringing Homer home."

INTERVIEWER
Is it possible to give us a little psychological portrait of Greek?

FAGLES
That's a pretty tall order. But let me try—in a few words! To begin with, Homer's Greek is paratactic. It sets things side by side. Its favorite way of joining the elements in a

sentence is to say "and" and "and" and "and." (Hemingway mastered the art, as you know.) And Homer's Greek is not only paratactic, it's remarkably forthright and direct, it has a terrific energy and momentum. What's more, Homer has a metric in him that's unstoppable and quite wonderful. Whether he's building a raft or hitching up a wagon or stringing a bow or winging an arrow, whatever Homer describes, however homely or humdrum, it always comes out as poetry—metrical, memorable. On the other hand, turning to English, my English at least, it's more hypotactic than paratactic. It deals in probable causes, in subordinations, and insubordinations. My English is hardly forthright and direct; it's more understated, lacking in forward drive, more phrase-bound, clausebound, fragmentary. What I try to say is never poetry, whether I'm describing a long hard sail in the Mediterranean or the reunion of a king and queen. My English, and much of the English I inherit, is far from cadenced, by and large, unless a Melville or a Faulkner makes it so. Well, so much for a brief character sketch of Homer's language, all too brief.

INTERVIEWER

Can you talk about the mystery whereby translations of the same author will inevitably reflect a translator's personal preoccupations?

FAGLES

I think I had some things on my mind, even on the brain. I wanted to bring out not only the surging action and violence of the *Iliad* but also its gravitas, the weight and majesty of the poem, especially in its more tragic moments. When I came to a great line that Priam speaks to Achilles, I labored over it quite a while. It sounds like this in Greek: *etlên d'hoi ou pô tis epichthonios brotos allos, / andros paidophonoia poti stoma cheir' oregesthai.* And a far cry in English sounds like this: "I have endured what no one on earth has ever done before / I put to my lips the hands of the man who killed

my son." Those lines, at least in Greek, represent the great
Iliadic experience. Hermes, who escorts Priam to Achilles'
tent to ransom Hector's body, never told the old king that
he had to kiss Achilles' hands—it's simply Priam's impulse.
But by doing so, he brings both men to tears, tears for their
own losses, and from their tears flows a reconciliation, however
brief, between the bereft king and the killer of his sons. It's
a moving, tragic moment, and I dwelt on it, long and hard.
A comparable, crucial moment in the *Odyssey* is when, in
the next to last book, Penelope challenges Odysseus by telling
the housekeeper to move his bed from the bedroom. Of course
it's not movable, it's built around the trunk of an olive tree.
He knows that, and so should she. So, in exasperation, he
goes back over the source of the bed, how he constructed
it, and where the olive stood. And he concludes by telling
Penelope, "This is our *sêma*, this is our sign." But *sêma* in
Greek means more than sign; it's also a mark of identification,
even something that stands for a person's life. So when I
came to the conclusion—it sounds like this in Greek: *houtô
toi tode sêma piphauskomai*—I expanded a little and came
up with, "There's our secret sign, I tell you, our life story."
I felt the bed could hold the biography of the couple, could
bring them back together again, and like the olive tree could
ensure the vitality of their reunion. Moments like that—if
they hit you hard enough, and you dwell on them long
enough—begin to open up a poem as momentous as the *Iliad*
or the *Odyssey*.

INTERVIEWER

Both epics contain battle scenes and love scenes. The combat is described in intense and inventive physical detail, noses
are lopped off, genitals are mutilated, teeth are knocked out.
But when we come to physical love, the act of erotic love,
it's hardly described in any physical detail at all. What do
you make of that?

FAGLES

It's true. It's hard to know what to make of it. We've
talked about it before, and I like your idea that lovemaking

can be described, at times, in terms of battle, and that's a cruel, savage irony. You also suggested, I remember, that it may be a question of Homeric decorum, a kind of conventionality that keeps him from being as physical about the act of love as he is about the act of killing. But if Homer is short on physical descriptions of lovemaking, he's fairly long on dramatic occasions for it, and these, I think, are really very telling. And you can find a way to bring them out, if only playfully. Homer doesn't title his books. That falls to the translator, if he wants to try his hand. I call Book Fourteen of the *Iliad*, where Hera seduces Zeus to keep him out of battle, "Hera Outflanks Zeus." (Perhaps for no good reason, but there it is.) I also think of some great moments that are Homer's way of making love dramatically. May I read you one?

INTERVIEWER

Please.

FAGLES

This is the simile that describes the reunion of Penelope and Odysseus in the next to last book of the *Odyssey*:

> The more she spoke, the more a deep desire for tears
> welled up inside his breast—he wept as he held the wife
> he loved, the soul of loyalty, in his arms at last.
> Joy, warm as the joy that shipwrecked sailors feel
> when they catch sight of land—Poseidon has struck
> their well-rigged ship on the open sea with gale winds
> and crushing walls of waves, and only a few escape,
>   swimming,
> struggling out of the frothing surf to reach the shore,
> their bodies crusted with brine but buoyed up with joy
> as they plant their feet on solid ground again,
> spared a deadly fate. So joyous now to her
> the sight of her husband, vivid in her gaze,
> that her white arms, embracing his neck
> would never for a moment let him go . . .

I find that very physical and, in its own way, erotic too. Watch how the simile works. The land to the shipwrecked sailor turns from Odysseus's feelings to the feelings of Penelope, and so the simile gives the couple a reciprocity, a mutuality that I find very heartening, and it presents their lovemaking, or at least the foreplay to it, in a very dramatic way.

INTERVIEWER

You've said that Odysseus is a character who has no consistency whatever, that he is as cruel as he is tender, as innocent as he is knowing, and as naive as he is experienced. Would you say this is also true of Penelope, or is she a different order of creation?

FAGLES

Let me begin by correcting myself. I never meant to say that Odysseus is inconsistent. I'd say he's remarkably complete. As Joyce put it, he's the "complete all-round" man, he's seen from every angle, seen with all his faculties intact. The best description of this kind of character comes from John Crowe Ransom, a critic whom few people read these days, unfortunately. Ransom refers to "character," not in the sense of habitual goodness, "but the Shakespearean, modern, passionately cherished, almost religious sense of the total individuality of a person who is rich in vivid yet contingent traits, even physical traits, that are not ethical at all." And as Ransom concludes, this kind of character "engages an auditor's love, and that is more than his ethical approval." That's the completeness of Odysseus. Do I think Penelope has the same sort of completeness? Absolutely. She goes from a creature of dreams to the hard-edged realist who can plan the contest of the bow that leads to the slaughter of the suitors and Odysseus's identification of himself. She's a weaver of fabrics—he's a weaver of plots. And together they complete the most natural marriage in fiction.

INTERVIEWER

Garry Wills has written that one of the great strengths of your translation of the *Odyssey* is its psychological subtlety

in the way Homer presents women characters. I wanted to
ask if you felt that the entry of women into classical scholarship
has changed the way we read the classics and translate them?

FAGLES

Indeed I do. I mentioned that passage about the *sêma* of
Odysseus's bed. I owe much of my sense of the word to one
of my colleagues at Princeton, Froma Zeitlin, who, among
other things, is one of the leading classicists with a feminist
leaning. Feminist criticism has identified exactly what Wills
is talking about. Yet remember that Wills describes the reunion of Odysseus and Penelope as "the greatest picture in
all literature of a mature love demanded and bestowed on
both sides equally." I think that equality is what you sense
in the famous simile in Book Twenty-three, the one I just
read, yet it's something as old as Homer, and it's typical of
his perspective on our lives. I think, in other words, that
feminist criticism offers a welcome clarification of many Homeric effects—effects which were always there.

INTERVIEWER

I'd like to propose a paradox for you to comment on. Many
readers, sophisticated, unsophisticated, come to Homer and
feel it's the best poetry they've ever read. Yet it takes no
special intelligence or training to read Homer. If you go to
Wallace Stevens or T.S. Eliot, you have to have your wits
about you. They ask a different kind of collaboration from
a reader. But Homer does so much work for the reader beforehand that he or she can just bring attention at the outset. I
would like to ask how is it possible that this best of poets,
whom you call "everything," requires the least of a reader?

FAGLES

I'm not so sure that Homer requires the least of a reader.
You suggest that what he asks of us—and it's the perfect
word—is *attention*. Our attention is riveted on Homer because Homer, thanks perhaps to the seeming simplicity of

his effects, is reality incarnate. In many ways I think that, far from asking the least of us, he may just ask the most—the most direct kind of participation, line by line, that kind of attention. Ruskin said this best, in *Modern Painters*, when he put words in Homer's mouth and had him say: "These are the facts of the thing. I see nothing else than these. Make what you will of them." The act of making what you will of Homer requires enormous attention, the utmost mental, physical, visceral energy from a reader or a listener—the ultimate participation.

INTERVIEWER

Here's another paradox. You've spoken eloquently of Homer as the great poet of the nature of human fate. I wonder how conscious you were as you undertook this work that you, as a translator, and we, as readers, are in fact the latest turn in Homer's fate, that he is at our tender mercies?

FAGLES

He's at our mercy all right, and I hope it's tender too. At times he gets some rough treatment, but Homer's so resilient he always springs back into shape and always, I think, seems to ask for more. It's true that a great poet becomes, in some sense, the later tradition that absorbs him. To take, or twist, a leaf from Borges, the greatest influence on the *Odyssey* is Joyce's *Ulysses*. The best aid for my own reading of the *Odyssey*, at least, is Joyce's novel. As a translator, I turn to him again and again, episode by episode. Perhaps that's a misleading, even dangerous thing to do, but I find it helpful. Homer's fate in the twentieth century is, in large part, the fate of James Joyce. Not such a bad fate to meet up with. You could do worse! So for those who don't speak Greek, Homer may live in our own language, and that's the latest twist of fate, one that just may offer him some kindness. For Homer will always have the last word—since the duty of a translator is to live up to the vivid drama that runs through Homer's lines and song.

INTERVIEWER

Moving from the paradoxical to the impossible, is translation a comic or a tragic activity?

FAGLES

I'll fudge the question and say it's something of both. Or I'll try to answer by saying—too simply—that when you're translating the *Iliad*, by God it's a tragic activity. When you're translating the *Odyssey*, it's wonderfully comic. Not only funny, what with the poem's sneezes, puns and fools, but there's something restorative about the *Odyssey*, a quality that belongs to the comic vision, as I mentioned before—the return home, the reclaiming of one's roots, and the sensation of rising back to strength and health and wholeness.

INTERVIEWER

I would indulge in a Barbara Walters moment because I happen to know that you are a football fan.

FAGLES

Who's a football fan?

INTERVIEWER

You are!

FAGLES

Can't keep any secrets.

INTERVIEWER

It would be great to work a fantasy football team out of the *Iliad* and the *Odyssey*.

FAGLES

Out of the *Iliad* and the *Odyssey*? Good. I know who'd be thrown off the team as captain. Agamemnon. He's a disaster as a leader! Achilles is the best broken-field runner. And the one I'd most like as a coach is Penelope. Good at

tactics, better at building morale, emotional when it counts.
I don't mean to be gallant. I'm not half-kidding.

INTERVIEWER

Just shrewd.

FAGLES

But not as shrewd as she.

—**Patricia Storace**

Kenneth Rosen

The Motto

By silence he meant it's bad enough
To squander words on paper. Don't waste them,
Along with your breath, on air. By exile
He meant the self-imposed, interminable
Theater of travel, the willed intensification
Of standard transience in which one's
Effortlessly the star of a not necessarily
Perilous adventure. He never meant banishment
Nor rejection, personal or political,
Neither Siberia nor *Tristia*. He meant Paris
And Trieste. By cunning he meant
Neither wisdom nor kindness. He meant
Avoid them, and practice the cleverness
And cruelty of a street beggar. If this
Doesn't seem to you the clue or path
To Homeric centrality, O blind man,
Blind woman, in love with the rhythms
Of utterance, noble, swift, yet plain,
Stay here, open your heart and your mouth
To me. See if you don't feel begin in you
An amazing wandering, a cyclops easily fooled,
A princess wet with pity, a dangerous song
From rocks in fog, a witch alone with a pig
Forever, a happy ending, a homecoming
In which everything is almost restored.

Three Poems by Kay Ryan

Dutch

Much
of life is Dutch
one-digit operations

in which
legions of
big robust
people crouch

behind badly cracked
dike systems

attached
by the thumbs

their wide, balloon-pantsed
rumps up-ended
to the Northern sun

while back in town
little black-suspendered
tulip magnates stride around.

Lime Light

One can't work
by lime light.

A bowl full
right at
one's elbow

produces no
more than
a baleful
glow against
the kitchen table.

The fruit purveyor's
whole unstable
pyramid

doesn't equal
what daylight did.

Crash

Slip is one
law of crash
among dozens.

There is also
shift—
moving a
granite lozenge
to the left
a little,
sending down
a cliff.

Also toggles:
the idle flip
that trips

the rails
trains travel.

No act
or refusal
to act, no
special grip
or triple lock
or brake stops

crash: crash
quickens
on resistance
like a legal system
out of Dickens.

Molly Bendall

Stunted Gardens

Dear Emile, I'm tolerating the tribute
of these flowers in the garden you once planted—
their modulating wits, the conspiratorial
turns and mockings of their heads.
I'm treating myself to a new plot
with glittery stems and fresh melodramas.
There were some salad moments of yours

still lurking—I'd enshrine them as you would
a lipstick print on an envelope. So,
I'm committed to redoing this longing bed
with a circle of snapdragons, then an angle
here, fast breezy star-blossoms over here.
A Balanchine design—hips forward
and Suzanne Farrell in the wings

with huge exaggerated eyelashes.
And as the dog days arrive, I'll remember
your élan, your delicate persecution. I wish
I knew the French names for flowers' sexual parts,
pronounced, I'm sure, deeper in the throat . . .
like *j'espère*. And these queens that
I've arranged with remembrances in mind

are oozing their jellied puffs of scent.
Finally, you know, when romance gives way,
sometimes there's the suggestion
of a petal's texture. I see it all in another season . . .
the slightly askew garden, its generous sapphire
and someone—maybe you, maybe me—
sweeping the shavings from imperishable gems.

Corey Marks

For Keats, After Keats

I.

Were I there, leaning against a London building's
filthy stonework, gazing by chance into a street
at the moment of *this* carriage's transit
from the city, its long exhalation toward Hampstead,

I'd watch the man clinging to the carriage-top
who stares at the driver's lash streaming in the air
as though each flick creates a new inscription
and not the patina of everything already undone.

This man, who doesn't understand the sun
whorled in sharp blue when he reels, or the city's
fevered inversion, doesn't understand the gravity
until the carriage-top licks hard against his cheek.

I'd watch the moment when he begins his blur
toward imperceptibility, when the cough comes,
scrawling its way through his lungs, each spasm
a foul adjective describing the noun of his body,

though untranslatable, like the scrawl of a child
who hasn't learned to write but writes anyway,
filling a page with interlacing loops already shaped
by his hand's shape, script already slanted,

crooked with what renders difference, makes
any word spiraling from his hand *his* word.
Only the child can tell what story's housed
in those sprawling ovals, and he remains

mute on the matter, bending close to the pen tip,
listening in some small room notched in the city
to the cut of each slow line against paper,
the immaculate sound of his body entering language.

II.

Perhaps the child's is the story of a room—a room
as empty as his wide scrawl, where the walls
have been washed again with white, and its articles
emptied into the city crosshatched beyond the window:

a bed, rolled and burned in a Roman alleyway
under the disinterested eye of a policeman, fueled
by a trunk of books, pages bending back into themselves
in flames, scoured first of words, then matter.

But the child will lose his own story in time, no matter
how he shapes the words. He'll never be the poet,
but the one left with another's words, never be
the one who hunches in a room writing a letter

when light rears from the ache in his lungs
like an incomprehensible utterance, light streaming
as an imagined visitation, a form so bloated
with luminescence it must burst, and does

when the lesions nettling his lungs wane,
sharpening the room's lines: *it's only morning;
and the dullard sun scrubs through the filthy windows.*
Instead, the child will become the man

who copies the letter in legible script. One morning
he'll sit in his own cold room, his back to a window,
and stitch a row of *X*s over the name Keats
penned so certainly in his final letter—*I shall write to . . .*

He listens for the tick as the pen snaps each line
across its opposite, listens as what was left undone
is undone, as outside the sun presses
like a faint and failing face against the glass.

III.

Were I that child, perhaps I would have laced
a different story into my chain of ovals, a story
I'd never have let go. Though more likely I too
would have diminished, sloughing my story's skin

to find myself at a desk mottled with Keats' papers,
the city leaning through the window at my shoulder.
I would have gazed mutely as my hand stitched over
the name in his letter with a coroner's imprecision.

But I never stared into the poet's unraveling, never saw
even the final tangle of possibility as it came undone,
still disturbing the world. My eyes blur, nothing else,
tracing the breathless cells Keats' words have become,

empty as a chain of loops inscribed across a page
empty as his lungs, half consumed and blackened
when the doctors cracked his chest in autopsy
to look on the disease they'd never read.

Nerves, they had told him, as though something
so vague could write him out of the story.
His words are text and texture on paper, or are excised
in a simple row of *X*s, a last retraction of possibility.

I want to copy what's illegible, make it clear,
though only my own words curl in my hand. My story.

There's no recovery—not even in the doctor's words
as he fingers Keats' vein, months before death,

and ticks the skin with a scalpel, releasing blood
to scrawl along the poet's arm toward free fall,
toward the bodiless, unencumbered moment:
Don't write. Don't write again.

Donald Platt

White Iris

Every year the flowers come back in the same order:
       first the crocus
like all the teenage girls on the block deciding

       on the same day to wear
purple high-top sneakers with yellow laces, then the whips
       of forsythia unbraid

into blossoms, and suddenly spring's a five-alarm
       fire that leaps
the streets. Daffodil and tulip flare up, a chicken-pox

       epidemic runs
through my daughter's daycare, the white winter faces of
   children erupt
       into rosettes that blister,

scab over and eventually fall off, petals of the ornamental
       cherry on the sidewalk
after rain, wisteria's low-grade fever, the jonquils'

       night-lights left on
all day, April's usual hysterics. My favorite's the white
       iris pushing through

the backyard's bad soil, detritus of smashed glass and old
   cracked concrete
       foundations, a stand
of thin phalli with uncircumcised buds shaped

like .38 caliber
bullets about to explode under the sun's triggering
    forefinger into

such vaginal blossoms, each with three
    frilled petals cupped
over the blue-veined styles, beneath which the sepals

    hang down
their dogs' tongues on a hot afternoon. What have I done
    to deserve and possess

this bounty growing wild in the backyard
    of a house I only
rent? Is it God or good luck? No, my neighbors say

    it's Mrs. Theresa della Rosa,
the renter before us, who had an option to buy, but lost
    her job in the meat department

at Smith's and had to move. It's she who, on a block
    of dark brick
    bungalows, painted our stucco
house white with lime-green stripes and fuchsia trim

    so it reminds
my wife of the pastel box of saltwater taffy she was given
    in childhood and hoarded

for half a year, eating one candy every week, a mouthful
    of sugared rubber bands.
As soon as she saw the house with its FOR RENT sign, she wanted

    to live there
and eat taffy forever. We still get bills and junk mail for
    Theresa della Rosa

or Current Resident. As I scrawl in my lopsided
      handwriting, "No longer
at this address / Return to sender," and put the bills

      back in the rusted mailbox,
I see my grandmother straighten up from weeding
      the zinnia bed, one hand

rubbing the hip she broke that's been mending
      slowly, the other
crumbling the black dirt she's just turned over.

      But Grandmother's seven years
dead, and Theresa della Rosa, though only a name
      I love, lives

in the white irises she planted, their perennial
      signature, anonymously
breaking through the dark illegible soil.

Two Poems by Constance Urdang

Atlantic Song

> *Ah, the Atlantic Ocean! You should have seen it then.*
> —Burt Lancaster, in *Atlantic City*

I walk along the shore,
Wind's salt tongue licks my face,
And see—beyond the swells
Of gray Atlantic, where
Seagull and petrel trace
The figures of their dances on the air—
The round earth's watery rim,
The jumping-off place.

Plunging from crest to crest
White horses in the foam
Dare me to ride them out
Far from the gritty shore,
Across the shuddering wastes
Where emptiness begins
Until there is no rest
And no returning home.

I walk along the shore
Where emptiness begins,
And see, beyond the swells,
White horses in the foam.
Seagull and petrel trace
Their dances in the air—
I cannot follow there.
Wind's salt tongue licks my face.

Salt Water

1.

Above: sun on the mountain
Below: mist on the water
The wise one waits

2.

At the rough edge of the continent
A meager harvest:
Sea wrack and saw grass, cold iron, crusted stone

3.

Let the lover come bearing a gift of seaweed
Pungent bladderwort, more aphrodisiac
Than all the perfumes of Araby

4.

The embroidery of little sails on the surface
Is quilting the tide, wakes foaming
Lacy as the train of a wedding dress

5.

A small powerboat interrupts
Stuttering across the chop
With a sound like the householder splitting wood for winter

6.

At half-past ten the salty freshness
Of morning is already diluted
As the water turns brackish at the mouth of the river

7.

Old Leteesha knew what she was doing
When she sent the children down to the beach
To bring back a medicine bottle filled with salt water

Rosanna Warren

Mud

for John Walker

It's not as simple as rhyming "mud" and "blood"
    as Owen did and does ("I, too, saw God through mud")
    in his "Apologia."
Or feces and "fecit," which is
    a kind of rhyme as in
    "Walker fecit," which he

did and does through
    mud, bruised flesh, pigment, glossy
    oil pressed from memory's trench:
"God" rhymes of course with
    everything. It's not enough
    to spread damp clay ("Was it for this

the clay grew tall?") across canvas: he can't
    bury fathers, uncles,
    sons, they keep
sprouting, worms their words ("Men went
    to Catraeth as day
    dawned"): Our words, his

words: Aneirin, Jones, a seethe on
    the surface we cannot
    possess. The dead belong
to no one, live their own
    maggoty life observed
    by the small, sheepskulled soldier;

by the father who clambers out of the painter's skull;
   by the easel which wants
   to be lantern and cross.
The Somme? July 1, 1916: men went, men
   want: all those men marched
   which century? Sixth? The

Welsh at Catraeth, three hundred dead: a sum:
   a song. Whose ribcage
   gapes? Whose numbers ooze
in the ditch of years? This painter comes
   too late. He hoists
   his loops of pods upon

a firmament of mud, he hangs dark swags
   of script and
   sacrament. (A
duchess approves. She likes chiaro-
   scuro in love and
   war). The painter has brought

a necklace—no, a rosary—of human
   kidneys, slick
   and soiled. It is
not as easy as rhyming "mud"
   and "blood." The words belong
   to no one. (Not that we

wanted. Not that we wanted to know.)

Albert Goldbarth

Sestina: As There Are Support Groups, There Are Support Words

The name of his native country pronounced on a distant shore
could not please the ears of a traveler more than hearing the
words nitrogen, oxidation of iron *and* hygrometer.
                                    —Alexander von Humboldt,
                              nineteenth-century scientist / explorer

When visiting a distant (and imponderable) shire,
one longs to hear the cry "Hygrometer!
Fresh hygrometer for sale!" Yes, and when the fair
sex sidles close and coyly murmurs "nitrogen"
into a burly masculine ear, I guarantee you: the translation
is *very* easy. The allurements of a local siren,

whispering the kind of patois a traveler like Lord Byron
favors, never fail to comfort and to reassure,
evoking pleasant memories of one's own beloved hygrometer
at home, kept fresh in Cosmoline and camphor
and awaiting one's rearrival back in his native xenon and
    nitrogen.
Without these occasional reminiscences, any translation

from nation to nation, tongue to tongue, becomes a
    translation
difficult to sustain. I think of my grandmother: "We're
    not hirin'
today" "Go away" "Dumb Jew"—*her* share
of the language that greeted her here in the land of alien
    hygrometer
and freedom, where she was only one more funny-skirted for-
eigner yearning to hear a lulling Hungarian nitrogen

hum her to sleep. Eventually, of course, the American
 nitrogen
sufficed. Her daughter could speak, in free translation,
both uranium and argon; and her granddaughter gigs with
 Fire 'n
Ice, a skinhead punk-grunge group that performs in sheer
black nighties and clown wigs—she plays mean electric
 hygrometer
in the first set and then, for a twofer,

(*very* American, that) plays paper-and-comb. Far
out. She's so fluent in various World Wide Webbery, that
 nitrogen
in a thousand different inflections is her birthright, and
 almost any translation,
mind to mind, gender to gender, is second nature. "I earn
my keep, I party, I sleep," is her motto. Though she's fortunate in having a lover who's CEO at Hygrometer,

Potassium, Klein & Wong: it helps to pay the "hygrometer
man" when he knocks at the door. I won't say that they fear
this guy exactly, but he's a major badass nitrogen-
 sucking cyberwired ninja-kicking shitheel (or, translation:
call him Sir). It makes one pine for a land where the birds
 all choir in
sweetly trilling melodies on a flower-scented shore,

and a translation sings all night. Row gen-
tly toward it. The tender forests sigh, and the soft whirr
of the hygrometer promises oxidation of iron.

Tugboat Syndrome

Jonathan Lethem

Context is everything. Dress me up and see. I'm a carnival
barker, an auctioneer, a downtown performance artist, a
speaker in tongues, a senator drunk on filibuster. My mouth
won't quit, though mostly I whisper or subvocalize like I'm
reading aloud, my Adam's apple bobbing, jaw muscle beating
like a miniature heart under my cheek, the noise suppressed,
the words escaping silently, mere ghosts of themselves, husks
empty of breath and tone. In this diminished form the words
rush out of the cornucopia of my brain to course over the
surface of the world, tickling reality like fingers on piano
keys. Caressing, nudging. They're an invisible army on a
peacekeeping mission, a peaceable horde. They mean no
harm. They placate, interpret, massage. Everywhere they're
smoothing down imperfections, putting hairs in place, putting ducks in a row, replacing divots. Counting and polishing
the silver. Patting old ladies gently on the behind, eliciting
a giggle. Only—here's the rub—when they find too much
perfection, when the surface is already buffed smooth, the

ducks already orderly, the old ladies complacent, then my
little army rebels, breaks into the stores. Reality needs a prick
here and there, the carpet needs a flaw. My words begin
plucking at threads nervously, seeking purchase, a weak point,
a vulnerable ear. That's when it comes, the urge to shout in
the church, the nursery, the crowded movie house. It's an
itch at first. Inconsequential. But that itch is soon a torrent
behind a straining dam. Noah's flood. That itch is my whole
life. Here it comes now. Cover your ears. Build an ark. I've
got Tourette's.

"Eat me!" I scream.

I grew up in the library of St. Vincent's Home for Boys in
downtown Brooklyn, on a street which serves as the off-ramp
to the Brooklyn Bridge. There the Home faced eight lanes
of traffic, lined by Brooklyn's central sorting annex for the
post office, a building that hummed and blinked all through
the night, its gates groaning open to admit trucks bearing
mountains of those mysterious items called letters; by the
Burton Trade School for Automechanics, where hardened
students attempting to set their lives dully straight spilled
out twice a day for sandwich-and-beer breaks, overwhelming
the cramped bodega next door; by a granite bust of Lafayette,
indicating his point of entry into the Battle of Brooklyn; by
a car lot surrounded by a high fence topped with wide curls
of barbed wire and wind-whipped fluorescent flags, and by
a red-brick Quaker meetinghouse that had presumably been
there when the rest was farmland. In short, this jumble of
stuff at the clotted entrance to the ancient, battered borough
was officially Nowhere, a place strenuously ignored in passing
through to Somewhere Else. Until rescued by Frank Minna I
lived, as I said, in the library.

I set out to read every book in that tomblike library, every
miserable dead donation ever indexed and forgotten there—a
mark of my profound fear and boredom at St. Vincent's as
well as an early sign of my Tourettic compulsions for counting,

processing and inspection. Huddled there in the windowsill, turning dry pages and watching dust motes pinball through beams of sunlight, I sought signs of my odd dawning self in Theodore Dreiser, Kenneth Roberts, J.B. Priestley and back issues of *Popular Mechanics* and failed, couldn't find the language of myself. I was closer on Saturday mornings—Daffy Duck especially gave me something, if I could bear to imagine growing up a dynamited, beak-shattered duck. Art Carney on *The Honeymooners* gave me something too, in the way he jerked his neck, when we were allowed to stay up to see him. But it was Minna who brought me the language, Minna and Court Street that let me speak.

We four were selected because we were the four white boys at St. Vincent's. I was surely undersold goods, a twitcher and nosepicker retrieved from the library instead of the school-yard, probably a retard, certainly a regrettable, inferior offering. Mr. Kassel was a teacher who knew Frank Minna from the neighborhood, and his invitation to Minna to borrow us for the afternoon was a first glimpse of the halo of favors and favoritism that extended around Minna—"knowing somebody" as a life condition. Minna was our exact reverse, we who knew no one and benefited nothing from it when we did.

Minna had asked for white boys to suit his clients' presumed prejudice—and his own certain ones. But he didn't show any particular tenderness that first day, a sweltering August weekday afternoon after classes, streets like black chewing gum, slow-creeping cars like badly projected science-class slides in the haze. Though he seemed a man to us, Minna was probably twenty-five. He was gangly except for a tiny potbelly in his pocket-T, and his hair was combed into a smooth pompadour, a Brooklyn hairstyle that stood outside time, projecting from some distant Frank Sinatra past. He opened the rear of his dented, graffitied van and told us to get inside, then slammed and padlocked the doors without explanation, without asking our names.

We four gaped at one another, giddy and astonished at

this escape, not knowing what it meant, not really needing to know. The others, Tony, Gilbert and Danny, were willing to be grouped with me, to pretend I fit with them, if that was what it took to be plucked up by the outside world and seated in the dark on a dirty steel truckbed vibrating its way to somewhere that wasn't St. Vincent's. Of course I was vibrating too, vibrating before Minna rounded us up, vibrating inside always and straining to keep it from showing. I didn't kiss the other three boys, but I wanted to. Instead I made a kissing, chirping sound, like a bird's peep, over and over: "Chrip, chrip, chrip."

Tony told me to shut the fuck up, but his heart wasn't in it, not this day, in the midst of life's unfolding mystery. For Tony, especially, this was his destiny coming to find him. He saw more in Minna from the first because he'd prepared himself to see it. Tony Vermonte was famous at St. Vincent's for the confidence he exuded, confidence that a mistake had been made, that he didn't belong in the Home. He was Italian, better than the rest of us, who didn't know what we were. His father was either a mobster or a cop—Tony saw no contradiction in this, so we didn't either. The Italians would return for him, in one guise or another, and that was what he'd taken Minna for.

Tony was famous for other things as well. He had lived outside the Home and then come back. A Quaker family had taken Tony in, intending to give him a permanent home. He'd announced his contempt even as he packed his clothes: They weren't Italian. Still, he lived with them for a few months. They installed him at Brooklyn Friends, a private school a few blocks away, and on his way home most days he'd come and hang on the St. Vincent's fence and tell stories of the private-school girls he'd felt up and sometimes penetrated, the faggy private-school boys who swam and played soccer but were easily humiliated in fistfights. Then one day his foster parents found prodigious Tony in bed with one girl too many: their own sixteen-year-old daughter. Or so the story went; there was only one source. Anyway, he was reinstalled at St. Vincent's, where he fell easily into his old routine of beating up and befriending me on alternating afternoons.

Gilbert Coney was Tony's right hand, a stocky boy just passing for tough—he would have beamed at you for calling him a thug. But he was tolerant of me, and we had a couple of secrets. On a Home for Boys visit to the Museum of Natural History, Gilbert and I had split from the group and returned to the room dominated by an enormous plastic blue whale suspended from the ceiling, which had been the focus of the official visit. But underneath the whale was a gallery of murky dioramas of undersea life, lit so you had to press close to the glass to find the wonders tucked deep in the corners. In one a sperm whale fought a giant squid. In another a killer whale pierced a floor of ice. Gilbert and I wandered hypnotized, and when a class of third graders was led away we found we had the giant hall to ourselves. Gilbert showed me his discovery: a small brass door beside the penguin diorama had been left unlocked. When he opened it we saw that it led both behind and into the penguin scene.

"Get in, Lionel," said Gilbert.

If I'd not wanted to, it would have been bullying, but I wanted to desperately. Every minute the hall remained empty was precious. The lip of the doorway was knee-high. I clambered in and opened the flap in the ocean-blue painted boards that made the side wall of the diorama, then slipped into the picture. The ocean floor was a smooth bowl of painted plaster. I scooted down the grade on my bended knees, looking out at a flabbergasted Gilbert on the other side of the glass. Swimming penguins were mounted on rods extending straight from the far wall, and others were suspended in the plastic waves of ocean surface that now made a low ceiling over my head. I caressed the nearest penguin, one mounted low, shown diving in pursuit of a fish, patted its head, stroked its gullet as though helping it swallow a dry pill. Gilbert guffawed, thinking I was performing comedy for him, when in fact I'd been overwhelmed by a tender, touchy impulse toward the stiff, poignant penguin. Now it became imperative that I touch *all* the penguins, or all I could, anyway—some were inaccessible to me, on the other side of the barrier of the ocean's surface, standing on ice floes. Shuffling on my knees I made the rounds, affectionately tagging each swimming bird before I made my escape back through the brass door. Gilbert was impressed, I could tell. I was now a kid who'd do anything, do crazy things. He was right and wrong, of course—once I'd touched the first penguin I had no choice.

Somehow this led to a series of confidences. I was crazy but also easily intimidated, which made me Gilbert's idea of a safe repository for his crazy feelings. Gilbert was a precocious masturbator, and looking for some triangulation between his own experiments and schoolyard lore. Did I do it? How often? One hand or two? Close my eyes? Ever rub against the mattress? I took his inquiries seriously, but I didn't really have the information he needed, not yet. My stupidity made Gilbert grouchy at first, and he spent a week or two glowering to let me know what galactic measures of pain awaited if I ratted him out. Then he came back, more urgent than ever. Try it and I'll watch, he said. It's not so hard. I obeyed, as I had in the museum, but the results weren't as good. I couldn't treat myself with the tenderness I'd lavished on the penguins, at least not in front of Gilbert. He became grouchy again, and after two or three go-arounds the subject was permanently dropped.

Tourette's teaches you what people will ignore and forget, teaches you to see the mechanism people employ to tuck away the incongruous, the disruptive—it teaches you because you're the one lobbing the incongruous and disruptive their way. Once I sat on a bus a few rows ahead of a man with a belching tic—long, groaning, almost vomitous-sounding noises, the kind a fifth grader learns to make by swallowing a bellyful of air, then forgets by high school when charming girls becomes more vital than freaking them out. This man's compulsion was terribly specific: he sat at the back of the bus, and only when every head faced forward did he give out with his digestive simulacra. Then, every sixth or seventh time, he'd mix in a messy farting sound. He was a miserable-looking black man in his sixties. Despite the peek-a-boo brilliance of his timing, it was clear to anyone he was the source, and so the other riders coughed reprovingly, quit giving him the satisfaction of looking. Of course, our not glancing back freed him to run together great uninterrupted phrases of his ripest noise. To all but me he was just an antisocial jerk fishing for attention. But I saw that it was unmistakably a compulsion, a tic—Tourette's—and I knew those other passengers would barely recall it a few minutes after stepping off to their destinations. Despite how that maniacal croaking filled the auditorium of the bus, the concertgoers were plainly engaged in the task of forgetting the music. Consensual reality is both fragile and elastic, and it heals like the skin of a bubble. The belching man ruptured it so quickly and completely that I could watch the wound instantly seal.

Similarly, I doubt the other boys directly recalled my bouts of kissing. That tic was too much for us all. Nine months or so after touching the penguins I had begun to overflow with reaching, tapping, grabbing and kissing urges. Those compulsions emerged first, while language was still trapped like a roiling ocean under a calm floe of ice, the way I'd been trapped in the underwater half of the penguin display. I'd begun reaching for door frames, kneeling to grab at skittering loosened sneaker laces (a recent fashion among the toughest boys at St. Vincent's, unfortunately for me), incessantly tapping the metal-pipe legs of the schoolroom desks and chairs and, worst, grabbing and kissing my fellow boys. I grew terrified of myself then and burrowed deeper into the library, but I was forced out for classes or meals. Then it would happen. I'd lunge at someone and kiss their cheek or neck or forehead, whatever I hit. After, compulsion expelled, I could try to explain, defend myself or flee. I kissed Greg

Toon and Edwin Torres, whose eyes I'd never dared meet. I kissed Leshawn Montrose, who'd broken Mr. Voccaro's arm with a chair. I kissed Tony Vermonte and Gilbert Coney and tried to kiss Danny Fantl. I kissed my own counterparts, other invisible boys working the margins at St. Vincent's. "It's a game!" I'd say, pleadingly. "It's a game." Since the most inexplicable things in our lives were games, with their ancient embedded rituals, British Bulldog, Ringolevio and Scully, it seemed possible I might persuade them this was another one, the Kissing Game. Just as important, I might persuade myself. "It's a game," I'd say desperately, as tears of pain ran down my face. Leshawn Montrose cracked my head against a porcelain water fountain; Greg Toon and Edwin Torres generously only shucked me off onto the floor. Tony Vermonte twisted my arm behind my back and forced me against a wall. "It's a game," I breathed. He released me and shook his head, full of contempt and pity. Danny Fantl saw my move coming and faked me out, then vanished down a stairwell. Gilbert stood and glared, deeply unnerved due to our private history. "A game," I reassured him.

Meantime beneath that frozen shell a sea of language was reaching full boil. It became harder and harder not to notice that when a television pitchman said *to last the rest of a lifetime* my brain went *to rest the lust of a loaftomb*, that when I heard "Alfred Hitchcock" I silently replied "Altered Houseclock," that when I sat reading Booth Tarkington in the library, my throat and jaw worked behind my clenched lips, desperately fitting the syllables of the prose to the rhythms of "Rapper's Delight," which was then playing every fifteen or twenty minutes out on the yard.

I found other outlets, other obsessions. The pale thirteen year old Mr. Kassel pulled out of the library and offered to Minna was prone to floor-tapping, whistling, tongue clicking, rapid head turns and wall stroking, anything but the direct utterances for which my Tourette's brain most yearned. Language bubbled inside me now but it felt too dangerous to let out. Speech was intention, and I couldn't let anyone else or myself know how intentional my craziness felt. Pratfalls, antics, those were accidental lunacy, and so forgivable. Practically speaking, it was one thing to stroke Leshawn Montrose's arm, or even to kiss him, another entirely to walk up and call him Shefawn Mongoose or Fuckyou Moonprose. So, though I collected words, treasured them like a drooling sadistic captor, melting them down, filing off their edges, before release I translated them into physical performance, manic choreography.

My body was an overwound watch spring, one which could easily drive a vast factory mechanism like the one in *Modern Times*, which we watched that year in the basement of the Brooklyn Public Library on Fourth Avenue. I took Chaplin as a model: obviously blazing with aggression, he'd managed to keep his trap shut and so had skirted danger and been regarded as cute. I needn't exactly strain for a motto: silence, golden, get it? Got it. Hone your timing instead, burnish those physical routines, your idiot wall stroking and lace chasing, until they're funny in a flickering black and white way, until your enemies don policemen's caps and begin tripping over themselves, until doe-eyed women swoon. So I kept my tongue wound in my teeth, ignored the pulsing in my cheek, the throbbing in my gullet, persistently swallowed language back like vomit. It burned as hotly.

We rode a mile or two before Minna's van halted, engine guttering to a stop. Then he let us out of the back and we found ourselves in a gated warehouse yard under the shadow of the Brooklyn-Queens Expressway, in a ruined industrial zone. Minna led us to a large truck, a detached twelve-wheel trailer with no cab in evidence, then rolled up the back to reveal a load of identical cardboard crates, a hundred, two hundred, maybe more.

"Couple you boys get up inside," said Minna distractedly. Tony and Danny had the guile to immediately leap into the truck, where they could work shaded from the sun. "You're just gonna run this stuff inside, that's all. Hand shit off, move it up to the front of the truck, get it in. Straight shot, you got it?" He pointed to the warehouse. We all nodded, and I peeped. It went unnoticed.

Minna opened the big panel doors of the warehouse and showed us where to set the crates. We started quickly, then wilted in the heat. Tony and Danny massed the crates at the lip of the truck while Gilbert and I made the first dozen runs, then the older boys ceded their advantage and began to help us drag them across the blazing yard. Minna never touched a crate; he spent the whole time in the office of the warehouse, a cluttered room full of desks, file cabinets, tacked-up notes and pornographic calendars and a stacked tower of orange traffic cones, visible to us through an interior window, smoking cigarettes and jawing on the telephone, apparently not listening for replies. Every time I glanced through the window his mouth was moving, but the door was closed, and he was inaudible behind the glass. At some point another man appeared, from where I wasn't sure, and stood in the yard wiping his forehead as though he were the one laboring. Minna came out, the two stepped inside the office, the other man disappeared. We moved the last of the crates inside, Minna rolled the gate of the truck and locked the warehouse, pointed us back to his van, but paused before shutting us into the back.

"Hot day, huh?" he said, looking at us directly for what might have been the first time.

Bathed in sweat, we nodded, afraid to speak.

"You monkeys thirsty? Because personally I'm dying out here."

Minna drove us to Smith Street, a few blocks from St. Vincent's, and pulled over in front of a bodega, then bought us pop-top cans of Miller, and sat with us in the back of the van, drinking. It was my first beer.

"Names," said Minna, pointing at Tony, our obvious leader. We said our first names, starting with Tony. Minna didn't offer his own, only drained his beer and nodded. I began tapping the truck panel beside me.

Physical exertion over, astonishment at our deliverance from St. Vincent's receding, my symptoms found their opening again.

"You probably ought to know, Lionel's a freak," said Tony, his voice vibrant with self-regard. He jerked his thumb in my direction.

"Yeah, well, you're all freaks, if you don't mind me pointing it out," said Minna. "No parents—or am I mixed up?"

Silence.

"Finish your beer," said Minna, tossing his can past us, into the back of the van.

And that was the end of our first job for Frank Minna.

But Minna rounded us up again the next week, brought us to that same desolate yard, and this time he was friendlier. The task was identical, almost to the number of boxes, and we performed it in the same trepidatious silence. I felt a violent hatred burning off Tony in my and Gilbert's direction, as though he thought we were in the process of screwing up his Italian rescue. Danny was exempt and oblivious. Still, we'd begun to function as a team—demanding physical work contained its own truths, and we explored them despite ourselves.

Over beers Minna said, "You like this work?"

One of us said *sure*.

"You know what you're doing?" Minna grinned at us, waiting. The question was confusing. "You know what kind of work this is?"

"What, moving boxes?" said Tony.

"Right, moving. Moving work. That's what you call it when you work for me. Here, look." He stood to get into his pocket, pulled out a roll of twenties and a small stack of white cards. He stared at the roll for a minute, then peeled off four twenties and handed one to each of us. It was my first twenty dollars. Then he offered us each a card. It read: *L & L Movers. Gerard & Frank Minna*. And a phone number.

"You're Gerard or Frank?" said Tony.

"Minna, Frank." Like *Bond, James.* He ran his hand through his hair. "So you're a moving company, get it? Doing moving work." This seemed a very important point: that we call it *moving.* I couldn't imagine what else to call it.

"Who's Gerard?" said Tony. Gilbert and I, even Danny, watched Minna carefully. Tony was questioning him on behalf of us all.

"My brother."

"Older or younger?"

"Older."

Tony thought for a minute. "Who's L & L?"

"Just the name, L & L. Two Ls. Name of the company."

"Yeah, but what's it mean?"

"What do you need it to mean, Fruitloop—Living Loud? Loving Ladies? Laughing at you Losers?"

"What, it doesn't mean anything?" said Tony.

"I didn't say that, did I?"

"Least Lonely," I suggested.

"There you go," said Minna, waving his can of beer at me. "L & L Movers, Least Lonely."

Tony, Danny and Gilbert all stared at me, uncertain how I'd gained this freshet of approval.

"Liking Lionel," I heard myself say.

"Minna, that's an Italian name?" said Tony. This was on his own behalf, obviously. It was time to get to the point. The rest of us could all go fuck ourselves.

"What are you, the census?" said Minna. "Cub reporter? What's your full name, Jimmy Olsen?"

"Lois Lane," I said.

"Tony Vermonte," said Tony, ignoring me.

"Vermont-ee," repeated Minna. "That's what, like a New England thing, right? You a Red Sox fan?"

"Yankees," said Tony, confused and defensive. The Yankees were champions now, the Red Sox their hapless, eternal victims, vanquished most recently by Bucky Dent's famous home run. We'd all watched it on television.

"Luckylent," I said, remembering. "Duckybent."

Minna erupted with laughter. "Yeah, Ducky fucking Bent! That's good. Don't look now, it's Ducky Bent."

"Lexluthor," I said, reaching out to touch Minna's shoulder. He only stared at my hand, didn't move away. "Lunchy-looper, Laughyluck—"

"All right, Loopy," said Minna. "Enough already."

"Loopylip—" I was desperate for a way to stop. My hand went on tapping Minna's shoulder.

"Let it go," said Minna, and now he returned my shoulder taps, once, hard. "Don't tug the boat."

To tugboat was to try Minna's patience. Any time you pushed your luck, said too much, overstayed a welcome or overestimated the usefulness of a given method or approach you were guilty of having tugged the boat. *Tugboating* was most of all a dysfunction of wits and storytellers, and a universal one: anybody who thought themselves funny would likely tug a boat here or there. Knowing when a joke or verbal gambit was right at its limit, quitting before the boat had been tugged, that was art.

Years before the word *Tourette's* was familiar to any of us, Minna had me diagnosed: Terminal Tugboater.

Distributing eighty dollars and those four business cards was all Minna had to do to instate the four of us as the junior staff of L & L Movers. Twenty dollars and a beer remained our usual pay. Minna would gather us sporadically, on a day's notice, or no notice at all—the latter possibility became incentive, once we'd begun high school, for us to return to St. Vincent's directly after classes and lounge in the schoolyard, pretending not to listen for the distinctive grumble of his van's motor. The jobs varied enormously. We'd load merchandise, like the cartons in the trailer, in and out of storefront basement grates all up and down Court Street, borderline shady activity that it seemed wholesalers ought to be handling themselves, transactions sealed with a shared cigar in the back of the shop. Or we'd bustle apartment loads of furniture in and out of brownstone walk-ups, legitimate moving jobs, where fretting couples worried we weren't old or expert enought to handle their belongings—Minna would hush them, remind them of the cost of distractions: "The meter's running." We put sofas through third-story windows with a makeshift cinch and pulley, Tony and Minna on the roof, Gilbert and Danny in the window to receive, me on the ground with the guide ropes. A massive factory building under the Manhattan Bridge, owned by an important unseen friend of Minna's, had been damaged in a fire, and we moved the inhabitants for free, as some sort of settlement or concession. The terms were obscure, but Minna was terrifically urgent about it, seething at any delay—the only meter running now was Minna's credibility with his friend-client. Once we emptied an entire electronics showroom into Minna's truck, pulling unboxed stereos off shelves and out of window displays, disconnecting the wires from lit, blinking amplifiers, eventually even taking the phone off the desk—it would have seemed a sort of brazen burglary had Minna not been standing on the sidewalk in front, drinking beer and telling jokes with the man who'd unpadlocked the shop gates for us as we filed past with the goods. Everywhere Minna connived and cajoled and dropped names, winking at us to make us complicit, and everywhere Minna's clients stared at us boys, some wondering if we'd palm a valuable when they weren't looking, some trying to figure the angle, perhaps hoping to catch a hint of disloyalty, an edge over Minna they'd save for when they needed it. We palmed nothing, revealed no disloyalty. Instead we stared back, tried to make them flinch. And we listened, gathered information. Minna was teaching us, when he meant to and when he didn't.

It changed us as a group. We developed a certain collective ego, a presence apart at the Home. We grew less embattled from within, more from without: non-white boys sensed in our privilege a hint of their future deprivations and punished us for it. Age had begun to heighten those distinctions anyway. So Tony, Gilbert, Danny and myself smoothed out our old antipathies and circled the wagons. We stuck up for one another, at the Home and at Sarah J. Hale, our local high school.

There at Sarah J. the St. Vincent's Boys were disguised, blended with the larger population, a pretty rough crowd despite their presumably having parents and siblings and telephones and bedroom doors with locks and a thousand other unimaginable advantages. There we mixed with girls for the first time—what mixing was possible with the brutal, strapping black girls of Sarah J., gangs of whom laid afterschool ambushes for any white boy daring enough to have flirted, even made eye-contact, with one inside the building. The girls were claimed by boyfriends too sophisticated to bother with school, who rode by for them at lunch hour in cars throbbing with amplified basslines and sometimes boasting bullet-riddled doors, and their only use for us was as a dartboard for throwing lit cigarette butts. Yes, relations between the sexes were strained at Sarah J., and I doubt any of us four, even Tony, so much as copped a feel from the girls we were schooled with there.

Minna's Court Street was the old Brooklyn, a placid ageless surface alive underneath with talk, with deals and casual insults, a neighborhood political machine with pizzeria and butcher-shop bosses and unwritten rules everywhere. All was talk except for what mattered most, which were unspoken understandings. The barbershop, where he took us for identical haircuts that cost three dollars each, except even that fee was waived for Minna—no one had to wonder why the price of a haircut hadn't gone up since 1966, nor why six old barbers were working out of the same ancient storefront; the barbershop was a retirement home, a social club and front for a backroom poker game. The barbers were taken care of because this was Brooklyn, where people *looked out*. Why would the prices go up, when nobody walked in who wasn't part of this conspiracy, this trust?—though if you spoke of it you'd surely meet with confused denials, or laughter and a too-hard cuff on the cheek. Another exemplary mystery was the "arcade," a giant storefront containing three pinball machines and six or seven video games, Asteroids, Frogger, Centipede, and a cashier who'd change dollars to quarters and accept hundred-dollar bills folded into lists of numbers, names of horses and football teams. The curb in front of the arcade was lined with Vespas. They sat without anything more than a bicycle lock for protection, a taunt to vandals. A block away, on Smith, they would have been stripped, but here they were pristine, a curbside showroom. It didn't need explaining—this was Court Street. And Court Street, where it passed through Carroll Gardens and Cobble Hill, was the only Brooklyn, really—north was Brooklyn Heights, secretly a part of Manhattan, south was the harbor, and the rest, everything east of the Gowanus Canal, apart from small outposts of civilization in Park Slope and Windsor Terrace, was an unspeakable barbarian tumult.

Sometimes he needed just one of us. He'd appear at the Home in his Impala instead of the van, request someone specific, then spirit them away to the bruised consternation of those left behind. Tony was in and out of Minna's graces, his ambition and pride costing him as much as he won, but he was unmistakably our leader and Minna's right hand. He wore his private errands with Minna like Purple Hearts, but refused to report on their content to the rest of us. Danny, athletic, silent and tall, became Minna's greyhound, sent on private deliveries and rendezvous, and given early driving lessons in a vacant Red Hook lot, as though Minna were grooming him for work as an international spy, or Kato for a new Green Hornet. Gilbert, all bullish determination, was pegged for the grunt work, sitting in double-parked cars, repairing a load of ruptured cartons with strapping tape, and repainting the van, whose graffitied exterior some of Minna's neighbors had apparently found objectionable. And I was an extra set of eyes and ears and opinions. Minna would drag

me along to backrooms and offices and barbershop negotia-
tions, then debrief me afterwards. What did I think of that
guy? Shitting or not? A moron or retard? A shark or a mook?
Minna encouraged me to have a take on everything, and to
spit it out, as though he thought my verbal disgorgings were
only commentary not yet anchored to subject matter. And
he adored my echolalia. He thought I was doing impressions.

Needless to say, it wasn't commentary and impressions,
but my verbal Tourette's flowering at last. Like Court Street,
I seethed behind the scenes with language and conspiracies,
inversions of logic, sudden jerks and jabs of insult. Now Minna
had begun to draw me out. With his encouragement I freed
myself to ape the rhythm of his overheard dialogues, his
complaints and endearments, his for-the-sake-of arguments.
And Minna loved my effect on his clients and associates,
the way I'd unnerve them, disrupt some schmooze with an
utterance, a head jerk, a husky *"eatme!"* I was his special
effect, a running joke embodied. They'd look up startled and
he'd wave his hand knowingly, counting money, not even
bothering to look at me. "Don't mind him, he can't help
it," he'd say. "Kid's shot out of a cannon." Or: "He likes
to get a little nutty sometimes." Then he'd wink at me,
acknowledge our conspiracy. I was evidence of life's unpredict-
ability and rudeness and poignancy, a scale model of his
own nutty heart. In this way Minna licensed my speech, and
speech, it turned out, liberated me from the overflowing
disaster of my Tourettic self, turned out to be the tic that
satisfied where others didn't, the scratch that briefly stilled
the itch.

"You ever listen to yourself, Lionel?" Minna would say
later, shaking his head. "You really are shot out of a fucking cannon."

"Scott Out Of The Canyon! I don't know why, I just—
fuckitup!—I just can't stop."

"You're a freak show, that's why. Human freak show, and
it's free. Free to the public."

"Freefreak!" I tapped his shoulder.

"That's what I said: a free human freak show."

"Makes you think you're Italian?" said Minna one day, as we all rode together in his Impala.

"What do I look like to you?" said Tony.

"I was thinking maybe Greek," said Minna. "I used to know this Greek guy went around knocking up the Italian girls down Union Street, until a couple their older brothers took him out under the bridge. You remind me of him, you know? Got that dusky tinge. I'd say half Greek. Or maybe Puerto Rican."

"Fuck you."

"Probably know all your parents. We're not talking the international jet set here—bunch of teen mothers, probably live in a five-mile radius, need to know the goddamn truth."

We learned to negotiate the labyrinth of Minna's weird prejudices blind, and blindly. Hippies, for instance, were dangerous and odd, also sort of sad in their utopian wrongness. ("Your parents must of been hippies," he'd tell me. "That's why you came out the superfreak you are.") Homosexual men were harmless reminders of the impulse Minna was sure lurked in all of us—and "half a fag," was more shameful than a whole one. Certain baseball players were half a fag. So were most rock stars and anyone who'd been in the Armed Services but not in a war. The Arabic population of Atlantic Avenue was as unfathomable as the Indian tribes that had held our land before Columbus. "Classic" minorities—Irish, Jews, Poles, Italians, Greeks and Puerto Ricans were the clay of life itself, funny in their essence, while blacks and Asians of all types were soberly snubbed, unfunny. But bone-stupidity, mental illness and familial or sexual anxiety—these were the bolts of electricity that made the clay walk, the animating forces that rendered human life amusing. It was a form of racism, not respect, that restricted blacks and Asians from ever being stupid like a Mick or Polack. If you weren't funny you didn't quite exist. And it was usually better to be fully stupid, impotent, lazy, greedy or freakish than to seek to dodge your destiny, or layer it underneath pathetic guises of vanity or calm.

Though Gerard Minna's name was printed on the business card, we met him only twice, and never on a moving job. The first time was Christmas day, at Minna's mother's apartment.

Carlotta Minna was an *old stove*. That was the Brooklyn term for it, according to Minna. She was a cook who worked in her own apartment, making plates of sautéed squid and stuffed peppers and jars of tripe soup which were purchased at her door by a constant parade of buyers, mostly neighborhood women with too much housework and single men, young or elderly, bocce players who'd take her plates to the park with them, racing bettors who'd eat her food standing up outside the OTB, butchers and contractors who'd sit on crates in the backs of their shops and wolf her cutlets, folding them with their fingers like waffles. She truly worked an old stove, too, a tiny enamel four-burner that was crusted with ancient sauces and on which three or four pots invariably bubbled. The whole kitchen glowed with heat like a kiln. Mrs. Minna herself seemed to have been baked, her whole face dark and furrowed like the edges of an overdone calzone. We never arrived without nudging aside some buyers from her door, nor without packing off with plateloads of food. When we were in her presence Minna bubbled himself, with talk, all directed at his mother, banking cheery insults off anyone else in the apartment, delivery boys, customers known and unknown, tasting everything she had cooking and making suggestions on every dish, poking and pinching every raw ingredient or ball of unfinished dough and also his mother herself, her earlobes and chin, wiping flour off her dark arms with his open hand. And she never once uttered a word.

That Christmas Minna had us all up to his mother's to eat at her table, first nudging aside sauce-glazed stirring spoons and baby-food jars of spices to clear spots for our plates. Minna stood at the stove, sampling her broth, and Mrs. Minna hovered over us as we devoured her meatballs, running her floury fingers over the backs of our chairs, then gently touching our heads, the napes of our necks. We pretended not to notice, ashamed to show that we drank in her nurturance as eagerly as her meat sauce. We splashed, gobbled, kneed one another under the table. Privately, I polished the handle of my spoon, quietly aping the motions of her fingers on my nape, and fought not to twist in my seat and jump at her. All the while she went on caressing with hands that would have horrified us if we'd looked close.

Minna spotted her and said, "This is exciting for you, Ma? I got all of motherless Brooklyn up here for you. Merry Christmas."

Minna's mother only produced a sort of high, keening sigh. We stuck to the food.

"*Motherless Brooklyn*," repeated a voice we didn't know.

It was Minna's brother, Gerard. He'd come in without our noticing. A fleshier, taller Minna. His eyes and hair were as dark, his mouth as wry, lips deep-indented at the corners. He wore a brown-and-tan leather coat, which he left buttoned, his hands pushed into the fake patch pockets.

"So this is your little moving company," he said.

"Hey, Gerard," said Minna.

"Christmas, Frank," said Gerard Minna absently, not looking at his brother. Instead he was making short work of the four of us, his hard gaze snapping us each in two like bolt cutters on inferior padlocks. It didn't take long before he was done with us forever—that was how it felt.

"Yeah, Christmas to you," said Minna. "Where you been?"

"Upstate," said Gerard.

"What, with Ralph and them?" I detected something new in Minna's voice, a yearning, sycophantic strain.

"More or less."

"What, just for the holidays you're gonna go talkative on me? Between you and Ma it's like the Cloisters up here."

"I brought you a present." He handed Minna a white legal envelope, stuffed fat. Minna began to tear at the end, and Gerard said in a voice low and full of ancient sibling authority: "Put it away."

Now we understood we'd all been staring. All except Mrs. Minna, who was at her stove, piling together a cornucopic holiday plate for her older son.

"Make it to go, Mother."

She moaned again, closed her eyes.

"I'll be back," said Gerard. He put his hands on her, much as Minna did. "I've got a few people to see today. I'll be back tonight. Enjoy your little orphan party."

He took the foil-wrapped plate and was gone.

Minna said: "What're you staring at? Eat your food!" He stuffed the white envelope into his jacket. Then he cuffed us, the bulging gold ring on his middle finger clipping our crowns in the same place his mother had fondled.

One day in April, five months after that Christmas meal, Minna drove up with all his windows thoroughly smashed, the van transformed into a blinding crystalline sculpture, a mirrorball on wheels, reflecting the sun. It was plainly the work of a man with a hammer or crowbar and no fear of interruption. Minna appeared not to have noticed; he ferried us out to a job without mentioning it. On our way back to the Home, as we rumbled over the cobblestones of Hoyt Street, Tony nodded at the windshield, which sagged in its frame like a beaded curtain, and said: "So what happened?"

"What happened to what?" It was a Minna game, forcing us to be literal when we'd been trained by him to talk in glances, in three-corner shots.

"Somebody fucked up your van."

Minna shrugged, excessively casual. "I parked it on that block of Pacific Street."

We didn't know what he was talking about.

"These guys around that block had this thing about how I was uglifying the neighborhood." A few weeks after Gilbert's paint job the van had been covered again with graffiti, vast ballooning font and an overlay of stringy tags. Something made Minna's van a born target, the flat battered sides like a windowless subway car, a homely public surface crying for spray paint where private cars were inviolate. "They told me not to park it around there anymore."

Minna lifted both hands from the wheel to gesture his indifference. We weren't totally convinced.

"Someone's sending a message," said Tony.

"What's that?" said Minna.

"I just said it's a message," said Tony.

"Yeah, but what are you trying to say?" said Minna.

"*Fuckitmessage*," I suggested impulsively.

"You know what I mean," said Tony defiantly, ignoring me.

"Yeah, maybe," said Minna. "But put it in your own words." I could feel his anger unfolding, smooth as a fresh deck of cards.

"*Put it in your fuckitall!*" I was like a toddler devising a tantrum to keep his parents from fighting.

But Minna wasn't distractable. "Quiet, Freakshow," he said, never taking his eyes from Tony. "Tell me what you said," he told Tony again.

"Nothing," said Tony. "Damn." He was backpedaling.

Minna pulled the van to the curb at a fire hydrant on the corner of Bergen and Hoyt. Outside, a couple of black men sat on a stoop, drinking from a bag. They squinted at us.

"Tell me what you said," Minna insisted.

He and Tony stared at one another, and the rest of us melted back. I swallowed away a few variations.

"Just, you know, somebody's sending you a message." Tony smirked.

This clearly infuriated Minna. He and Tony suddenly spoke a private language in which *message* signified heavily. "You think you know a thing," he said.

"All I'm saying is I can see what they did to your truck, Frank." Tony scuffed his feet in the layer of tiny cubes of safety glass that had peeled away from the limp window and lay scattered on the floor of the van.

"That's not all you said, Dickweed."

Dickweed: it was different from any insult Minna had bestowed on us before. Bitter as it sounded—*dickweed*. Our little organization was losing its innocence, although I couldn't have explained how or why.

"I can't help what I see," said Tony. "Somebody put a hit on your windows."

"Think you're a regular little wiseguy, don't you?"

Tony stared at him.

"You want to be Scarface?"

Tony didn't give his answer, but we knew what it was. *Scarface* had opened a month before and Al Pacino was ascendant, a personal colossus astride Tony's world, blocking out the sky.

"See, the thing about Scarface," said Minna, "is before he got to be Scarface he was *Scabface*. Nobody ever considers that. You have to want to be Scabface first."

For a second I thought Minna was going to hit Tony, damage his face to make the point. Tony seemed to be waiting for it too. Then Minna's fury leaked away.

"Out," he said. He waved his hand, a Caesar gesturing to the heavens through the roof of his refitted postal van.

"What?" said Tony. "Right here?"

"Out," he said again, equably. "Walk home, you muffin asses."

We sat gaping, though his meaning was clear enough. We weren't more than five or six blocks from the Home, anyway. But we hadn't been paid, hadn't gone for beers or slices or a bag of hot, clingy zeppole. I could taste the disappointment—the flavor of powdered sugar's absence. Tony slid open the door, dislodging more glass, and we obediently filed out of the van and onto the sidewalk, into the day's glare, the suddenly formless afternoon.

Minna drove off, leaving us there to bob together awkwardly before the drinkers on the stoop. They shook their heads at us, stupid looking white boys a block from the projects. But we were in no danger there, nor were we danger-ous ourselves. There was something so primally humiliating in our ejection that Hoyt Street itself seemed to ridicule us, the humble row of brownstones and sleeping bodegas. We were inexcusable to ourselves. Others clotted street corners, not us, not anymore. We rode with Minna. The effect was deliberate: Minna knew the value of the gift he'd withdrawn.

"*Muffin ass*," I said forcefully, measuring the shape of the words in my mouth, auditioning them for tic-richness. Then I sneezed, induced by the sunlight.

Gilbert and Danny looked at me with disgust, Tony with something worse.

"Shut up," he said. There was cold fury in his teeth-clenched smile.

"Tellmetodoit, muffinass," I croaked.

"Be quiet now," warned Tony. He plucked a piece of wood from the gutter and took a step towards me.

Gilbert and Danny drifted away from us warily. I would have followed them, but Tony had me cornered against a parked car. The men on the stoop stretched back on their elbows, slurped their malt liquor thoughtfully.

"*Dickweed*," I said. I tried to mask it in another sneeze, which made something in my neck pop. I twitched and spoke again. "*Dickyweed! Dicketywood!*" I was trapped in a loop of self, stuck refining a verbal tic to free myself from its grip. Certainly I didn't mean to be defying Tony. Yet *dickweed* was the name Minna had called him, and I was throwing it in his face.

Tony held the stick he'd found, a discarded scrap of lattice with clumps of plaster stuck to it. I stared, anticipating my own pain like I'd anticipated Tony's, at Minna's hand, a minute before. Instead Tony moved close, stick at his side, and grabbed my collar.

"Open your mouth again," he said.

I grabbed Tony back, my hands exploring the neck of his T-shirt, fingers running inside it like an anxious, fumbling lover. Then, struggling not to speak, I pursed my lips, jerked my head to the side and kissed his knuckles where they gripped my collar.

Gilbert and Danny had started up Hoyt Street in the direction of the Home. "C'mon, Tony," said Gilbert, tilting his head. Tony ignored them. He scraped his stick in the gutter and came up with a smear of dog shit, mustard-yellow and pungent.

"Open," he said.

Gilbert and Danny slinked away, heads bowed. The street was brightly, absurdly empty. Nobody but the men on the stoop, impassive witnesses. I jerked my head as Tony jabbed with his stick, and he only managed to paint my cheek. I could smell it though, powdered sugar's opposite, married to my face.

"*Eat me!*" I shouted. Falling back against the car behind me, I turned my head again and again, twitching away, enshrining the moment in ticceography. The stain followed me, adamant, on fire.

Our witnesses crinkled their paper bags, offered ruminative sighs.

Tony dropped his stick and turned away. He'd disgusted himself, couldn't meet my eye. About to speak, he thought better of it, instead jogged to catch Gilbert and Danny as they shrugged away up Hoyt Street, leaving the scene.

We didn't see Minna again until five weeks later, Sunday morning at the Home's yard, late May. He had his brother Gerard with him; it was the second time we'd laid eyes on him.

None of us had seen Frank in the intervening weeks, though I know the others, like myself, had each wandered down Court Street, nosed at a few of his usual haunts, the barbershop, the arcade. He wasn't in them. It meant nothing, it meant everything. He might never reappear, but if he turned up and didn't speak of it we wouldn't think twice. We didn't speak of it to one another, but a pensiveness hung over us, tinged with orphan's melancholy, our resignation to permanent injury. A part of each of us still stood astonished on the corner of Hoyt and Bergen, where we'd been ejected from Minna's van.

A horn honked, the Impala's, not the van's. Then the brothers got out and came to the cyclone fence and waited for us to gather. Tony and Danny were playing basketball, Gilbert ardently picking his nose on the sidelines. That's how I picture it, anyway. I wasn't in the yard when they drove up. Gilbert had to come inside and pull me out of the library, to which I'd mostly retreated since Tony's attack. I was wedged into a windowsill seat when Gilbert found me, immersed in a novel by Allen Drury.

Frank and Gerard were dressed too warmly for that morning, Frank in his bomber jacket, Gerard in his patchwork leather coat. The back seat of the Impala was loaded with shopping bags packed with what looked like Frank's clothes and a pair of old leather suitcases. They stood at the fence, Frank bouncing nervously on his toes, Gerard hanging on the mesh, fingers dangling through, doing nothing to conceal his impatience with his brother, an impatience shading into disgust.

Frank smirked, raised his eyebrows, shook his head. Danny held his basketball between forearm and hip; Minna nodded at it, mimed a set shot, dropped his hand at the wrist and made a delicate *o* with his mouth to signify the *swish* that would result.

Then, idiotically, he bounced a pretend pass to Gerard. His brother didn't seem to notice. Minna shook his head, then wheeled, aimed two trigger fingers through the fence, and grit his teeth for *rat-tat-tat*, a little imaginary schoolyard massacre. We could only gape. It was as though somebody had taken Minna's voice away. And Minna *was* his voice— didn't he know? His eyes said yes, he did. They looked panicked, like they'd been caged in the body of a mime.

Gerard gazed off emptily into the yard, ignoring the show. Minna made a few more faces, wincing, chuckling silently, shaking off some invisible annoyance by twitching his cheek. I fought to keep from mirroring him.

Then he cleared his throat. "I'm, ah, going out of town for a while," he said at last.

We waited for more. Minna just nodded and squinted and grinned his close-mouthed grin at us as though he were acknowledging applause.

"Upstate?" said Tony.

Minna coughed in his fist. "Oh yeah. Place my brother goes. He thinks we ought to get a little country air."

"When are you coming back?" said Tony.

"Ah, coming back," said Minna. "You got an unknown there, Scarface. Unknown factors."

We must have gaped at him, because he added, "I wouldn't wait under water, if that's what you had in mind."

We were in our second year of high school. Till now I'd counted my future in afternoons, but with Minna leaving, a door of years swung open. And Minna wouldn't be there to tell us what to think of Minna's not being there, to give it a name.

"All right, Frank," said Gerard, turning his back to the fence. "Motherless Brooklyn appreciates your support. I think we better get on the road."

"My brother's in a hurry," said Frank. "He's seeing ghosts everywhere."

"Yeah, I'm looking right at one," said Gerard, though in fact he wasn't looking at anyone, only the car.

Minna tilted his head at us, at his brother, to say *you know*. And *sorry*.

Then he pulled a book out of his pocket, a small paperback. I don't think I'd ever seen a book in his hands before. "Here," he said to me. He dropped it on the pavement and nudged it under the fence with the toe of his shoe. "Take a look," he said. "Turns out you're not the only freak in the show."

I picked it up. *Understanding Tourette's Syndrome* was the title. It was first time I'd seen the words.

"Meaning to get that to you," he said. "But I've been sort of busy."

I reached for him through the fence and tapped his shoulder, once, twice, let my hand fall, then raised it again and let fly a staccato burst of Tourettic caresses.

"Eatme, Minnaweed," I said under my breath.

"You're a laugh and a half, Freakshow," said Minna, his face completely grim.

"Great," said Gerard, taking Minna by the arm. "Let's get out of here."

Tony had been searching every day after school, I suspect. It was three days later that he found it and led us others there, to the edge of the Brooklyn Queens Expressway at the end of Baltic. The van was diminished, sagged to its rims, tires melted. The explosion had cleared the windows of their crumbled panes of safety glass, which now lay in a spilled penumbra of grains on the sidewalk and street, together with flakes of traumatized paint and smudges of ash, a photographic map of force. The panels of the truck were layered, graffiti still evident in bone-white outline, all else, Gilbert's shoddy coat of enamel and the manufacturer's ancient green, now chalky black, and delicate like sunburned skin. It was like an X ray of the van that had been before.

We circled it, strangely reverent, afraid to touch, and then I ran away, toward Court Street, before anything could come out of my mouth.

Como Conversazione

On Literary Biography

The following excerpted discussion on the subject of literary biography is one of a continuing series of private seminars held at the Casa Ecco on Lake Como, chaired by Drue Heinz and Grey Gowrie. This is the third conversazione published in these pages after "Humor" (136) and "Travel and Travel Writing" (147). A conversation on religion is forthcoming, and this fall a seminar is planned on the art of translation, its findings to be published next year. The Panel and their most recent works are listed below.

DRUE HEINZ	Publisher of *The Paris Review*
GREY GOWRIE	Head of the Arts Council of England; Chair of the proceedings at Lake Como
JAMES ATLAS	*Delmore Schwartz: The Life of an American Poet; Bellow* (forthcoming)
R.F. FOSTER	*W.B. Yeats: A Life*, vol. 1
DAN FRANKLIN	Publishing Director of Jonathan Cape
ROBERT GIROUX	Editor at Farrar, Straus & Giroux
VICTORIA GLENDINNING	*Elizabeth Bowen; Edith Sitwell; Vita; Rebecca West; Jonathan Swift*
SELINA HASTINGS	*Nancy Mitford; Evelyn Waugh; Rosamond Lehmann* (forthcoming)
LUCY HUGHES-HALLETT	*Cleopatra: Histories, Dreams and Distortions*
JAMES KNOWLSON	*Damned to Fame: The Life of Samuel Beckett*
JEREMY LEWIS	*Cyril Connolly: A Life*
GEORGE PLIMPTON	*Truman Capote: In Which Various Friends, Enemies, Acquaintances, and Detractors Recall His Turbulent Career*
HILARY SPURLING	*The Unknown Matisse; Ivy: The Life of Ivy Compton-Burnett*

TOPIC: *BIOGRAPHY—ART OR CRAFT?*

GLENDINNING: All our lives are in a sense novelistic in that they have their highs and their lows, quiet bits and loud bits. There's a dynamic in a life. The danger in the perfectly documented, perfectly recorded life is that it misses out on the dynamics. I don't think biography is an art so much as a craft. In any craft you want to make a shape. We're all afraid our lives are random. One of the reasons we both write and read biographies is to make a structure and a framework: our lives may be random, but we need the illusion that there is a shape, a meaning.

ATLAS: We often leave out the art and just get to the biography, and that makes for a very ponderous book. One is always working very hard at not only selection but issues of organization within the text so that chapters and the narrative have a beginning and an end. A matter that we don't sufficiently take into account is that we're held to the same standards, the same aesthetic standards, as the novelist. As Leon Edel points out in that wonderful book *Telling Lives*, you can do everything but invent. We do try, of course, not to invent or make it up as we go along. But the greatest biography creates the same illusion that a novel creates—of really being a very organized narrative. That's something we tend to forget in our obsession with research and getting everything in.

GOWRIE: James [Knowlson], did being a close confidant of Samuel Beckett make life easier or more difficult?

KNOWLSON: Undoubtedly more difficult. One has to say that, of course, you are lucky if you have seen your subject in many different situations. You've seen him directing; you've had dinner with him three, four, five times a year; you've even got drunk together. You have seen him making eyes at a particular actress; you have seen him call out—"Where is that fucking waiter!" So you know, for instance, that there is an element of suppressed violence in your friend. My response to all this was transformed, to some extent, by the fact that it was Beckett himself who said to me, "Let's have a clause that will give you more freedom—that your book will not be published within my lifetime or that of my wife." So that freed me in a sense. The big test, of course, is how strong your commitment is to being objective, because you may be accused of being . . . affectionate. I would accept that. I accept it as better than the opposite.

LEWIS: I love memoirs and autobiographies—the firsthand accounts—but I'm not a great reader of biographies, although I loved writing one: all too often biographies, and literary biographies in particular, seem to me to be second-rate as well as secondhand. Many of them are perfunctory about building up subsidiary characters without making things up: biography needs the novelist's gift of creating character and incident and getting the story rolling. Cyril Connolly himself was a tremendously obsessive autobiographical writer and everything he wrote was explicit or covert autobiography. He said somewhere that the difference between any two biographies about subject X was always the autobiographical element. Writing about Connolly was a very strange experience. Though I had very little in common with him, what I absolutely loved about writing his biography was that it was almost like writing a volume of autobiography. The autobiographical element, the involvement with your own character, is something that can bring a book to life.

GOWRIE: Did you start behaving like the Connollys?

LEWIS: No. I did become extremely fond of him and I absolutely love his writing, but I did want to give him a sharp kick a lot of the time—when I found him sulking like a baby, or being particularly disloyal to one of the women in his life or failing to deliver to some long-suffering publisher a book he had no intention of writing. One of the most fascinating things about writing a biography is that extraordinary thing of getting to know someone in the round, if not very deeply. I got to know something about every aspect of his life. People who'd known him terrifically well would know in depth about segments of his life. I'd say, Did you know that Connolly did this or that, and a great friend would say, Oh, really! I never knew that. So you get that extraordinary feeling of being, albeit at a rather superficial level, the only one who knows the whole of his life. A very strange sensation, never having met him.

ATLAS: Eventually you discover that a life has a theme. In all their randomness lives do, I think, enact the working out of certain recurring conflicts. I remember after I'd written a thousand pages about Saul Bellow and I had come to the end of my book, my editor said to me, "Now this is all very interesting— but what is it about? What is his life about?" I realized that that was the one thing I had yet to deal with, that his life—if I can say it in a sentence—is about, and without being too psychoanalytic about it, the struggle, within his family of powerful brothers and an overbearing father, to achieve his own freedom and identity. Even when he's talking about political issues or literary issues or social issues, he goes back, over and over, to the same theme about this primal struggle. That doesn't mean that it's repetitive or tedious; it means it gives his life story a very true and satisfying unity that I think we all have in our lives, however chaotic they are.

LEWIS: I found that, with Connolly, these motifs in his life came through, rather like Wagnerian motifs: falling in love with two or more people at once, whether school friends from Eton or beautiful women, making excuses in advance for the masterpieces he would never get around to writing, indolence and failure followed by guilt and remorse . . .

FOSTER: I'm slightly bothered about this autobiographical empathetic approach to biography, which I think can be responsible for a lot of false trails, but it is an assumption that's made. The great critic Denis Donoghue was asked to write the authorized

life of W.B. Yeats in the 1960s. He gave it up, he said in a
very long article in the *TLS* in 1964, because he quarreled with
the estate about access and so forth. Then a few years later
I opened up an in-flight magazine in which, writing about
biography, he admitted he gave up the Yeats project because
he didn't want to have to become like Yeats and not recognize
his own children on the street and be very lofty about everything.
A rather worrying version of why he gave it up. Then I met a
friend of Denis's who said, "Oh not at all. Denis told me he
gave it up because he was too vain to stay out of print for as
long as it would take to write a biography." You can take
your pick.

I suspect that the in-flight magazine one was the right one.
I think he assumed that to write about Yeats you had to take
on a Yeatsian aura or to identify with Yeats's often difficult,
not to say repellent, political views. I think you can be empathetic
but detached rather than necessarily autobiographically implicated. The rather grisly kind of possessiveness of a certain school
of biography with the subject's first name used intensively on
every page is the kind of thing that gives biography, often
rightly, a bad name as a second-rate intellectual exercise.

GLENDINNING: Sometimes I've written a paragraph, often rather late at night, that seems to me full of insight, say, one
paragraph in which it seems to me I've got to the nub of
something. Then I read it in the morning and I think, I wasn't
really writing about him, I was writing about me. You put a
line straight through it. I think when you're writing biography
you have to watch for that the whole time, and take it out if
you're in any doubt at all.

SPURLING: With any given subject, you start out with a ground-
ing of knowledge, of assumptions, of preconceptions, which
point you in a certain direction. Later on there comes a stage
at which, having collected as much material as you can, you
have to stop collecting. You've been listening to the various
instruments: now you become the composer; and at a later

stage, once you begin to orchestrate the book, you become the conductor. Or to use another metaphor, it's very like what goes on in acting. You've studied the part, you've got the text, you know the ground that's to be covered. But you can't know how to play it until you actually put on the clothes of whomever you're writing about and attempt to see it through that person's eyes. If you can't do that then your biography isn't going to be worth very much in the end. Any great actor draws on all parts of his personality. The greater the actor the deeper he will draw on what he has in himself to flesh forth whatever character he's playing. That's why a dozen actors can play Lear and it'll be a different Lear every time. When it comes to sitting down to write the biography, if you can't actually to some extent assume the role of the person you're writing about—recreate that part, breathe life into it—your biography won't work. There is also an equal, and absolutely ruthless, element of objective analysis. This is a very cold and surgical thing. It's why I myself find it quite impossible to write about people I know and above all to write about people still alive. I was invited to do that by a friend whose novels I greatly admire. We both thought that question-and-answer sessions would be a good idea but it turned out totally impossible. I had an absolute block, which I couldn't understand, which was painful for him too. I had to think about it hard in order to explain to him and myself why I couldn't do this. I decided in the end that it was for the same reason that a surgeon doesn't operate on his friends or family. Your own emotions get in the way. I didn't want to dissect him because I was too fond of him.

FOSTER: Andrew Motion is one of those people who take on the color of the person he's writing about without vulgarization. He wrote about Philip Larkin's life as a lugubrious, horribly funny and at the same time deeply sorrowful story, like a Larkin novel, using the strengths of Larkin's own vision. I think it's a masterpiece.

GOWRIE: I don't know if this comment will be relevant, but both Drue and I knew an extraordinary man, John Brearley.

He was the greatest restorer of oil paintings in the world, and he received a terrifying commission to restore the *Meninas* of Velázquez, which is really a relic, an icon of Spain. He had to have secret-service people because he was under such threat: the idea of someone touching the painting, and the idea of someone who wasn't Spanish touching it. Slowly word started to trickle out that his work was wonderful. He ended up an enormously famous and fêted person in Spain with the order of every kind of fleece. I asked him how he worked. He said, "Well, painting is really very tactile, perhaps more like a sport. It's the stroke. I look and look and practice and practice until I get his strokes. The way I put on my own stuff has to be done in the identical rhythm." I wondered if that was at all like writing biography.

FOSTER: I agree with you. But it can become too readily like pastiche. Richard Ellmann's *James Joyce* is the template of literary biography, but I think Ellmann's *Oscar Wilde* is not successful because the style of Wilde creeps rather heavily into the style of Ellmann. There are rather lumbering epigrams from time to time and a sub-Wildean taste which doesn't do Ellmann himself justice. Someone's trying to do the strokes. Sometimes the more pronounced the style of the person you're writing about, the more you have to abstract yourself—from Jamesian strokes if you're Edel or Wildean if you're Ellmann.

A subject we haven't taken up is how far you bring the subject's work into the life. The exemplary instance is Ellmann's use of the short story "The Dead" in his Joyce book, where he devotes, I think, a whole chapter to it, showing that where and how it was written reflects the reality of Joyce's relationship with Nora. He says infinitely more in his analysis of that short story about Joyce and Nora than, for my money, Brenda Maddox does in a long and rather speculative book. But, again to take Ellmann, he turns aside and does a marvelous chapter on "The Decay of Lying" in the Wilde book, but it reads as a tributary, a plunging off into another alley. It breaks the narrative because Ellmann wanted to write in a rather Wildean way about Wilde's writing.

HASTINGS: When I came to the end of writing about Nancy Mitford I hadn't realized how much it was an act of creation. I had spent four years, in a way, creating a character. I thought I was putting Nancy Mitford on the page as she lived, though I didn't know her, and at the very end, just as I was coming to the end of the last chapter, I suddenly remembered that I hadn't looked at the BBC archives. There was quite a long filmed interview with her. I went to look at it and I got a terrible shock, because what I was seeing on film was nothing at all like the person I'd been writing about.

GOWRIE: So what did you do?

HASTINGS: I'm trying to forget it.

SPURLING: But this is just the kind of shock you get when you see yourself in a full-length mirror not having expected it, isn't it?

HASTINGS: Exactly. I can't bear that sort of emotional identification.

ATLAS: I think one of the most exhausting things about dealing with Bellow—having written a biography of someone whom I never knew, Delmore Schwartz, and then someone whom I did know, Bellow—was that when I was around Bellow I had to practice an exhausting detachment, which I came to see as a kind of analytic retreat from being in a relationship with him. What interested me was to observe him in an almost clinical manner: listen to his speech and how he told stories. It was necessary not to become part of the drama of his life, yet after a few hours I found this suppression of self very tiring, not out of a sense of egotism, not that I wanted attention, but just that I had to be almost no one to really get at who he was.

SPURLING: Like a bird-watcher.

ATLAS: Yes, really. I had to fade into the woodwork. At one point he said to me—we were having dinner—"Well, you're pretty quiet," which is the last thing that I am, but I had become this retiring, shy sort of wallflower.

HASTINGS: I had the same kind of experience with Rosamond Lehmann, whom I'm writing about now and whom I knew all my life. It was a friendship of ups and downs. The moment she asked me to be her biographer, on the understanding that nothing was to be written in her lifetime, we met for numerous sessions with the tape recorder—I long to write a story called "The Captive Biographer," because from that moment I could not answer back! I couldn't say, "Oh that's rubbish, that's simply not true." I just had to sit there and tape whatever she chose to give me, which was largely hours and hours of rehearsing her grudges.

GLENDINNING: I think this has something to do with writing about people of an earlier generation. I remember I'd finished Vita Sackville-West before I heard her voice on tape. I was absolutely shocked to the quick by this deep gin-sodden aristocratic English, in which all the vowels were positively distorted, "fescinating" instead of "fascinating." A kind of upper-class English that in my childhood you sometimes heard in the corridors of trains shouting for a porter, but nowadays I think not at all. I mean it's easier with Jonathan Swift. I know that words meant different things in the eighteenth century and I can accept that he wore a periwig. But we have to take into account the sort of subtle but also abysmal differences between us and them a generation and a half ago.

SPURLING: I personally find the twentieth century so fascinating because it's the period I live in, and the people I write about are the people who shaped it. There are still people alive who constitute the last oral link you can have with history. The period you're writing about now, Swift, it's all in books.

FOSTER: Sometimes you know that a piece of your subject's work speaks to you about his or her life in a way that is new. The interesting thing is that very often it's not what the world conceives to be a major or an accessible part of that person's work. "The Dead," of course, is a known masterpiece. But the piece of Yeats that I suppose I pivoted my first volume on is an essay called "J.M. Synge and the Ireland of His Time," Yeats's first essay in autobiography, not an elegy for a dead friend but autobiographical in that he was also explaining why he was turning away from conventional Irish nationalism. I found that the themes in it take up jottings made very early on in his notebooks. But it certainly isn't a piece of Yeats you would find in the anthologies. People who read the draft thought I had rather overplaced weight on it. My point was not that this is the greatest thing Yeats ever wrote but that this was the key to his mind at a pivotal stage of his life. That's why it's there. What's not polished to a level of highest art can tell you more about where the writer is in his or her life than something that's accumulated the levels of patina and varnish that adhere to the great poem or the staggering play.

GOWRIE: How do you get a real sketch of the character when you're dealing with social anthropology and political events and everything else as well?

FOSTER: I suspect it's rather like the fact that you can only be a good abstractionist after you've gone through life drawing. I suspect that you can only write the short biography when it is the tip of the iceberg of thirty years immersion in every detail. A short biography would have to be written by people who know everything that they weren't saying. I think if one was to do the nightmare scenario of a short biography of Yeats, it would have to be after having been able to do the two volumes. The great obstacle with Yeats—now I don't want to relate this entirely to my own work—was the question of the occult. I'm a very un-occult person, but I did realize just from a superficial reading of Yeats's oeuvre that the occult informed everything.

I began reading about the 1880s, and especially about art school and bohemian circles, and discovered just how widely spread theosophy was. This was the key. It led to an idea I developed that Irish Protestants of the nineteenth century are particularly susceptible to supernatural beliefs for various sociological reasons, which was the way into dealing with Yeats's belief in it. It bears out the point about the importance of understanding the historical context.

GLENDINNING: Something that always concerns me with a sort of anxiety is something to do with double vision. It's about whether we're looking at our man or our woman in close-up with a magnifying glass, all the idiosyncrasies and strange mind-sets, or whether we start with a wider context, such as Roy Foster said about what was going on in the 1880s, because it's no good finding all sorts of strangenesses and curiosities in our subject if in fact a lot of people were feeling like that at the same time. There's this awful sort of double pull between the context and the sort of individualism of that person. Swift was a problem in optics—he was very interested in optics—because he was either too big or too small for the company he was keeping. That was what he was writing about anyway—people being too big and too small.

HUGHES-HALLETT: I'm currently writing about el Cid. I have great problems in that el Cid lived and was written about, or sung about, at a period when the idea of objective truth existed, of course, but was not very highly valued. I think that possibly represents a more honest approach to biography than the con-temporary one, where most people around this table are at-tempting to translate something from one medium to another. It's an impossible translation: just as flesh and blood is not the same as a painted image, so lived experience is not the same as narrative prose. However hard you work to establish facts, you're always creating a character.

GOWRIE: It's coming round again in chaos theory—the fact that we don't have certainties.

GLENDINNING: It's incredibly important in that it is how biography began. Biography is probably the oldest literary art. It began with people round a camp fire or in a baronial hall singing or reciting, usually in verse (this before written literature) the stories of ancient kings and leaders and chieftains and warriors . . . this to hold them in memory.

GOWRIE: We've just seen this on a world scale, which is the mythopoeticizing of Diana, the Princess of Wales. In other words, there's Diana the person, who many of us knew, and Diana this new extraordinary saint.

TOPIC: *A LOOK ACROSS THE CHANNEL*

SPURLING: English biography until after the war was a sort of gentleman-amateur kind of thing with no source notes, and done by people who had dabbled themselves, maybe men of letters in the worst sense rather than the best. The good thing about the entrance of academe into biography is that it makes everybody more rigorous and professional. I sometimes think that the reason Anglo-Saxons do biography—and it's really a strength of our weakness—is that I think Anglo-Saxons are incredibly bad at general ideas, large thought, abstract notions. We're pinned down to personality. Thomas Carlyle said, I think, "All history is the biography of great men," which is one way of looking at it, but only one very twisted way of looking at it.

GLENDINNING: I read a French biography about Sartre; it was really a book about philosophy.

SPURLING: This is a great and serious weakness of French biographers. When I was first approached to write the life of a Frenchman, I read the available books—virtually all in English (mostly by Americans). There was no biography of Henri Matisse in any language. The only serious text in French was a majestic work by Pierre Schneider who had access to the family archive, which nobody else had ever had, and whose preface contains a sentence

I have never forgotten. It said, "History will be treated as the enemy throughout this book." When I read that, I thought, Well, perhaps there is room for an English biographer. We would be complementary, and so it has turned out; we are now the best of friends.

There aren't many things the English do better than the French but biography is one of them, and when I crossed the Channel I thought there might be some interest in producing a good workaday biography of their greatest painter. But it didn't turn out like that. I began in the north, in Matisse's home, where I quickly discovered it was wiser never to mention his name because people were still ashamed of him there: a man who couldn't paint, who may have taken those loonies in Paris, London and America to the cleaners, but not us. I learned to avoid his name, at any rate with the older generation. Most people of middle age had never heard of him, so it wasn't a problem with them. I also learned not to mention the word *biographer*. That goes down extremely badly in France. When a local historian or a provincial archivist or museum official asks what I am doing, I always say *research* because at *biography* they just curl their lip. I didn't understand this for a long time. In France there are a lot of things one stubs one's toe against but which nobody ever explains. It is basically a philosophical distinction, what they call Cartesianism. We have the philosophers we have because we are that kind of people. If the French hadn't had Descartes, they certainly would have invented him. Their biographical Cartesianism means: I think, therefore it is. The reason they don't do biography is not that they can't, but that they won't, because they despise it completely. They think it is the intellectual pits, a manifestation of this very primitive Anglo-Saxon obsession with the facts. No self-respecting French writer would be caught dead doing it. It is a self-fulfilling expectation because the biographies they do produce are often exceedingly dull, being based on fantasy rather than reality, and too often the commonplace fantasies of a banal imagination. If they took the trouble to find out what actually happened, their books would be more interesting.

FRANKLIN: It's also the Calvinist point of view. The Dutch
neither write nor publish biographies. There is no Dutch biography of Rembrandt. Simon Schama has just written one.
Whether he will get it published there—on the principle that
no one should be elevated above anybody else—is problematic.

GLENDINNING: When the British in the British Consulate
staged that weeklong conference, called *Vies Extraordinaires*, a
few months ago in Paris, a lot of Frenchmen turned up, but
rather as if they were going to the zoo.

SPURLING: The English who attended were all the top English
biographers. English people are always delighted with an excuse
for a week in Paris. The French delegates were not anything
like the same caliber.

GLENDINNING: They were serious, but they weren't serious in
our sense. Pierre Assouline, who wrote the life of Georges Si-
menon, gave an excellent lecture, and that was it, the only
serious contribution.

TOPIC: *BIOGRAPHER AS INVESTIGATOR, THE EARLY YEARS
IN PARTICULAR . . .*

GLENDINNING: When doing a twentieth-century subject recently "gone to Heaven," sometimes I feel like a policeman.
You go around seeing all the survivors, the witnesses. Each sees
himself or herself as a center, and is slightly unconsciously upset
that you're not asking directly about them. So sometimes you
get the feeling that, even with the best will in the world every
story, every memory is slightly smarted to put themselves inside
the frame or outside the frame, depending on which is to their
advantage. People will be absolutely sure that so and so left a
party with so and so. It turns out it was not so. What do you
do with these different voices and visions? This is not just a
problem in current biography. After Swift's death, in the next
forty years, about half a dozen people who collected myths and

anecdotes around him, and had strong opinions, went into print in the later eighteenth century with their memories of Dean Swift, all of which contradict each other, and all of which are as much about the writer of these memories as they are about Dean Swift. The four gospels are completely different versions of the life of Christ.

ATLAS: Never mind the accounts that come from other people, you certainly can't trust the subject matter either. There are so many times I've gone to so and so and gotten honorable, erroneous information—not that he's lying, but because he doesn't remember. Although sometimes his memory is in the service of self-image.

FOSTER: Skidelsky got a lot of flack for his life of Oswald Mosley. In the second edition he wrote a very interesting introduction, defending why he took what seemed to some an over-sympathetic view of a repellent subject. The sentence that I remember is that he said that a biographer's function is to be somewhere between the defense counsel and the judge. Of course, that's a territory that you can't occupy. By definition there is no territory between defense counsel and judge.

SPURLING: But can you alternate the roles?

ATLAS: To make something of your data you have to have a strong authorial point of view. The fact that Bellow was a compulsive adulterer is hardly a moral issue; it's not for the biographer to step in with personal feelings. You can't say, "Well, you're a bad fellow; you mustn't do this." But you also can't just say, "This is what happened." You have to be an interpreter. You have to step in and explain what might or might not have been at work there, and why.

LEWIS: Connolly was obsessive about keeping things, even bus tickets and menus—let alone the letters he'd written to friends. All his life he had this yearning for paradise lost, a kind of Eden

from which he'd been expelled. Though he was frightfully
bullied at Eton, particularly when he was young, as soon as he
left the place he began to build it up as a kind of lost paradise.
He found Oxford frightfully dull and didn't like it at all and
was very got down by the sound of bells and by the pipe-
smoking Rugbians who peopled Oxford. Soon as he left Eton
he started writing to his Eton friends, begging them to return
to him the enormous numbers of love letters he'd written to
them, so that he could use them to recreate this paradise lost.
In the 1960s he came back to this idea of recreating in print
this lost Eden from which he'd been expelled. Again, he started
pestering all these old fellows, his Eton friends, who were now
in their sixties: "Have you still got the letters I wrote to you
when I was at school?"

SPURLING: Childhood, for several of my subjects, has turned
out to be the last thing that I or anybody else would have
expected. My first subject was Ivy Compton-Burnett, who spent
all her life writing novels about what went on in English manor
houses, seedy manor houses. There wasn't enough money coming in, and the inhabitants lived a totally enclosed life with
their servants, children and governesses. A good deal of violence
goes on behind the scenes: adult incest, child abuse, murder
and mayhem. Some of Ivy's friends were extremely angry with
me when I discovered that, far from having grown up in a
manor house, she never even set foot in one until she was well
into her forties. Her grandfather was an agricultural farm laborer.
Ivy had a strong imagination, and manor-house life was the
setting that suited her, an enclosed world in which she could
explore the struggle for power under laboratory conditions, so
to speak. She actually belonged to the lower middle class.
     Then I wrote a life of Paul Scott, who spent his life writing
about India in a series of novels later televised as *The Jewel and
the Crown*. I knew I would have to go to India to investigate
Paul's background. I thought this would be the exact opposite
from the claustrophobic world that Ivy wrote about. I would be
dealing with an imperial canvas spanning two continents, a

world war and the breakup of the empire. But, blow me, it turned out that Paul Scott was born in North London, grew up in a narrow, inward-looking, rigidly conformist suburb, never went to India until he was conscripted and posted off there against his will in 1942.

The third time I thought, Well this time I'll really have a change. I'll write about Matisse, the great poet of the Mediterranean. All anyone could tell me about Matisse's background was that he was what the French call *grand bourgeois cossu*, that's to say, solidly established in the upper ranks of the middle classes. Well, blow me again, he turns out to have struggled up from the working class. His grandfather was a weaver. The Matisses had been weavers from the beginning of time, living not much above subsistence level in a tiny one-room hovel filled by the loom at which the head of the household would work up to eighteen hours a day for a wage that was never enough to feed the children. Matisse's father broke away to run a corner shop that grew into a wholesale seed merchant's business. But nobody, till I started digging around, would have imagined these backgrounds for these particular people.

GLENDINNING: I think the truth is that the creative imagination grows best in the suburbs. There everybody plays princes and princesses in the way that they want—either in India or in manor houses. If you were actually a prince or princess and grew up in a manor house, your imagination doesn't need too much.

HASTINGS: The biography I'm working on at the moment, Rosamond Lehmann, her childhood was the source of great romantic inspiration and I think what sparked her off throughout. Although her own family was interesting and her father was very literary and her grandparents knew Thackeray, Dickens and George Eliot and so on, she as a fairly small child used to be invited by Lady Desbrough to children's parties at Taplow, and she saw the Grenfell boys, much older than she was, in their white flannels with their Brideshead-type Marchmain lock of hair over the forehead. She thought this was completely wonderful. All those young men in her novels come from what she understood Julian Grenfell and his friends to be. She always felt the outsider and yearned to be a duke's daughter. She thought that if you were a member of the aristocracy you had a golden key to another world, to which people like her never had access. This certainly was what she searched for all her life and, in a slightly different way, so did Waugh.

FOSTER: In his forties Yeats certainly began to reinvent his childhood, when he was becoming progressively disillusioned with middle-class arriviste Catholic Ireland. He turns his highly unreliable first autobiography into a sort of elegy for a Victorian Ireland that was archaic, when in fact his relatives weren't archaic at all—they were property developers and seed merchants and hardheaded modern businessmen. He describes them as merchants and sailors instead of entrepreneurs. He never mentions that the lost domain of childhood at Rosses Point in Sligo was in fact to be developed as a sort of Coney Island by his family, though they didn't have the money to sustain it. It's a reinvention that is all to do with how he sees Ireland in 1913 and 1914 and very little to do with the actual conditions of Sligo in the 1860s and 1870s when he was young.

KNOWLSON: When he was a little boy, Beckett used to take stones from the beach, pebbles from the beach, and hide them. In the course of the first hour I met him I said, "Tell me about stones, tell me about stones." He said, "I'm sure it's something to do with Freud, Jim." Everything he'd said up to then to future biographers—Laurence Harvey and Deirdre Bair, who met him three times—was about a happy childhood. But for me that image of the little boy at Greystone Harbour, with those biggish stones, gray stones . . .

ATLAS: I've always wondered with Bellow. He claimed that he knew from the beginning that he was singled out in some fashion: one of his first images was of the iridescent pool of water on a street, and somehow he imagined that seeing this image with such great clarity, he realized, at the age of three, that he was going to be an artist and that everything that happened afterwards impelled him in this one direction. He certainly had a curious sense of destiny without any evidence for it. I wonder if that isn't really a feature of genius.

GIROUX: Writers who start out as orphans are a special class, like Ben Jonson. Another orphan is the American poet Elizabeth Bishop. She was a baby when her widowed mother, who became mentally disturbed, took her from her birthplace (Worcester, Massachusetts) to her maternal grandmother in Great Village, Nova Scotia, where she had a reasonably happy childhood. Then her paternal grandfather wanted her back at Worcester, where the Bishops were a leading and very wealthy family who had built the Boston Library and part of West Point. Elizabeth wrote a wonderful story, "The Country Mouse," about being kidnapped at age six and living like a stranger in their big house. There were no other children. She said she identified with the Bishop's Boston bull terrier, Beppo, who was so well trained that when he did something wrong he consigned himself to solitary confinement in the closet. Elizabeth felt herself an outsider, like the dog.

ATLAS: One of the horrifying things about Hemingway's childhood was that his mother sent him this package that had in it the pistol with which his father had shot himself.

GOWRIE: There are a lot of fantasies about nannies. Auden once said to Robert Lowell, "Mental illness, Cal, very tiresome and silly. My nanny wouldn't have allowed it."

SPURLING: I madly wanted to write Ivy's life and I could not believe her when she said her life had been too dull to write about. I thought, Well how come she knows so much about murder, about incest, about the abuse of power? But her friends assured me it was true: her life had been blameless and boring; she never did anything, and there was no way of finding out about her because there were no papers of any sort. I wrote to her two surviving sisters and went to see them, taking two potted plants with me, one of which they unwrapped with enthusiasm while the other got left behind on the sideboard. The first moment I began to feel my hunch might be right was when I heard Miss Juliet Compton-Burnett say to her sister Miss Vera, "Oh look, Vera, the poor little flower's been forgotten. Just like a stepchild." It turned out Ivy was the middle child of thirteen children. Her father's first wife had born him six children in eight, nine years—very quickly—and she died giving birth to the sixth. Within a year he married again and Ivy was on the way. He was madly in love with Ivy's mother. He had met her and must have fallen in love with her before his first wife died in childbirth. I slid over that a little bit in my book because I didn't want to distress Miss Vera and Miss Juliet. Their father went on and had seven more by his second wife.

The catastrophe of their life, and it was a tragedy for all of them, was that the second Mrs. Compton-Burnett could not stand small children. She was extremely beautiful, born in Dover, with big ideas about where she was going, adored her husband who was a doctor, a highly successful one, but a homeopath, which meant that he was outlawed by the whole medical profession. His practice was in London but he kept his children and his wife on the seacoast near Brighton because the children were delicate, and for her that was a disaster. She loathed children, loved society, adored her husband, and here she was marooned in a large suburban house with increasing numbers of children—six of whom weren't even hers. The stepchildren, in mourning for their real mother, hated her as the supplanter. Her own first child was Ivy, after which she went on to have a baby at regular intervals for the next fifteen years. Her husband died suddenly when Ivy was seventeen, with no warning at all, of a heart attack brought on by overwork, all the strain. After that, Ivy's mother went mad. That, again, I think I understressed in my book. I was an apprentice biographer learning my trade and again I didn't want to distress the sisters too much. I underplayed the madness of the mother who became a total tyrant. There was no escape from that house. They went to the local school but none of the Compton-Burnetts were allowed to play with other pupils. Every Sunday Mrs. Compton-Burnett set out at the head of a procession of children for the graveyard. She was dressed in black with a long veil and a long mourning train, with the children, down to the baby in its pram, all dressed in black, all bearing flowers to lay on Dr. Compton-Burnett's tomb, which remains to this day the largest and shiniest tomb in the whole graveyard. This was Ivy's youth.

Her father had believed in education for girls, but when he died, that was dropped—Ivy had no future. There was no way out. They never met anyone. They had no society, no world of their own. Her brother escaped to Cambridge and that was Ivy's sole window on the world; she adored her brother, who was at King's College, where he was a friend of Rupert Brooke. He moved into Brooke's rooms when Brooke moved out. They both were favorites of the same Goldsworth tutor, Lowes Dickinson. I always thought I could hear in Ivy's dialogue echoes of that incredibly smart, clever, golden generation at Cambridge in the years immediately before the First World War. But I could never put my finger on it, until I found a stray reference in a letter to Ivy about her having been at Cambridge in May Week, 1911. Even then I could find no outside corroboration of what she'd made of it. No letters. No recollections anywhere. Finally I went to see Philip Noel Baker, a distinguished politician who had been at King's in those days. Of course he remembered Noel Compton-Burnett. Everybody had liked and admired Noel, so brilliant, expected to go on to become a great poet, a great literateur. He died instead in 1916 in the Battle of the Somme. I asked if there had been a sister. "Oh yes," he said, "I remember Ivy, it was May Week." There were no girls at Cambridge in those days; all the boys were in love with each other, but not Philip Noel Baker. "Oh yes," he said, "I saw her crossing the quad, the sister, on Noel's arm, she was stunning. *She knocked the college sideways.*" I don't know if any of you have ever seen a photograph of Ivy Compton-Burnett—but that is very far from the impression she produced in later life.

The core of my biography was an attempt to reconcile the golden-haired stunner of 1911 with the stern, severe Victorian governess who produced a stream of alarmingly subversive novels that made her a literary legend in her lifetime. That seems to me to be the point and the purpose of biography: to show how art is rooted in the life, often in lives the artist did not lead, or led only in the imagination.

TOPIC: *SECONDARY SOURCES*

GOWRIE: I wonder if anybody has got transfixed, when they were writing their biographies, by the less famous or the less known ancillary person.

HASTINGS: When I was writing Waugh, I managed towards the end to find the two little girls, as they then were, who'd lived next door to him in North Hampstead. They had played with him and had known him throughout his London childhood. They weren't faintly interested in the fact that he'd become a great novelist. They remembered him as the naughty little boy who used to climb through the fence at the bottom of the garden and lead them on terrible escapades on Hampstead Heath. It was wonderful talking on this level. The great novelist didn't come into their picture at all. He was simply the person who used to go and frighten Pavlova's swans at her garden in Ivy Lodge or who used to chop up cabbages in the garden of the grand lady of the manor and so on—it gave one a proper perspective because one must remember that ordinary life goes on, and one's subject had an ordinary life and it's very easy to lose sight of this.

GIROUX: Did you know that Waugh's father was a book publisher? Early in this century he was the editor of Chapman & Hall, the nineteenth-century house that published Charles Dickens.

HASTINGS: Oh, yes. I did.

GIROUX: I always wondered what Evelyn thought when Papa Arthur Waugh denounced T.S. Eliot as a "drunken helot" when *The Waste Land* first appeared in 1922. He found the text incomprehensible, a lot of gibberish, and didn't hesitate to say so. He never knew that "He Do the Police in Different Voices" comes right out of Dickens.

GLENDINNING: Very often my subject's mother has tended to take over the whole book. Vita Sackville-West's mother, the daughter of a Spanish dancer, married into the English aristocracy. She made slaves of deeply sophisticated, cultured and cultivated gentlemen like Wallace of the Wallace Collection and Edmund Lutyens the architect—and her daughter, who I was trying to think of as the center of my book. Edith Sitwell's mother was a deeply silly and disturbed woman, who had Edith much too young, gambled compulsively and was sent to prison for debt. Her husband refused to buy her out. So I have had problems with mothers getting bigger and bigger and bigger. What was rather good with Jonathan Swift was that his mother virtually abandoned him when he was a baby, and he didn't meet her again until he was twenty. So she became like the magical mystery tour of my book; because she wasn't there, I had to go in search of her. When you're really interested in family dynamics, the problem is keeping the balance when somebody is such a strong character that the focus of the book shifts too far and you lose track altogether.

HENIZ: How do you balance it out if he didn't see her for twenty years?

GLENDINNING: He was brought up by what you might call a committee of uncles in Dublin, and had no significant female loving person. He sought his mother out when he was twenty. She went to live in Leicester. He walked all the way from Holyhead to Leicester to find her. After that he went to see her every year until she died, wrote to her once a month.

GOWRIE: The Trollopes were always walking.

GLENDINNING: Everybody walked.

HEINZ: That's why they thought so much better and clearer; they thought while they walked.

LEWIS: When I was writing Connolly, one person I really loved in the book was Connolly's father, who was a drunken major. He was a world authority on postal stamps and potted meats and snails. Connolly was tremendously ashamed of him. Major Connolly was very useful to me because he wrote up masses of family history, clapping fiercely away on the red ribbon of his ancient typewriter. He used to write to Connolly, reproaching him for one thing or another, and I found his letters so touching because he always ended them saying, *Much love, Dad*, and then he'd type underneath in brackets, *Major M. Connolly*. He was such a wonderful man. Connolly was ashamed of the major for most of his life. His mother deserted the major and ran off with his commanding officer to live in South Africa, and so Connolly had spent a lot of time at home with the major, who was always drunk and belching and weaving around the house. Connolly was always writing to his friends about the ghastliness of his father. He always idealized his mother, who I must say I didn't have much time for. I think the fact that his mother deserted him induced in Connolly a pattern of falling in love not only with two people at once but of forcing the women in his life to desert him. He would sit and lick his wounds: How dreadful. I miss you, how awful life is, how sorry I feel for myself . . .

TOPIC: *LITERARY AUTOBIOGRAPHY*

GLENDINNING: There are all sorts of reasons why a person might write an autobiography. One reason is certainly to conceal certain things; another is to present a certain image. A further point should be made that there will be things a biographer will know about someone if they've gone deep enough that the autobiographer couldn't have known. To take a simple example: imagine yourself being violently kicked into a lake. You don't turn around and catch sight of who did it; you're struggling in the waters, coping with the consequences of the kick. It's the people who watch, especially if they were watching from a window some way away, who will have understood the scene— seen the person creeping out of the bushes. All that sort of stuff is the biographer's business.

FOSTER: Trollope and Yeats are examples of deeply disingenu- ous autobiographies written for reasons to do with the people they were when they wrote biography, aged sixty and nearly fifty, and are much more useful as guides to their psychologies in 1878 or 1914 when they wrote the books than they are to the facts of their early lives.

GLENDINNING: Trollope's autobiography has the most infuriat- ing sentence. All he said on the subject of marriage: My marriage was like the marriage of other people, and as such of no interest to anyone except my wife and myself.

In a sense an autobiography is just for the biographer—just another ingredient. Just as his novel may be another part of his work.

SPURLING: I'll give you a very simple example concerning Ivy Compton-Burnett, who was a terrifying woman. Four different people claimed that this story happened to them at very different periods of her life. The first was Francis Birrell, the second was the novelist Olivia Manning, next a journalist from the *Express*, and the last was Philip Toynbee. Roughly speaking the story goes that this young journalist (or fan) is invited to dinner at the Compton-Burnett establishment and, being nervous, knowing what a stickler she was for punctuality, arrives a little early, then realizes that the evening can't be faced without a stiff drink. Besides, there isn't going to be much in the way of drink once they've got past the front door. So whoever it is goes and has a couple of whiskeys. The guest comes back a little late and rings the bell. The door is opened by the maid, who says, "You're late. The ladies have gone in to dinner." So in he goes and, as Philip Toynbee told the story, Miss Compton-Burnett and her friends have proceeded from the soup to the fish. The conversation goes on without him. He isn't really ever accepted into the scene, people pass things over his head. Things go from bad to worse until this youth wakes up to find that although at some stage he had passed out, the meal had continued over his head, to and fro, taking its course to the end when the ladies left, leaving the light on for him. Francis Birrell said he woke up with his face in the fish, having smashed the arm of an eighteenth-century chair. He got up and found the ladies had gone to bed (it was half past eleven), put the light out and let himself out of the flat. Much the same happened to Olivia Manning more than twenty years later. It happened again to a journalist who wrote about it in the *Express*. Finally it happened to the young Philip Toynbee in the late fifties. Now are we to believe that Ivy literally petrified her young admirers time after time, or is this an apocryphal story that tells the truth?

GLENDINNING: There are certain charismatic figures—Swift was definitely one—to whom myths accrue. There are a great many folk stories, very old jokes if you like, which the dean is credited with. In Ireland people make a little joke and they'll say, "As the dean said." Even in his lifetime this happened.

PLIMPTON: Truman Capote never wrote an autobiography, but I can't imagine it would have been taken seriously. Fantasy had taken over. He once told me that he was working on a murder case in Nebraska that he'd been led to by one of the detectives in *In Cold Blood*. It involved this landlord trying to increase his holdings along the creek by murdering off his neighbors. In one case he had put rattlesnakes into a couple's car who had gone to church. They came out on a hot July day, stepped into the car and, according to Truman, had been done away with by these rattlesnakes. I said, "Truman, that does seem rather unlikely." First of all, rattlesnakes have rattles, they're lethargic and their poison is hematoxic, which means it works through the bloodstream. These people presumably could get to the hospital and get themselves fixed up. The next time I heard the story it had been changed substantially. The couple had suddenly become in their nineties, extremely elderly, just teetering on the edge of life. The rattles had been removed from the rattlesnakes and the lethargy problem had been taken care of by their being laced with amphetamines. Truman told the new version on the Johnny Carson TV show. The audience gave out that awful sound of derision and disbelief, *oooh*. Truman was really taken aback.

HUGHES-HALLETT: If we're talking about apocryphal stories, when I wrote my Cleopatra book I looked into the question of the drinking of pearls. As you know, Cleopatra's supposed to have dissolved a pearl in wine and drunk it—a story told not only about her, but also about Nero and two other wealthier Romans. It would have been understood by readers in the earlier period, not as something that necessarily happened, but as something that told you something about the protagonist. It couldn't be true. Any liquid capable of dissolving a pearl would also dissolve the stomach if you drank it.

GLENDINNING: It wasn't ever intended to be believed. It conveyed information but at a nonliteral level.

I'd like to make a sort of general point: for a major figure such as Swift, a lot of the material will have been looked at already—by a great many writers and scholars, by people writing articles. His letters are published in five scholarly volumes, unread by most people but on the shelf if you want to find them. This was also true of Trollope, whose letters were published. Every biographer would be picking something different depending on what their inner trajectory really was. George Weidenfeld told me ages ago that there's always room for another biography on any really interesting figure. There is no such thing as a definitive biography because we will all pick up something different from the same body of material and so everybody's on their different quest.

SPURLING: I think there is always an element of portrait paint-ing in a biography, but the historical element is absolutely crucial. Facts so quickly become legend that you spend a lot of time sorting one from the other. This is what the French have refused to accept. They cannot attach any importance to what they call *les donneés*, the given facts, which are no more than the crude foundation on which you base your portrait, you paint your picture, you develop your philosophy; and it's the intellectual brilliance of that structure, the number of philosoph-ical fireworks that you can throw up, that will establish the value of what you're doing. A perfectly respectable theory, but where the French fall down is that the facts from which they start are so often false, conventional and secondhand.

A biographer is a historian too, writing about lives that don't make sense outside their historical context. For instance, if you're writing about an illegitimate child born in 1894, you have in some tactful way to sketch in the fact that this was an almost impossible situation for the mother, that most illegitimate chil-dren born to working-class girls in urban Europe died. The child had to be more or less kept in a cupboard; any landlady would put an unmarried mother on the street; you would lose your job as well. Only a small portion of fostered children grew to be adults. You must sketch that in; you must also sketch in the pressure of bourgeois opinion that made it impossible for a mother to keep the child. Otherwise very simplistic moral judg-ments are passed that have nothing to do with the circumstances.

GLENDINNING: Unless you get the facts reputable and in con-text you can't begin to make a serious portrait, a portrait with any depth or profundity.

ATLAS: I think you have to know consciously or unconsciously what it is that you're looking for. This can be a very ill-defined shadowy kind of quest indeed. You have to have some sense of why you were drawn to this figure, or what it was about this figure that kindled your interest.

KNOWLSON: I've always felt that Beckett's work was very strongly influenced by painting. Working on this work for twenty-five years, it dawned on me that not only was he very aware of classical painting, an expert on seventeenth-century Dutch art for example, but that his own images had behind them some kind of ghostly traces of Rembrandt and Caravaggio. I was aware of the whole visual dimension only when I found his diaries for 1936 and 1937, when he was going round Germany and writing for himself—rather more trustworthy than autobiography. The quest therefore is constantly being reformulated. I can remember very clearly having a dinner with Samuel Beckett when I said to him, "Your bookshelves must be full of psychoanalysis and psychology." He thought for a moment and said, "No, no, no, Jim." That was a shock to me. But then after he died, out of his trunk came all his notes on "Erogenous Jones" as he called him, Wilhelm Stekle, or angst, Otto Rank's *Trauma of Birth*, with underlining and exclamation marks. Well, he was telling the absolute truth: he did not have on his shelves books of psychoanalysis. I know now that he was reading them in the British Library, in the British Museum in 1934-1935. So that again for me was a process of readjustment.

ATLAS: I remember I went to see one of Bellow's many girlfriends. I was in a very shy, early stage of my research. She said, "Well, he had his sexual dos and don'ts." The next question anyone except me would ask is, And what were those? So I said, turning deep red, "Oh, what year did you meet?"

SPURLING: There is a kind of ruthlessness in this quest. Personally, I don't think I would undertake a biography and all the miserable years of drudgery that it involves if I weren't basically a nosy parker. I need to know. You become a questing nose. If it seems that there is something over there, you dive across, and then you come back and investigate behind something else.

What did he mean by that? There must be something under this carpet. You're always lifting up the carpet—but I wouldn't want to do that to someone who's part of my life.

GLENDINNING: I had the same trouble with Rebecca West. I knew her for the last ten years of her life. We talked about me writing about her. I became completely inhibited from even going to see her as much as I should have. After she had died, I was reading her diaries. There was this awful little entry: *Victoria hasn't been to see me. I don't think she's very interested.*

HASTINGS: I remember once going to interview somebody who'd known Mr. Nichols, Charlotte Brontë's husband, and I was asking her about it. She said, "Why on earth do you want to know what Charlotte Brontë had for breakfast." I'd have given my right arm to know what Charlotte Brontë had for breakfast.

D. Gregory Griffith

O Orpheus

I can bang at the lyre, but make it sing?
Each time the muse whistles through my spine,
she numbs like a drug, and I nod
through my inspiration.

I never lead dreams out of sleep;
they fall back as I rise. I remember
faces like old snapshots: mute, flat,
black and white—

expressions blurred by old glass, limbs
cropped for the frame, or cut off
by photo edges. If I can't sing someone
whole across the threshold, I'll turn

each face to the past with a stare.

Two Poems by Derick Burleson

One Million One

Refugees flee their homes. Exiles
move back in, thirty-year echoes
of mortar shells rattling windows.

    Down the river bloated bodies bob.
    Little brother, which body is yours?

Relief planes bomb refugees
with food and a few more perish
under the crashing crates of manna.

    Blowflies buzz, such bliss!
    Dogs grow fatter than ever.

Experts jet in—medical, forensic.
They distribute white suits,
surgical masks and white gloves.

    Refugees are being immunized.
    The water they drink is purified.

Bright yellow bulldozers belch
black clouds of diesel smoke,
digging the bottomless trench.

    All down the river sun-bleached limbs dance.
    Little brother, which leg is yours?

Exiles smile to be home, harvest
beans that the refugees planted.
These new citizens patrol old borders.

Vultures cluck, such joy!
Hyenas giggle, fatter than ever.

The dead are aligned, so many
fence posts, each wrapped and tied
in mats living women weave: dead banana leaves.

A million eat charity, injected
with health. The river water is purified.

Pairs of white-suited workers pitch
bodies into the trench, a layer of wrapped bodies,
a layer of lime.

All down the river torsos swell.
Little brother, which belly is yours?

Perched at trench edge, separate
abacus beads strung on kilometers of wire,
experts count one million.

Maggots bloom out of bellies.
Crows whet beaks on bones, such glee!

Relief workers distribute plastic tents.
Defeated soldiers dance
round fires of food crates.

An army is being immunized.
The river it drinks has been purified.

Generals speak. Refugees listen,
held hostage at gunpoint,
planning the counterattack.

Exiles are being immunized.
The water they drink is purified.

One million flee for their lives
again. Their army on the run,
refugees would rather die at home.

    Blowflies have never known such love.
    Vultures are fatter than ever.

Grass grows over the airstrip. Grass grows
over the grave. And here come herdsmen
driving cows to pasture, never so green.

    All down the river severed heads sing.
    Little brother, which song is yours?

Ethnologist's Lament

All day I measure noses.
People are brought before me.
My brass calipers never lie.

If the nose is long enough,
I give that person a card.
If not, I shrug and smile.

I keep meticulous records.
Research: self is a science.
Nature's laws are exact.

The sun is savage here,
burns my nose quite raw.
I haven't caught brain fever,

yet many have: a few
even died. The women here
are lovely. I shouldn't say so.

Noses of Tutsis are identical
to ours. Outrage! you cry.
Color is the only difference.

I can show you my records.
I wonder how you'd measure up.
We know the length of nose

is a sign of finer perceptions
noble blood bestows. Our card
shows those capable of receiving

gifts we bring, gifts of God
and science to create, we anticipate,
an oasis of advanced civilization

beneath this savage sun.
Yet my work is full of sorrow.
I pity those Hutus whose noses

are only almost long enough.
Nature's laws never lie.
My brass calipers are quite exact.

I work for the good of my King.
I work for the good of our colony,
beautiful among a thousand hills.

I miss my wife back home.
My work is full of sorrow.
Few noses are long enough.

The sun rises and sets at six.
All night I dream of noses.
Noses just too short

to learn God's laws and
science's. I wear a helmet
against the sun.

Anthony Deaton

On the General Principles of Knot-Tying: An Elegy for the Body

Port with the tossed deck, whipping
Sheep-bends between the coiled lines,
We lean. Our faith in bracing and ballast,

And the sky washes down upon us, cloud
Into spindrift. "To know knots
You must know danger,"

Our skipper said. "Safe passage
Is a day's work." Hauled salmon.
The hold brims humpies and sockeye,

Their wriggle-flop bodies of fin
And petaled skin we sweep below.
While one would be enough for me,

One stilled eye enough to hold back
From the long fresh-water feed of coastal streams,
We bend to commerce. And the water rises,

As if to beg us quit. And the water
Rises until a body is finally
Caught at cross-purposes between

The ship's steady toil
And the unstoppable spillage of net
Into the wake of our endeavor—

A body. My body,
Snatched, rigged right up the boom,
As if it were a flag,

An exquisite signature. O,
What now? Now, white hospital light.
Who dreamed it would end here among the hemostats,

Nasal cannuli? The scooped arc
Of the spatula-needle noses through-
And-through its long transaction, closes

The serried, open wound. Swage
Follows. Needle point. Over and again. This
Is the knot that finally binds.

Two Poems by Malcolm Farley

Lunch Hour

The dim prospects from this window make me ask
if should I hold you in the half-light—when morning

swaddles me in partial truth, when the difficulties
of high noon still mumble in their beds—and say:

"Now ask about the changeling underneath your quilt,
the one who shies away from truth and other steel,

who won't be touched, who lies beside you speechlessly
as though he were blue distance." But I'm a minor bureaucrat

worrying too much how scandals happen—today,
a cloud that gags the nearby tower with roiling vapor.

Conscience stirs the murk to my left, uncovering
the blunt imperatives on Sixth Avenue, below,

capitals that blare: MOVING/KEEP/LANE/FIRE.
Great wisps of fog reach down, unswirl, embrace.

Post-Modern Grimm

Once upon a time a girl named December Thought
sat alone at the top of a tree of frosted glass
where she brooded over cigarettes and coffee,
recuperating from a long disease.

Each night a boy who tasted just like Thirst
peered through his dented kaleidoscope
and saw her in the tessellated reds and citrons.

All chimes in his chest went off at once,
making a din he hoped the sky would hear.
Many heroic obstacles and recognitions later,
Thirst coaxed her down and won her love,

but found they didn't melt or recombine
to form a classical hermaphrodite. She became
a fieldstone wall. He, the thistle in her shadow.

Two Poems by Irving Feldman

These Memoirs

Stumbling midnight tipsy in Jackson's studio,
who knocked black paint over into tomorrow
and throbbing rainbows of our morning after?
Well, thanks to these *Memoirs*, now we know.

When howling sounded over Rockland State,
whose Parker jotted the holy phonemes down?
'Fess up, Allen, and give the man back his pen!
—because these *Memoirs* tell us, and now we know.

In that smoky predawn dive *who* taught Balanchine
to do the twist, quoted since on scores of stages?
No thanks to Mr. B. we know about this
—down to the bubbles in the Veuve Clicquot.

There could have been dull Nothing, you never know
—bland canvas, numb poem, torsos untorsed.
Who, then, was the quirk at the lip of Oblivion,
the droplet that set the trembling source aflow?

But by what inversion of Fate the Ironist
have his loveliest strokes become his erasure?
Surest to remember is soonest forgot.
That's the awful truth, as these *Memoirs* show

—fitfully, from darkening pages, where one reads
how, years ago, overlooked, *his* drained goblet lay
tipped over, losing light, filling with silence,
far below the lid of Cage's black piano.

"And lies there still, flowing, lost, overflowing,"
our nameless author wrote. His last words are:
"Absurd though all this will seem, yet in these pages
Oblivion toasts Memory now—as we know

"this moment, overflowing, flowing, lost."

Laura Among the Shades

Honor, and excellence, and transcendent best,
I was the laurels I denominated:
diadem and queen and diadem's bearer.
Disdaining tribute from inferior hands,
I crowned myself *The Greatest Poet Alive*.

And died to pursue opponents far worthier.
I bore my distinction against the famous dead,
and grimly—not their rival, their enemy.
My evergreen shall overgrow their names
grimed on the black page of Oblivion.

My conceit was always larger than myself.
Not vainglory, it was ambition, and meant
to show my complete contempt for poetry.
Accursed the leaves I plucked and poison to me,
my laurels mingled with berries of the nightshade.

Two Poems by Dorothea Tanning

Report From the Field

Sublimation, a new version of piety,
Hovers the paint and gets her going.
Everything drifts, a barely heard sigh is the

Sound of wind in the next room blowing
Dust from anxiety. A favorite receptacle
Holds her breath and occasional sewing.

Only the artist will be held responsible
For something so far unsaid but true,
For having the crust to let the hysterical

Earnest of genuine feeling show through,
And watching herself in the glassy eyeing
Of *Art as seen through a hole in her shoe.*

Painter and poet, sometimes said to be lying,
Agonizingly know it is more like dying.

Insomnia, my cousin,

you ride the night machine
witlessly in bedlam,
breathing on my screen,
my panting outdoor movie,
its paid admission being
my square root,
my flash bulb
socket-pinned and joyless.

Insomnia, my cousin,
you have sired nightly
indecent vertigo.
I lie haggard as you drag
your insane engine past
across the floor,
slamming doors
on all my four dimensions,

leaving me high day
to shred the clotted dream.
Cousin, I repeatedly
betray you with its debris.

Two Poems by Shawn Sturgeon

The Word on Alexandria

Urging our oxen toward the risen sun,
our stick plows stirring up the dust in waves,
also, in waves, we taste those words come back,

as ash will or craft of the reedy Nile:
so many sounds can set the tongue on fire,
so many words can set the temples aflame.

Let them burn!—and the library's in flames,
and parchment scraps float in the full-blown sun,
so many sounds can set the tongue on fire.

Our senses draw back from the mind as waves
in a time of drought, by the reedless Nile,
when we pray again those words, *Come back*

a spring, in spring—the waters coming back.
So many words set the temples aflame,
and we feel the ground swell, and read the Nile,

and think we ourselves are the risen sun,
that we drown in our words, in molten waves,
as if such waves could set the tongue on fire,

as if such cries could make of soul a fire,
until we hope those souls may never come back
as earth or sky on which we stand and wave,

knowing those waves set the temples aflame,
knowing those temples find the risen sun
here, in Alexandria, by the reed-blown Nile.

And still, we listen to the reed-blown Nile—
so many songs can set the tongue on fire—
and it is this we hear is our risen sun,

whom we've heard, we have heard, is coming back,
with words that will set the temples aflame,
and the dead will swell from the ground in waves,

and we'll feel ourselves drowning in the dusty waves,
as ash will or craft of the reedy Nile—
so many cries will set the plows aflame,

so many cries will set the tongue on fire,
until these words dissolve, until they never come back,
until I am the word of the risen sun,

and these words are waves, and these waves are fire,
and the Nile burns, and the library comes back
with words that are flames of the shriven sun.

An Etruscan Farewell

The day our wives left, we gathered their things
in brown, worsted sacks and burned them
in the garden, scattering the ashes
as seed before a razing wind.

They never returned, but the garden has
shown improvement, though the wisteria
comes and goes. Such life, as we know, returns
fragrantly, but as each season

reduces us to a still finer dust
we feel within us a passion

for losing ways—the rustle of footsteps
on the path, our hands aflutter

with the dry sleep of blossoms. Perhaps one
should expect rain, that the sun dries
the precipitous nights. Flowers feed by
such lights. Vines devour what walls remain.

Renée and Theodore Weiss

Footwork

I.

My father? He was into shoes.
But also into pins and needles,
pots and pans: a five-and-ten,
for its small town ambitiously
called The Weiss Emporium.

O yes, he was into dresses too.
Mustache pointed and upcurled,
he, donning felt slippers,
capered among the svelte girls
as he draped and posed them,
featured in his store window.

(Like the figures lounged about,
showing off secondhand goods,
in well-lit, roomy windows
on certain notorious streets
in certain European cities.)

But, his feet not meant for standing
still, mainly he was into shoes,
boxed two by two—like birds
he kept—and wrapped in tissue.
Each shoe wore, ornately lettered
on its inner sole, *Doctor Weiss.*

II.

For the little Hungarian village
where he grew up, shoes were
special, trotted out only
on grand occasions.
                              Otherwise
folks squished their toes in mud
or marched in boots to timeless
drill.
        But wooded birds nearby,
responding to my father's gypsy
tunes, winged through his trills.

One October dawn, his boots
swinging round his neck, Father
slipped into the mists swirled
from the shadowy Black Forest.
His eyes fixed on his dreams,
tweetings lit the path he took.

Heaving weeks on weeks of ocean
washing away his past, he landed
footloose in a maze of roads,
among buildings storied skyward,
their denizens rushed by.
                              How walk
unshod on such jammed streets?
With all America on the move,
shoes must lead him to his fortune.

III.

Fortune nothing: chores and bills
that drove him from one small town
to another; each glowing future,
beckoning him, quickly dimmed.

Even so he stole time, hunched
over a backyard stoop, for looking
after his flock.
                    Forcing whiskey
down a squawking old hen's gullet,
he set her on an orphaned nest.
Come to, soberly she took it
for her own.
                    And when a chick,
struggling through its shell,
wobbled on its twisted leg,
father carved it a twig crutch;
soon it fluttered among the rest.

So with his last shoe store,
stuck in the middle of a downtown
screeching traffic, he lined
the store's back wall with cage
on cage of paired canaries.
                                Then,
when he sang those gypsy tunes,
feet stamping, near the cages,
the birds twittered forests
round him.
                Till, assured of his
boyhood skills, he rode a spunky
horse, belonging to a farmer
friend, that sped him to the wood
there is no leaving.

In the Air

Noah Hawley

Joy Ray lives on Great Jones Street upstairs from Sticky Mike's Frog Bar, a nightclub in front of which Rocket, drunk and loping towards the subway, was once robbed at gun point. There is a synchronicity to this that does not escape us whenever we rehash our pasts in the smoky bars and Cuban-Chinese diners of Eighth Avenue. After Rocket had been mugged and assaulted—not shot, but pistol-whipped—and was lying on the sidewalk getting his bearings back, Joy Ray, wearing a black tube dress under a long, brown camel-hair coat, exited a cab in front of her apartment. In passing Rocket's supine body she dropped fifty-seven cents in change onto his back. Then, having made her substantial blow for the day against homelessness, she made her way upstairs to continue working on a portrait she would later title *Hamaji in Yellow and Green*, the very painting in front of which Rocket would be standing, five weeks after my brother Neil died, when I met him for the first time. All these circumstances we consider with much astonishment in the back of Sam Chao's Chinese-Cuban All Night.

"A head wound," says Rocket, "and then I look up and there's this black-haired beauty stooping over me and the next thing I know, dimes and nickels raining down."

Rocket lives and works in a warehouse space in the Fort Greene section of Brooklyn among the truck yards and highway overpasses of the BQE. He is a sculptor of no minor talent, cutting figures from steel and stone, welding ideas into form, fastening love to hate and misery to joy. Physically, he is a lumbering giant whose thin hair recedes. An epileptic, he suffers from grand mal seizures, which strike him like bolts of lightning, and then one must be careful to get hold of his tongue so he doesn't bite it off or swallow it. He has told me that in the brief seconds before a seizure he will experience a feeling of euphoria, a sense of lightness that brings with it a moment of divine inspiration. It is from these moments that he constructs his images, which so often have to do with the themes of losing control and the betrayal of bodies.

We meet regularly for midnight meals, Rocket, Joy Ray and I, slumming on the outskirts of the new elitist Chelsea. Eating red beans and rice or greasy dim sum, drinking beer from sweaty cans, we pick flecks of other people's meals from our silverware and discuss Rocket's drinking problem in the clinical tones of pop psychology. We toy with the language of television miracles. We decree that Rocket, by consuming alarming quantities of domestic beer, is trying to *fill a void*. We describe his bouts of hostile depression as *indicative of unresolved issues left over from childhood*. Rocket corrects us by saying that sometimes a cigar is just a cigar, but we smile our knowing smiles. From dangerously high levels of talk-show exposure we understand that it is always the guests themselves who are the last to know the condition from which they suffer, though it is there for us to read in the one or two cryptic sentences that squat beneath their chins. By refusing to succumb to our psychoanalytic conclusions, we tell Rocket, he is living in denial.

Having established the absolutism of the fascistic Freudian state—i.e. *you would not be here if you were not sick* (here in this case being Sam Chao's All Night Cuban-Chinese diner on West Eighteenth Street) we move on to discuss Joy Ray's fear of intimacy—which has rendered her chronically single—and my own untamed kleptomania, though what we look for in this exercise of turning our own lives into antiseptic case histories is not therapeutic insight, but the salvation of absurdity. This is how we combat our fear. Our fear of failure or loneliness, of death and mediocrity. The fear, expressed and secret, of losing our youth, of hidden tumors and late night subway dismemberments; fear of insanity, fear of contagious disease and sudden drug addiction; the fear of one day discovering the Virgin Mary lurking in the abstract imagery of our art, and the religious implications this would raise.

On nights when we are not out sampling the schizophrenic delicacies of the Cuban orient, we can be found drinking in the seedy pockets of the Lower East Side, where Rocket smokes too many cigarettes and tries, often successfully, to pick up girls. There is an animal magnetism about him, not unlike the thrill of murder. He says, "I need to be in love to feel like I'm alive." Who am I to say that this is untrue? So I let him buy us beers—because I am invariably unemployed and low on physical cash—and he does, shelling out drink money for the red heads and peroxide blondes who hang off his arm, revealing more than they should of their bodies, their own insecurities and desperations visible in the folds of their cleavage and the lift of their skirts. Joy Ray joins us more often than not, but always late, apologizing for this or that. She is a wearer of interesting hats.

Inside these crowded bars, Rocket informs me of plans he has for an installation piece. It springs from the need he feels to make people uncomfortable. He envisions a room in which the hinges of the doors are on the floor, so that the doors themselves open downward; a room where the bed is a skylight that looks into subway tunnels and sewers and the pillows are soft sculptures of the homeless curled up into fetal positions. There is a big bay window, but the view is blocked by crowds who press up against the glass, looking in, their eyes wide. He tells me he has stood in this room already. In a vision. The temperature in the room must be 98.6 degrees. The temperature of the human body. The walls will be pigskin. The room will have no corners. In fact it won't be a room at all. It will be a cavity.

At the end of our dystopic evenings, alcohol ingested, truth and beauty dispatched, we go our separate ways: Rocket lugging squealing, risk-addicted women into the streets, putting them on the back of his rusty Honda, Joy Ray reapplying lipstick and hailing a cab to take her to this opening or that, a disco, a nightclub, an off-off-Broadway show.

Sometimes, when they are too drunk to find their way home, Rocket and Joy Ray will crash with me, Rocket's body thrown violently across the cramped interior of my bathroom, a leg in the tub, a hand trailing out into the hallway. He will need to be in there later when the purging begins and so has learned to collapse on my crooked bathroom tiles. In this way we consider him a trainable animal. Housebroken, says Joy Ray. I offer her my bed, though some nights she pulls at me to stay with her, grabs at my shirtsleeves, tugs my hair, but I shrug her off, often losing the shirt, letting her fall back with it as I slip away into the main room, where I tumble into an old reclining chair.

Outside, the city screams its never ending electric opera; sirens harassing the unconscious with prophecies of disaster, egged on by the narcoleptic car alarms of the millennial consumer—lost, lonely, afraid of the dark. Sacked out in our separate rooms, we pretend we are numb to the racket, to the artificial glare that coats the city like a luminous skin.

We purport to sleep soundly, to thrive on the mania of millions, but inevitably dawn finds us groggy and half-conscious and we arise unrested, troubled by freshly forgotten dreams, Joy Ray somehow resurrecting her beauty from the graveyard of exhaustion, as Rocket struggles to his knees and vomits into the porcelain bowl.

I was born and raised in this discordant metropolis. To Rocket and Joy Ray this grants me a kind of morbid celebrity, like the survivor of a great holocaust.

"Listen," I tell them. "Before it was the capital of the world, before home computers and MTV, there were two little boys living in one enormous, exotic concrete playground. Brothers, who were too young and unbowed to be scared of anything, navigating the great sea of legs, racing each other across five lanes of oncoming traffic."

I don't tell them how homesick I am for that younger New York, the innocence of it. I don't tell them how bitter I am that the city of my childhood has been replaced by the squalor of newspaper headlines, rent payments and crime statistics. I keep my mouth shut on the subject, because Rocket and Joy Ray are suspicious of nostalgia, insulated as they are by double thick layers of aloofness and bravado. But then they know nothing about Neil's suicide, nothing about how it turned this city into a ghost town for me; all the old schools, all the secret places we used to go, the insubstantial memories of countless moments spent on every block and crumbling corner. Today, I wander the streets surrounded by hazy visions of the past, jostled by pedestrians with transparent faces and steam-colored clothes. I lurk near flower stands and newspaper kiosks, drinking coffee from cardboard cups and spying on the specters of my past.

After Neil's death I moved into a tiny one-bedroom apartment on Avenue A and Sixth Street, where the floors slant at steep angles. This is where I fumble with my own fickle art; the kinetic medium of language. From the back windows I can see the ashtray gardens of my neighbors, blots of grass littered with the stubby ends of rusted lawn furniture and cracked cement tables. There are graffiti-scarred trees that rustle when the wind blows, a plague of feral tabby cats and pigeons that walk the narrow roofs of fences that dissect each plot of cluttered ground. Inside, the latest coat of paint peels from the walls. Downstairs, I can hear the families from Ecuador and Nicaragua yelling at each other in Spanish to either turn down or turn up their televisions.

It is a part of the city where Neil and I never lived, a clot of streets we never walked down, and, therefore, thankfully ghostless and unfamiliar.

Of the three of us Joy Ray has achieved the most success. Her portraits are shown in two Soho Galleries, and, she has been told, Julian Schnabel himself recently bought a portrait she painted of me, a sale that kept her high for weeks. If you have to pin her down to some style of painting, then Joy Ray is something of an absurdist. She likes to paint portraits in which people's occupations, their "functions" come through. In this way she implies that people are simply pieces of a greater whole, cogs and computer chips in a societal machine. For example, the portrait in front of which I first met Rocket, *Hamaji in Yellow and Green*, is a painting of Hamaji Baru, a Pakistani cab driver. In it, his head is yellow, checkered with white, his face bumpered. The teeth of his smile are numbered like a license plate. She uses heavy strokes of oil, blends colors and textures. The images rise up out of the canvas, but not so clearly that there is no room left for interpretation. The trick is to capture the features and feel of the person in the object. She likens it to the way that people's pets grow to resemble them. Using canvas and brush, Joy Ray attempts to portray the essential "Hamajiness" of her taxi driver. Her work is meant to make us reflect on who we are, on how we define ourselves if not by our professions.

The portrait of me, the one that supposedly hangs in Julian Schnabel's living room, is painted in grays and browns. She has taken an old spinal X ray of mine, the rivets of my vertebrae connecting my shadowy pelvis to my skull, and mounted it on a board, five by two. She has stroked the suggestion of my torso. Over my skull she has painted a large manual typewriter, angled as is my head, so that the keys are legible, the old style As and Os, the QWERT POIUY of my consciousness. She has given me a shadowy figure, upon which are certain printed words, barely legible against the dark soup of background and body. The words themselves are unimportant. They are meant to show that the cells of my body are made up of the letters of the alphabet.

For Joy Ray, who grew up in Maryland, New York is like the duplicitous invention of a mad scientist. She is impressed by the contrast of life and death, wealth and poverty, sickness and health. She comes from rich parents, has never felt the stinging panic of impending hunger—this is where Rocket, who grew up the son of an auto mechanic and a waitress, will attack her when we fight about art. He is famous for telling a packed gallery opening filled with upper echelon collectors and famous artists that he wanted to hold art burnings.

"Assemble all of the motel watercolors, the office lobby oil paintings of lobster traps and New England fishing boats," he said. "I want a pile so high we all start speaking in tongues."

When asked politely to leave, he decorated a bronze bust of Elvis with macaroni salad and stumbled drunkenly to the street, where he managed, through some miracle, to drop into an epileptic seizure, allowing him to be escorted from the premises by ambulance rather than police car.

"Being a cerebral cripple has its advantages," he says. In the bucks and jerks of his body we can see the death that shadows him. More than once he has told us that he envies Jackson Pollock. "Those last seconds after the crash. His body flying through the air. What are the images he must have seen? What kind of visions? That's the art I want to make. To quantify the dying thoughts of great artists."

I hide my confessions in my apartment, my ghosts and memories. I sit on the window ledge, watch the alley cats walk the narrow fence tops. My typewriter lurks in the background like an accusation. The moon rises and sets.

When a person makes his way up through the under-lit interior of a twenty-six story building, I wonder, when he pushes open an insulated metal fire door and clambers out onto the roof, is his head filled with memories and regrets? When a nineteen-year-old boy kicks gravel across the bald dome of a skyscraper and spits into the breeze, is he really mouthing *if only?* And when he stares down at the traffic, when he places first one foot and then the other on the narrow concrete ledge, muscling all his weight up into a single, swaying perpendicular, what is he thinking? What strange mixture of elation and fear seizes hold of his mind?

In the kitchen the refrigerator stutters. Joy Ray turns, but does not wake. Outside the lights in other buildings, other apartments begin to flicker out.

When my brother stood shivering on the edge, poised on the cusp of an irreversible leap, did he say my name, did he let the vowels, the syllables catch on the wind? Did he know then that by taking his own life he was reshaping mine, altering my aspirations, inspiring an obsession that to this day makes me feel as if the only story worth writing is the one that explains why he did what he did on that balmy night in late September? Perhaps if he had not written a note, if he had not put down on paper his final, disjointed thoughts in the same way a writer sits down before a blank white sheet to wrestle with his imagination, to forge a shaky truth from a pack of outright lies. But he did leave a note, did express his unhappiness with a few cursive lines meant to convey the sentiment that life, for him, had become coarse and uninspiring. Uninspiring. As if the rest of us face every day with a Mr. Rogers sensibility. As if the rest of us are not routinely hobbled by feelings of melancholy and doubt. That night there was a jackknife high dive, followed by a routine, bureaucratic phone call and, afterward, a continual sense of helplessness. Imagine the words below my chin, *Continual sense of helplessness. Man racked by grief and guilt. Brother of a sad, mute ghost*. What can we do in this world if we can't even keep each other alive?

In the morning I lie in bed and watch Joy Ray dress, the embrace of her underwear white against her dark legs, the plane of stomach, stretch of arm, turn of hip. In the bathroom, Rocket begins to make noises of distress. Joy Ray fastens her bra, slips a T-shirt over her head. She brushes her hair with long even strokes. Today she will sell three paintings for a total of forty thousand dollars. Art for her will take on new meaning.

She phones in the afternoon to give me the news. Her voice is breathless, ebullient. I suggest we meet at Sam Chao's to celebrate. She says she wants to take us to Vong. Let's splurge one night, she says.

At Vong, Rocket is surly, distant. He arrives drunk, underdressed. He refuses to let Joy Ray buy him a drink. We sit for the most part embarrassed, unable to capture the excitement and sense of future that Joy Ray wants on a night such as this. I make the effort to be jocular. Rocket interprets this as a sign of abandonment and begins calling me names in a dry, caustic voice. Joy Ray checks her watch, retreats to the ladies' room. For her the struggle has paid off. There will be parties and receptions, the freedom to concentrate on work, the temporary alleviation of anxiety. Sitting beside the abusive Rocket, I question the fairness of what has happened. I recognize that what we have had, the three of us, has not so much been a friendship as a competition. When she returns, I smile and squeeze her hand, but it is not the smile of a well-wisher. For Rocket and I, alone, abandoned, there is only the enmity of the loser.

The next night, Joy's agent arranges a small party for her at the Hollis Gallery. Rocket arrives sloppy and mean. He shoves the agent into a folding table covered with chopped vegetables. This is all crap, he shouts. His face is purple. Joy

Ray stands in a corner shaking her head. I take him outside
to calm him down, put my hand on his arm. We have too
much in common to fight, but between losers there is no
allegiance, only resentment—when we look at each other all
we can think of is our own failure, so I am not consoling or
kind. I do not utter words of comfort or camaraderie. I tell
him to stop being such a horrible bastard. I call him a stupid
drunk. Then I find myself lying in the street staring up at
his knees, because out of nowhere he has hit me with a closed
fist in the jaw. He leaves me there, stunned on my ass, and
lopes off into the night.

"Fuck him," says Joy Ray after I have composed myself
and returned inside. I can't help but wonder if she would
cut me loose as quickly, even after what we had. "Some friend
he turned out to be," she says. I consider coming to his
defense, but she should know better. Hasn't she sat there
all those nights with us in Sam Chao's Cuban All Night?
Doesn't she understand the depth of Rocket's symptomology,
the kind of tough love we have always been required to
dole out?

In January, Rocket is thrown out of his studio. He hasn't
paid his rent in six months. I see him drinking in a bar on
Avenue A. He wants to know if I can put him up for a while.

"Just until I get some pieces sold," he says.

He stays only a few days, long enough to eat whatever
remains in my fridge, to piss on my bathroom floor and
menace me when he comes home drunk or stoned. Joy Ray
calls. She wants to know if Rocket has returned to earth. I
tell her that if she were his friend she'd ask him herself. After
that I don't speak to her for close to a month.

I begin to feel panicked by New York, the crush of buildings
blocking out all but a small patch of sky. And the ghosts.
There are so many places I will not go, past the university,
down into the subway. For a while I tell myself that in a city
of this size there will always be new corners to frequent, new
restaurants and bars, but it's a lie. I find myself coming back

to all the old places. I am looking for myself, trying to warn the younger me about the violence that lies ahead. Out on the corner of Sixth Avenue and Eleventh Street I watch the children boil from the doors of PS 41. They take to the streets, directed by school monitors and crossing guards, moving en masse toward the welcoming windows of Ray's Pizza. What good is the past, I think, if it remains always just out of reach? I blow on my fingers, warm them on my coffee cup. While I'm standing there, caught up in vision, a police officer stops and tells me it's illegal to loiter within a hundred yards of a school. He implies that I'm some kind of pervert. I'm just waiting for my brother, I tell the officer, but my voice is shaky and unreliable.

Cowboys and Indians, stoop ball and skateboards. When Neil was looking at colleges I told him to get out of the city. Take the opportunity and go to an ivy-covered school in New England, where the leaves turn colors and a sense of small-town quiet pervades. I had gone to Haverford in Pennsylvania, had welcomed the departure from concrete. But Neil wanted to be near me. He thought there were things I could teach him. Me, who was, by this point, completely estranged from my parents, exhausted by their whole destructive act. They were fighters, my parents. They gave us nothing but faulty reasoning and low self-esteem. *We were their enablers. Codependents. They warped us with their unhealthy lifestyle.* Neil stayed home till he was eighteen, becoming quiet, nervous, afraid of people and the confrontations they required. I used to see him on weekends, sometimes school nights. He was so underappreciated. In the last month of his life he talked about transferring. He wanted to know what I thought about Connecticut or maybe Boston. Would I visit? I told him he needed to make friends of his own. He accepted this as if it meant something more than just, Find your own place, your own life. This one is mine.

After Rocket moves out, I run into him several times in the beverage pockets of the East Village. The things we used to have in common now serve as a wedge between us. My own association with Joy Ray makes me some kind of accomplice in *the persecution of Rocket*. I try to point out to him that I am no better off than he, that I have been relegated to temp work in ominous office towers uptown, to collecting unemployment in between assignments, to fending off the bill collectors and landlords with a combination of procrastination and a great sense of denial. I try to tell him how my own words have betrayed me, how my typewriter sits under a great weight of New York City soot. The truth is, he is jealous that I have slept with Joy Ray and she has never shown even the slightest interest in him. He tells me one night that he is in love with her, wakes me up at three in the morning to sit on the sloping floors of my studio with his head in his hands. He speaks in short bursts, quietly.

In July, Rocket goes into the hospital. Doctors have discovered a brain tumor the size of a Concord grape pressed against his thick, unyielding skull. His parents fly out from Detroit, the father with grease-stained hands from the auto plant, the mother fluttering, unable to relax. Rocket's head is shaved. There are bandages from the operation. After the radiation therapy he loses so much weight his face is just a thinly veiled skull.

Joy Ray tries to visit, but he won't see her. Six months later he is dead. The news comes by phone. Another merciless communication from beyond. I have been sitting in my apartment staring at it, waiting for it to ring, which is strange because it never does. After I hang up, I drop the phone in the trash, pack a few small items. Joy Ray comes to the funeral, but she and I have little to say to each other. We have split in many ways like cells, evolved into different species.

At Rocket's funeral I read the poem I have written for him. It is the first thing I have been able to write since Neil died. A hate letter to the irreversible nature of time. Nearby the highway emits a steady hiss. We stand under a swollen sun, stupefied by grief. A fat priest with a comb-over reacquaints

us with the concept of Jesus. When it is my turn I start to
sweat. I pull a crumpled sheet of paper from my pocket, stare
down at my own text. I read to the fallen faces of Rocket's
relatives, the subdued huddle of former friends. The words
are not so much statements as oversized questions. I am asking
them to explain.

Portfolio

Four Engravings

Nicola Tyson

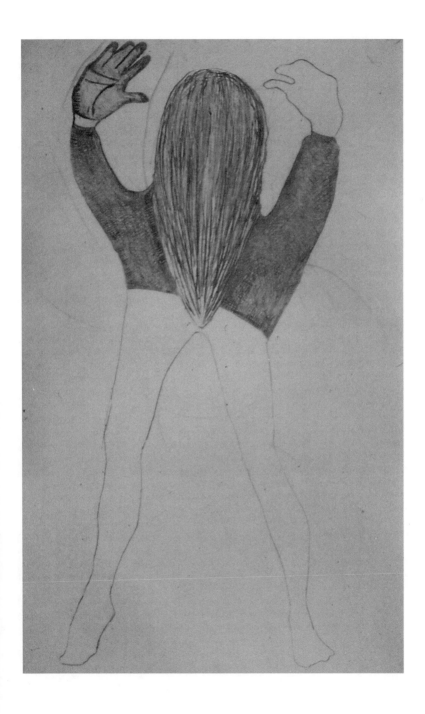

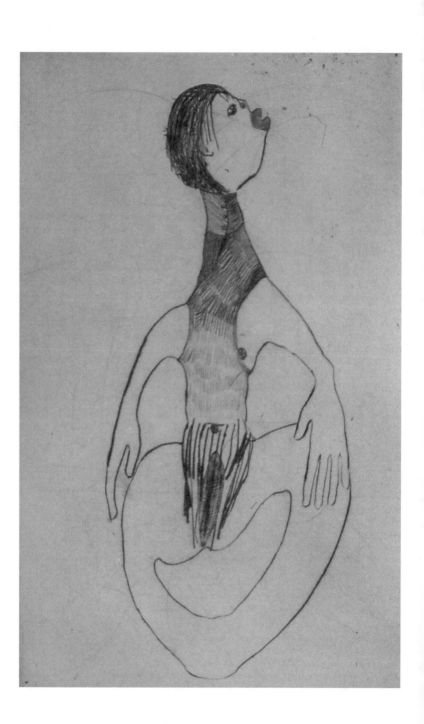

W.G. Sebald: A Profile

James Atlas

"It was an escape route, something entirely private," Max Sebald mutters as he rummages through a thick folder of old photographs. A boy in a white gown and caftan; a graveyard with tilted headstones; a turn-of-the-century spa: they're the kind of photographs you'd come across in a junk shop, leafing idly through a box of postcards. Which is more or less where Sebald found them. He had been collecting photographs for years before he began to write, he explains, scouring the shops in the seaside towns of East Anglia, where he's lived since emigrating from Germany in 1970, for images to put in his books—or rather, to serve as their catalysts. "Not even people in the house knew what I was up to; I'd just retire to my workshop and potter about. I think it was these photographs that eventually got the better of me."

They had got the better of me, too. In fact they were a large part of the reason I was sitting over a coffee in Sebald's comfortable, book-lined study in Norwich. I had come on a literary pilgrimage. *The Emigrants*, his English debut, pub-

lished three years ago by New Directions, in an elegant translation by Michael Hulse, was like no other book I'd ever read.
Interspersed with the text—a sequence of biographical narratives about Germans exiled by the Holocaust—were cap-
tionless photographs that, out of context, made no sense.
Why a grass tennis court with leafless winter trees in the background? Why a Jewish cemetery overgrown with vines? Why
the spire of the Chrysler Building and the Brooklyn Bridge?
And who were the people in these photographs, who seemed
to have no connection to one another? A family around a dinner
table; children in a classroom; a quartet of goggled passengers
in a roadster: they have the musty air of snapshots in a family
album, where long-forgotten faces, anonymous and indistinct,
gaze up from the yellowing page—"what one imagines lost souls
look like," in Sebald's haunting description.

© The Emigrants.

His new book, *The Rings of Saturn*, supposedly a compilation of random notes begun when the author was in a mental
hospital, is a continuation of this peculiar hybrid form. The

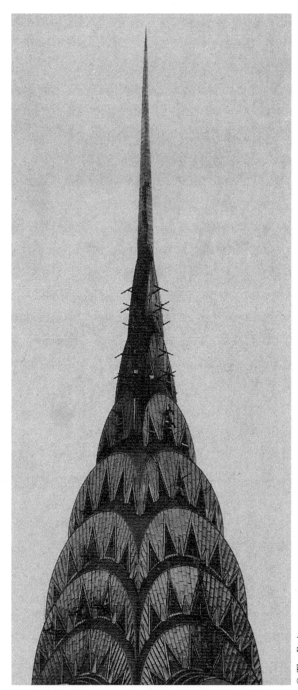

elusive narrator, a meticulous amateur historian of East Anglia, wanders the countryside with a rucksack on his back,
recounting in the digressive but hypnotic prose that is Sebald's
trademark the lore he's gathered about the area's medieval
past, the long-vanished inhabitants of its derelict manor
houses, the archaeology of its quaint seaside villages. Like *The
Emigrants*, *The Rings of Saturn* is illustrated with mysterious
photographs that play off and clarify the equally mysterious text.

And like its predecessor, it's told in the voice of a nameless
I whose identity is indeterminate, his odd soliloquy on the
ravages of history counterpointed by passages from the works
of Swinburne, Chateaubriand, Borges ("I asked Bioy Casares
for the source of this memorable remark, the author writes
. . .") and Joseph Conrad, who once sailed the North Sea
coast in the days when he was still the sailor Józef Korzeniow-
ski. From a detailed summary of Conrad's early life, Sebald
segues to the novelist's traumatic journey into the deepest
recesses of the Belgian Congo, which would inspire his masterpiece *Heart of Darkness*—then abruptly returns to an account
of his own travels, his forward narrative progress interrupted
by associations with Belgium:

> At all events, I well recall that on my first visit to Brussels in
> December 1964 I encountered more hunchbacks and lunatics
> than normally in a whole year. One evening in a bar in Rhode
> St Genèse I even watched a deformed billiard player who was
> racked with spastic contortions but who was able, when it was
> his turn and he had taken a moment to steady himself, to
> play the most difficult cannons with unerring precision. The
> hotel by the Bois de la Cambre where I was then lodging for
> a few days . . .

And so on, proceeding from a brisk inventory of the hotel's
ponderous furniture to a consideration of the ugly monument
the Belgians erected to commemorate the Battle of Waterloo.
For Sebald, the discontinuities of the unconscious are the
mainstay of his art.

Sebald, who is fifty-four, speaks with a pronounced German
accent, but his English, after nearly three decades, is sophisti-

cated and precise. (How many native English speakers know
how to use the word *apodictic* in a casually tossed-off sentence?) With his thinning mane of white hair, rimless glasses
and bushy mustache, he resembles the Frankfurt theorist Walter Benjamin. On this late winter day he's dressed in non-
descript corduroys and a bulky sweater; only the mustache
and the cigarette he's smoking in a holder give off a hint of
his Continental origins. He introduces himself by his nick-
name—Max.

Sebald's books elude easy classification. Are they fiction or
nonfiction? History or a Borgesian fabrication built upon fact?
His publisher, hedging, has resorted to the dual category of
fiction-literature. "It's hard on publishers," he concedes.
"You have to make sure it doesn't get in the travel section."
When I try to pin him down, he becomes slyly evasive. "Facts
are troublesome. The idea is to make it seem factual, though
some of it might be invented." In the end, truth as a historian
or biographer understands the term is irrelevant to him. "I
just want to write decent prose. Whatever it is—biographical,
autobiographical, topographical—doesn't matter. I have an
aversion to the standard novel: 'She said, and walked across
the room'—there's something trite about it. You can feel
the wheels turning."

•

Sebald's books are resolutely plotless. Their narrative line
follows the contours of the unconscious. His method is to
build up a collage of apparently random details—stray bits
of personal history, historical events, anecdotes, passages from
other books—and fuse them into a story; Sebald, borrowing
the term from Claude Lévi-Strauss, calls it *bricolage*. The
effect is a kind of organized free association, as if one were
reading a sequence of dreams instead of a linear narrative.
The Emigrants begins: "At the end of September 1970, shortly
before I took up my position in Norwich, I drove out to
Hingham with Clara in search of somewhere to live." But
Clara will soon be left behind, and the narrator—*I*—will

never be more than a shadowy pronoun, like the narrator of *The Rings of Saturn*, who opens his story: "In August 1992, when the dog days were drawing to an end, I set off to walk the county of Suffolk, with the hope of dispelling the emptiness that takes hold of me whenever I have completed a long stint of work."

Who was this authorial presence, this enigmatic *I*? The biographical note appended to *The Emigrants* was fuller than most. It revealed that Sebald was born in Wertach im Allgaü, Germany, in 1944; that in 1966 he became an assistant lecturer at the University of Manchester; that he'd taught at the University of East Anglia since 1970; that he'd served as Director of the British Centre for Literary Translation from 1989 to 1994. But it still left a great deal unsaid; even the author's full name—Winfried Georg—could only be teased out by consulting the copyright page. What fascinated me was the incontrovertible fact yielded up by his birthdate: Sebald wasn't Jewish. How many Jews born in Germany in 1944 survived Hitler's ovens? *The Emigrants* wasn't the work of a survivor, then; it was something far more rare: the work of a disinterested moral witness. Or was he? "Such a life is somehow still touched with a smudge, or taint, of the old shameful history," Cynthia Ozick observed in a review of *The Emigrants*; and "the smudge, or taint—or call it, rather, the little tic of self-consciousness—is there all the same, whether it is regretted or repudiated, examined or ignored, forgotten or relegated to a principled indifference."

The Emigrants is an anomaly in so-called Holocaust literature, a book that goes to the heart of that catastrophic event by hovering on its periphery. Like Aharon Appelfeld, whose novels tend either to prefigure the Holocaust or to dwell on its lingering aftermath, Sebald chronicles the ripple effect of recent German history on four indirect victims: a retired English doctor who fled the pogroms in Eastern Europe and, never having felt at home in his adopted land, eventually commits suicide; a German primary-school teacher in the 1950s who also ends a suicide; a cluster of the author's relatives

who emigrated to America in the 1920s; and a Jewish refugee
painter whose parents were murdered by the Nazis. Each of
these stories is tangential to the Holocaust, yet each of the
protagonists is fatally implicated in it, caught up, however
obliquely, in the eradication of the Jews. Visiting an abandoned Jewish cemetery in Kissingen, the anonymous narrator
encounters "a wilderness of graves, neglected for years, crumbling and gradually sinking into the ground amidst tall grass
and wild flowers under the shade of trees, which trembled
in the slight movement of the air." Soon the graves themselves
will vanish.

The great theme of *The Emigrants* is the hidden consequences of the Holocaust—not only the trauma of the survivors, the allocation of guilt, the Germans' struggle with their
Nazi past, or even the new insights about human nature that
it forced upon us, but its eerie aftereffects, the veneer of
normality that encourages us to forget. "I felt increasingly
that the mental impoverishment and lack of memory that
marked the Germans, and the efficiency with which they had
cleaned everything up, were beginning to affect my head and
nerves," Sebald writes in the last chapter, recounting his visit
to the abandoned graveyard at Kissingen: "It was not possible
to decipher all the chiselled inscriptions, but the names I could
still read—Hamburger, Kissinger, Wertheimer, Friedländer,
Arnsberg, Auerbach, Grunwald, Leuthold, Seeligmann, Frank,
Hertz, Goldstaub, Baumblatt and Blumenthal—made me
think that perhaps there was nothing the Germans begrudged
the Jews so much as their beautiful names, so intimately
bound up with the country they lived in and with its language." Like Daniel Goldhagen, the controversial author of
Hitler's Willing Executioners, Sebald believes the Holocaust
was uniquely German; it was no accident that it happened
there. "There is something about Germans, which for lack
of a better word we'll call cowardice," he says, groping for
an explanation of the collective blindness that enabled the
Nazis to flourish. "They have a habit of avoidance. People
don't want to know. It's as if it never happened. In England,

the sixteenth, seventeenth, eighteenth and nineteenth centuries are still visible; in London, there are tangible layers of history. In Germany, partly because of the destruction of the cities and partly because of the way in which Germany deals with its own past, their history is much less present. It has been, as it were, neutralized. The cities all look like each other—pedestrian zones, wretched malls with trees growing out of concrete pots, the same shops . . ."

Yet for all his moral outrage, Sebald isn't a polemicist; his intent is less to build a prosecutorial case against Germany, as Goldhagen does, than to puzzle over the transience of human life. However murderous the Nazis' intent, they were only accelerating the inevitable. "From the earliest times, human civilization has been no more than a strange luminescence growing more intense by the hour, of which no one can say when it will begin to wane and when it will fade away," he writes in his new book. All things pass; nothing endures. This is the lesson so powerfully brought home in *The Rings of Saturn*. Where *The Emigrants* showed how widely the Holocaust emanated from its epicenter, how efficient was the destruction it unleashed, *The Rings of Saturn* forces us to loosen our grip on the illusion that *anything* is permanent. As he sifts through history, cataloging one historical catastrophe after another, Sebald conjures up the image of a globe engulfed in serial chaos: low-lying ports are swallowed up by storms; rainforests are leveled by fire; entire populations are massacred in obscure distant wars. East Anglia itself, Sebald's quaint and docile corner of England, was only half a century ago the staging ground for the war against Hitler:

> Time and again, as one walks across the wide plains, one passes barracks, gateways and fenced-off areas where, behind thin plantations of Scots pines, weapons are concealed in camouflaged hangars and grass-covered bunkers, the weapons with which, if an emergency should arise, whole countries and continents can be transformed into smoking heaps of stone and ash in no time.

Saturn, formally speaking, is like *The Emigrants*: the signature photographs of people and landscapes described in the text; the rambling, nearly free-associative meditations and long incantatory sentences unwinding with slow serpentine grace; the ruminative first-person voice. But the narrator is a more visible figure, more bodied forth as a literary character on the order of Dostoyevsky's Underground Man or Kafka's Gregor Samsa, to whom he compares himself. As I made my way through its densely allusive pages, I was put in mind of Mallarmé's dictum that everything in the world exists to be put in a book. The depredations of Dutch elm disease, the lifespan of the silkworm and the social transformation wrought by the silk industry in the eighteenth century, even a five-page discourse on the physiology and migratory habits of herring, all find their way into Sebald's weave. The leitmotiv that binds his digressive excursions into the past in *The Rings of Saturn* is the same one that dominated *The Emigrants*—"scenes of destruction, mutilation, desecration, starvation, conflagration." It's not a pretty picture.

•

Sebald's self-exile makes him exotic—"How many German writers live in East Anglia?" he notes—but it also makes him a representative case. From Eliot in England to Joyce in Paris and Nabokov in the United States, the writers who dominate the contemporary canon have been essentially stateless, citizens of a domain that requires no cultural passport; George Steiner has named this condition "unhousedness." Or, as Sebald himself put it to me in his occasionally clumsy but invariably accurate English: "Paradigmatically postmodern writers are often operating on linguistic borderlines." To this experience he has brought a prose so lapidary, so particular, so loaded with concrete detail that it has the impact of a photograph. "I heard the woodwork of the old half-timber building, which had expanded in the heat of the day and was now contracting fraction by fraction, creaking and groaning," he writes in *The Rings of Saturn*, recounting a night spent in a country inn. He goes on:

> In the gloom of the unfamiliar room, my eyes involuntarily turned in the direction from which the sounds came, looking for the crack that might run along the low ceiling, the spot where the plaster was flaking from the wall or the mortar crumbling behind the panelling. And if I closed my eyes for a while it felt as if I were in a cabin aboard a ship on the high seas, as if the whole building were rising on the swell of a wave, shuddering a little on the crest, and then, with a sigh, subsiding into the depths.

Like his great stateless predecessor in the famous preface to *The Nigger of the Narcissus*, he wants, "above all, to make you *see*."

•

Others before me had fallen under the spell of Sebald's work. The paperback edition of *The Emigrants* carried effusive blurbs from Susan Sontag and A.S. Byatt, and it had showed up on several writers' Best Books of 1997 lists in England. But hardly anyone I canvased in America had heard of him; the book seemed to be circulating samizdatlike from hand to hand. (I'd heard about it from a friend.) Like Bernhard Schlink's *The Reader*, a small gemlike novel about a love affair in Nazi Germany and its eerie postwar reverberations, Sebald's masterpiece had acquired a readership in the old way, without publicity or drumbeating on the part of its publisher, a venerable literary house that tends to concentrate on poetry. No one seemed to know much about the author. When I asked his London agent, Victoria Edwards, what he was like, she said she'd never met him. Like his peripatetic narrator, he liked to go for walks in all weather; twice when I called, his wife told me he was "out with the dogs." The notion of a literary profile bewildered him. "I am glad you liked *The Emigrants* and quite astounded that you propose to come all the way to talk to me," he'd written in reply to my request for an interview.

He had turned out to be less forbidding than I'd anticipated. When I arrived in Norwich that morning on the train
from London, Max had been waiting at the gate. I recognized
him from the photograph on the back of *The Emigrants*. He
was shy at first as we drove through the streets of Norwich in
his rattletrap Peugeot, but he soon grew talkative, pointing
out the eleventh-century Norman cathedral that towers im-
mensely over the town and going on about his dealings with
publishers, agents, advances—a writer's shoptalk. "My publishers would say to me that they had sold foreign rights to
France or Italy—'We got you five hundred pounds'—and
then I'd never hear another thing about it again," he complained, grousing like a journalist at Elaine's. He struck me
as worldly, in a quiet, unobtrusive way, possessed of a steely
ego and not afraid to engage in public debate on highly
charged issues. When he gave a series of lectures on the history
of the Allies' air war against the Reich in Zurich last year,
he told me, it provoked intense coverage in the German
media. "I felt that I'd touched on a raw nerve," he said
without apparent regret.

Sebald's house, The Rectory, is a redbrick Victorian manor
with tall windows and a manicured lawn in a suburban cul-
de-sac on the outskirts of Norwich. He renovated it himself,
by hand, over half a dozen years. Trim and tidy, it seemed
the very antithesis of his dark, broodingly apocalyptic prose.
While we settled down in the study to talk, his wife, Uta, a
handsome fiftyish blond—they met as students at the University of Freiburg—was visible through the windows, mowing
the lawn with a tractor mower. Morris, their big black dog,
dozed on a cushion. The pristinity of the room—volumes of
German literature neatly arranged on the shelves; a blindingly
white rug; a leather club chair and couch; a wood-burning
stove painted fire-engine red—unnerved me for some reason.
The only eccentric touch was the row of hats hanging on the
wall: they reminded me of one of those somber, depopulated
museum installations of Joseph Beuys, where the once-living
form is represented by an old coat or a scrap of fur. Otherwise

he could have been a bourgeois shopkeeper in his suburban domicile. "I like to try to lead a normal life," he told me—and for all intents and purposes he does. Uta, who brings us tea and cookies, is engaging and friendly; the Sebalds' daughter, Anna, twenty-six, is a schoolteacher living nearby. "She's not all that interested in my work," Sebald maintained.

I asked him about a sentence from *The Emigrants* that had stayed with me: "When I think of Germany, it feels as if there were some kind of insanity lodged in my head." In the fifties and early sixties, he explained, when he was growing up, the Nazi era was regarded as an almost normal episode in German history. "In 1939, my father was unemployed. He had the good fortune, as he saw it, to be admitted to the Weimar One Hundred Thousand Man Army. Once you got in there, you had prospects, a job." His father fought in the Polish campaign, and was briefly interned in a French POW camp toward the end of the war, but rarely talked about his experiences. Sebald's childhood was, by his own account, ordinary. "I never thought much about anything at all. I had a *penchant* for reading," he says, giving the word a French pronunciation, "but otherwise I was the same as everybody else—skiing and all the rest of it." He painted a rather withering portrait of his parents as bourgeois burghers. "My father was a clerk in an office until the fifties, and then joined up in the army again. He retired early, as one does in that profession, and has done nothing for the last forty years but read the newspaper and comment on the headlines. He has a critical bent of mind, and very pronounced opinions about the issues of the day." What does he think of his son's work? "He took a certain interest when there was public attention; then he seemed to be jolly pleased about it."

It wasn't until Sebald entered the University of Freiburg that he became aware of the war's unspoken legacy. "Conditions for students were very poor," he recalls. "German colleges in those days were unreformed, completely overrun, undersourced. You would sit in lectures with 1,200 other people and never talk to your teachers. Libraries were practically nonexistent." But what troubled him more than the overcrowded conditions was the conspiracy of silence surrounding the Nazi era. "All my teachers had gotten their jobs during the Brownshirt years and were therefore compromised, either because they had actively supported the regime or been fellow travelers or otherwise been silent. But the strictures of academic discourse prevented me from saying what I wanted to say or even investigating the kinds of things that caught my eye. Everyone avoided all the kinds of issues that ought to have been talked about. Things were kept under wraps in the classroom as much as they had been at home. I found that insufficient."

He transferred to a university in Switzerland, and then applied for a teaching job in Manchester. "I knew nothing about Manchester. I hardly knew English, and had no intention of staying. I thought I would just be there for a year." In *The Emigrants*, Sebald provides a vivid account of his arrival in that sooty industrial metropolis aboard a night flight from Kloten:

> Once we had crossed France and the Channel, sunk in darkness below, I gazed down lost in wonder at the network of lights that stretched from the southerly outskirts of London to the Midlands, their orange sodium glare the first sign that from now on I would be living in a different world. . . . By now, we should have been able to make out the sprawling mass of Manchester, yet one could see nothing but a faint glimmer, as if from a fire almost suffocated in ash. A blanket of fog that had risen out of the marshy plains that reached as far as the Irish Sea had covered the city, a city spread across a thousand square kilometres, built of countless bricks and inhabited by millions of souls, dead and alive.

Sebald was forty-five when he began to write. "I had quite a demanding job. There was never time to write." I asked him if he had ever been in therapy: his work is so apparently random in the way it leaps from subject to subject that it mimes the process of free association. "I never got round to it," he answers. "My therapy consists of reading other case histories." But in the seventies and eighties he spent summers at a mental clinic near Vienna, a sort of therapeutic vacation from the rigors of teaching that would also serve as research; the director, Leo Navratil, encouraged his patients to draw or paint, and had published a book of poems by one of his inmates, Ernst Herbeck, that Sebald found "mind-boggling." He continued: "I thought it would help me understand some of the basic conditions in creativity to go there." He hadn't gone as a patient? "Oh, no, no. Writing itself is an insane occupation: hard, compulsive, most of the time not pleasurable. There is always the desire to find out how one is made up, to get to those layers that are out of sight; but I would find it hard to write anything confessional. I prefer to look at the trajectories of other lives that cross one's own trajectory—do it by proxy rather than expose oneself in public."

•

I was startled to encounter in *The Rings of Saturn* a description of someone I actually knew, the poet and translator Michael Hamburger, who retired from London some years ago to a rural cottage in Middleton, a hamlet about twenty miles from Sebald's house. I had met him in the early seventies, when I was a student at Oxford; but I hadn't seen him in more than twenty years, and proposed to Sebald that we go for a visit.

On the way, we stopped off in Southwold for lunch at the Crown Hotel. It was a snug establishment, with rough-hewn wooden tables and small-paned bay windows that looked out on the main street of the town. On this wintry February day, it was full of elderly people in cardigans; Southwold is a popular retirement community for BBC executives, Sebald explained. He seemed at ease in the comfortable dining room. He said that the Crown was one of his regular haunts, and that he often stopped in for a night or two "to get away from the routine." It was a curious thing: his work is so relentlessly grim that it verges on the comic, but Sebald himself appeared wryly cheerful, even when he was discussing the work of Primo Levi or describing a book on euthanasia in Nazi Germany that he'd just read. ("An asylum in Kaufbeuren was still dispatching victims three weeks after the Americans arrived.")

Like most writers I know, he showed a lively interest in real estate; as we strolled around the town after lunch, he lamented that he should have bought one of the grand old houses on the village square when he first arrived in the area; now they're too expensive. "In his writing, he comes across as a melancholy man," Michael Hulse told me, "but he's really a very funny man." When I commented on this apparent contradiction between his somber world view and his equable disposition, he shrugged. "One is born with a certain psychological constitution," he said, referring to himself in the third person as if to deflect any insinuation of egotism, "and then one discovers that life is partly dispiriting and partly exhilarating in its oddness." He invoked Flaubert's famous advice to be a bourgeois in life and a madman in art. "I want to hold on to my job, so I'm not condemned to this activity. If left to my own instincts I might well have become a recluse."

He wanted to show me the Sailors' Reading Room on the promenade. I instantly recognized the navigational instruments and barometers on the walls, the battered leather armchairs and ships' models, from Sebald's description in *The Rings of Saturn*. Two old men were playing pool in the backroom. It felt odd to be touring the very locales so vividly conjured up in *The Rings of Saturn*—it was almost as if I myself had stepped into the pages of his book. A writer in exile, Sebald had acquired as deep a sense of place as any writer I know. Tramping the lanes and meadows of East Anglia, he had steeped himself in its lore. "The intriguing thing for me about Suffolk is that it is untouched by history, as the whole country is in a sense," he remarked. "There hasn't been a war on English soil since the seventeenth century." I asked if he ever felt homesick for Germany. He answered: "Yes, until I go there. When I first came here I had no intention of staying in Manchester. I still go over several times a year, and have made repeated attempts to return to Germany, but I always end up coming back here." At one point in the late 1980s he worked for a German cultural institute, and last year he was offered a position in creative

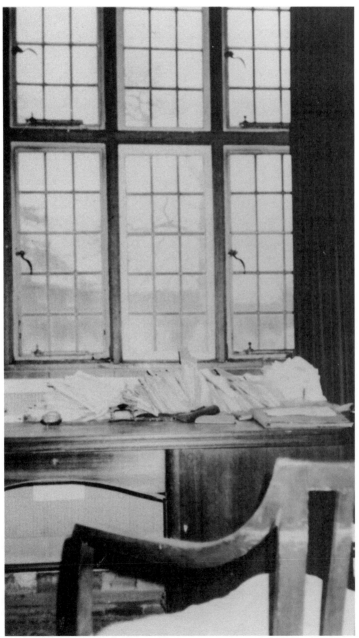

writing at the University of Hamburg. "I did not want to be
drawn into the German culture industry. I do feel uncomfortable in Germany. It feels like a cold country."

It was growing dark as we left town and pulled into a
muddy driveway beside an ancient farmhouse. Michael, in a
worn corduroy jacket, opened the heavy wooden door. He's
in his mid-seventies now, but he looked nearly the same as
he did when I last saw him, frail and wrenlike; even his hair
is still dark. His beautiful wife, the poet Anne Beresford, had
also aged well. He welcomed us into a cold, dank room with

© Rings of Saturn.

a low heavy-beamed ceiling, leaded windows, and a charred stone fireplace—a room out of a Brontë novel. There were books everywhere—in a closet, on floor-to-ceiling shelves, piled up by the stairs that lead to the study. The house is "part Stuart, part Tudor," he said. "It's falling down around us, but it will probably see us out."

It was dark now. The wind rattled the windows. Suddenly I felt far away from home, the way I used to feel when I lived in England twenty-five years ago, before there were phones everywhere and central heating and people flew back and forth across the Atlantic for a weekend. But a few minutes later, it was time to go; the spell was broken. Back in the car, we headed for the Norwich train station. Sebald was talking about the family tragedies that had lately befallen so many of his friends. "For years I didn't know anyone who was ill," he said. "Now it's all around me."

That night, back in my room in London, I looked up the pages about Michael in *The Rings of Saturn*. I had read the book in galleys, and hadn't seen the photographs before. There were two of Michael's study—one showed his book-crowded writing desk and the ancient small-paned bow window behind it; the other showed a mass of books piled up beside a door. It was strangely moving to find images so recently imprinted on my own consciousness staring up at me from the page. Suddenly I thought of a book I'd read as a child: C.S. Lewis's *The Lion, the Witch and the Wardrobe*, in which a gang of children climb through a closet door and find themselves transported to some other world. That's what being with Max was like.

The photographs in Mr. Atlas's profile appear courtesy of New Directions Publishing Corporation.

NOTES ON CONTRIBUTORS

FICTION

Noah Hawley is the author of the novel *A Conspiracy of Tall Men*. He lives in San Francisco.

Jonathan Lethem is the author of *Gun, with Occasional Music*; *Amnesia Moon*; *As She Climbed Across the Table*; *Girl in Landscape*, as well as a collection of stories, *The Wall of the Sky, the Wall of the Eye*. The piece published in this issue is an excerpt from his forthcoming novel, *Motherless Brooklyn*.

José Saramago won the Nobel Prize for Literature in 1998. His books include *The Stone Raft*, *The History of the Siege of Lisbon*, *The Gospel According to Jesus Christ* and, most recently, *Blindness*. His Art of Fiction interview appeared in issue 149 of *The Paris Review*. He currently lives in Lanzarote, Spain. His translator, **Margaret Jull Costa**, received the 1992 Portuguese Translation Prize for her version of Fernando Pessoa's *The Book of Disquiet*. Her translation of Saramago's novel *All the Names* will be published next year.

Kate Walbert is the author of the story collection *Where She Went* and is currently at work on her first novel, *The Gardens of Kyoto*. Her fiction previously appeared in issue 144 of *The Paris Review*.

FEATURE

James Atlas is the editor of the Lipper/Viking Penguin "Lives" series of brief biographies by celebrated writers. He participated in the Como Conversazione: On Literary Biography that appears elsewhere in this issue.

POETRY

Molly Bendall is the author of *After Estrangement*, a collection of poems. She teaches at the University of Southern California.

Michael Benedikt is a former poetry editor of *The Paris Review*. His poetry is represented at many web sites.

Peg Boyers is the executive editor of *Salmagundi* at Skidmore College.

Derick Burleson taught English at the National University of Rwanda from 1991–1993 and is completing a PhD in creative writing at the University of Houston. He received a 1999 NEA fellowship in poetry.

Anne Carson received both the Lannan Foundation Poetry Prize and the Q-Spell Poetry Prize in 1996. Her books include *Plainwater; Glass, Iron and God* and *Wild Workshop*, an anthology.

Robin Davidson teaches at the University of Houston. Her prizes include the 1994 Creative Artist Award from the Houston Cultural Arts Council and the 1996 Abiko International Poetry Prize. She lives in Houston.

Peter Davison is poetry editor for *The Atlantic Monthly*. His most recent book is *The Poems of Peter Davison, 1957–1995*.

Anthony Deaton is working on a PhD at the University of Houston. His poetry has appeared in *The Southern Poetry Review*.

Annmarie Drury's poems have appeared in *Western Humanities Review* and are forthcoming in *Raritan*. She currently lives in London, where she is completing an MA in comparative literature at the School of Oriental and African Studies.

Malcolm Farley received an MFA in creative writing from Columbia University. He lives and works in New York City.

Irving Feldman teaches at SUNY Buffalo in the department of English. He was a MacArthur Fellow in 1992, and is the author most recently of *The Life and Letters*.

Gary Fincke has published several books, including *The Technology of Paradise*, a poetry collection, and *Emergency Calls*, a collection of stories.

Albert Goldbarth lives in Wichita, Kansas. His most recent books include a collection of poems, *Troubled Lovers in History*, and a collection of essays, *Dark Waves and Light Matter*.

Mary Gordon has received the Lila Acheson Wallace-Reader's Digest Award and a Guggenheim Fellowship. Her novels include *Final Payments*, *The Company of Women*, *Men and Angels*, *The Other Side*, and, most recently, *Spending*. She is a professor of English at Barnard College in New York City.

D. Gregory Griffith lives in Cincinnati, Ohio. He is a graduate student and teacher at the University of Cincinnati.

William Logan teaches at the University of Florida. He is the author of a number of books of poems, including *Vain Empires*, and a book of essays and reviews, *All the Rage*. His new book of poems, *The Night Battle*, and a book of criticism, *Reputations of the Tongue*, are forthcoming.

Corey Marks has published poetry in the *Antioch Review*, *Black Warrior Review* and *New England Review*.

Campbell McGrath was awarded the Kingsley Tufts Poetry Prize for 1996 for his most recent book, *Spring Comes to Chicago*. He received a MacArthur Fellowship this year.

Christian Nagle's poems have appeared in the *Antioch Review* and are forthcoming in *Southwest Review*. He was a featured playwright in Edward Albee's New Play Series for 1998.

Donald Platt received the Verna Emery Poetry Prize for his first collection, *Fresh Peaches, Fireworks, & Guns*. He is an assistant professor of English at the State University of West Georgia.

Kenneth Rosen received a Fulbright Award to teach modern literature in the American Studies program at the University of Sofia in Bulgaria. He is the author of *No Snake, No Paradise* and the forthcoming *A Portion for Foxes*.

Kay Ryan's most recent book is *Elephant Rocks*. She received an Ingram-Merrill Award in 1995.

Martha Silano is the author of *What the Truth Tastes Like*, which received the William & Kingman Page Poetry Book Award. She teaches English at Edmonds Community College in Lynnwood, Washington.

Shawn Sturgeon teaches English at the University of Cincinnati.

Terese Svoboda's most recent books are *A Drink Called Paradise*, a novel, and *Mere Mortals*, a collection of poems.

Dorothea Tanning is a painter and sculptor. Born in Galesburg, Illinois, she has lived and worked in Arizona, New York and, for twenty-eight years, in France. In 1979 she returned to New York City, where she continues to paint and write.

Constance Urdang is the author of *American Earthquakes*, *The Woman Who Read Novels*, *Peacetime*, and a book of poems, *Alternate Lives*. She died in 1996.

Rosanna Warren's prizes include the American Academy of Arts and Letters Award and the Lila Wallace-Reader's Digest Fellowship. The poem published in this issue is from her forthcoming volume *Arbor Vitae*.

Charles H. Webb is a professor of English at California State University–Long Beach. His book *Reading the Water* won the 1998 Kate Tufts Discovery Award. A forthcoming collection, *Liver*, won the Felix Pollak Prize in Poetry.

Renée and **Theodore Weiss** have served as editors of the *Quarterly Review of Literature* for over fifty years and were awarded the PEN Lifetime Achievement Award in 1997. They recently have begun writing poems together and have just finished their first collection.

INTERVIEWS

Carter Coleman (Shelby Foote) is the author of *The Volunteer*, a novel.
Donald Faulkner (Shelby Foote) is the associate director of the New York

State Writer's Institute and the author of two collections of poetry, *At Dunkard Creek* and *In Dyers Wood*.

William Kennedy (Shelby Foote) is the founding director of the New York State Writer's Institute and a professor of English at SUNY Albany. His books include *Very Old Bones*, as well as the three novels known as the Albany cycle, *Legs*, *Billy Phelan's Greatest Game* and *Ironweed*, which received the 1984 Pulitzer Prize. His Art of Fiction interview appeared in issue 112 of *The Paris Review*.

Patricia Storace (Robert Fagles) is a former poetry editor of *The Paris Review* and the author of a book of poems, *Heredity*, and a travel memoir, *Dinner with Persephone*, which won a Runciman Award. She has won a Whiting Writers Award.

ART

Catherine Murphy's work appears courtesy of Lennon, Weinberg gallery in New York City.

Vik Muniz was born in São Paulo, Brazil and now lives in New York City, where he is represented by the Brent Sikkema Gallery.

Valerie Sadoun is a French painter living in New York City.

Nicola Tyson's work appears courtesy of Brooke Alexander Editions in New York City.

ERRATUM: Some of the information included in Phoenix Nguyen's contributor's note in issue 150 was incorrect. She was born in Lac Son, but it was not considered a strategic hamlet. Her father was a farmer, not a fisherman. Her father was a village chief, not a district chief. North Vietnamese troops marched into Saigon on April 30, 1975. Her work has been published previously in *St. Louis Magazine* and *The Webster Review*.

CAFÉ LOUP

Open 7 Days

Casual, Art-filled

**Delicious Food
at moderate prices**

**105 West 13th Street
New York City, 10011
Tel. 212 AL5-4746**

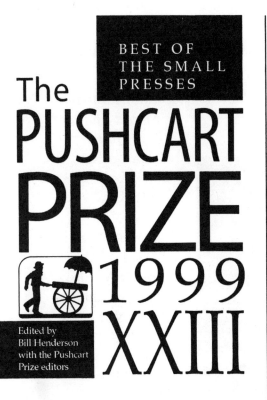

The

PUSHCART
PRIZE

BEST OF
THE SMALL
PRESSES

1999
XXIII

Edited by
Bill Henderson
with the Pushcart
Prize editors

"A distinguished annual
literary event."

ANNE TYLER
NEW YORK TIMES BOOK REVIEW

"The cream of the small
press crop."

WASHINGTON POST

THE PUSHCART PRIZE has
been selected many times as
a notable book of the year
by The New York Times Book
Review, and has been
chosen for several Book of
the Month Club QPB
selections. Pushcart Press
and its Prize were named
among the "most influential
in the development of the
American book business
over the past century and a
quarter."

PUBLISHERS WEEKLY

**"THE BEST READ ANNUAL THAT IS PUBLISHED –
READ AND NOT MERELY SOLD AND COLLECTED
ON A SHELF."** Russell Banks

THE 1999 PUSHCART PRIZE is one of the largest in
the history of the series—over 600 pages of
stories, essays and poems as selected from
hundreds of presses with the help of over 200
distinguished Contributing Editors.

HARDBOUND $29.50
PAPERBACK $15.00

PUSHCART PRESS
P.O. Box 380
Wainscott, N.Y. 11975

the modern writer as witness

Special Issue
American Families

Volume XII Number 2 $7   1998

Contributors
Marcia Aldrich
Pete Fromm
Dan Gerber
Jean Ross Justice
Julia Kasdorf
Anna Keesey
Maxine Kumin
Thomas Lynch
Joseph McElroy
Roland Merullo
Kent Nelson
Linda Pastan
Maureen Seaton
Floyd Skloot
Paul West

"From its inception, the vision that distinguishes Witness *has been consistent: it is a magazine situated at the intersection of ideas and passions, a magazine energized by the intellect, yet one in which thought is never presented as abstraction, but rather as life blood. Each issue is beautifully produced and eminently readable."*

Stuart Dybek

Call for Manuscripts:

Witness invites submission of memoirs, essays, fiction, poetry and artwork for a special 1999 issue on **Love in America**.
Deadline: July 15, 1999.

Writings from *Witness* have been selected for inclusion in *Best American Essays, Best American Poetry, Prize Stories: The O. Henry Awards,* and *The Pushcart Prizes.*

THE PARIS REVIEW
BOOKSELLERS ADVISORY BOARD

Available now from the Flushing office
BACK ISSUES OF THE PARIS REVIEW

Please add $3.00 for postage and handling for up to 2 issues; $4.75 for 3 to 5. Payment should accompany order. For orders outside the U.S. please double the shipping costs. Payments must be made in U.S. currency. Prices and availability subject to change. **Address orders to: 45-39 171 Place, Flushing, N.Y. 11358**

MASTERCARD/VISA # _____ EXP. DATE _____